The Origins
of Biblical Law

Also by Calum M. Carmichael

Biblical Laws of Talion

Law and Narrative in the Bible: The Evidence of the Deuteronomic Laws and the Decalogue

The Laws of Deuteronomy

Women, Law, and the Genesis Traditions

The Origins
of Biblical Law

*The Decalogues and the
Book of the Covenant*

Calum M. Carmichael

Cornell University Press

Ithaca and London

THIS BOOK HAS BEEN PUBLISHED WITH THE AID OF A GRANT FROM THE HULL MEMORIAL PUBLICATION FUND OF CORNELL UNIVERSITY.

First published 1992 by Cornell University Press.

International Standard Book Number 0-8014-2712-6
Library of Congress Catalog Card Number 92-6908
Printed in the United States of America
Librarians: Library of Congress cataloging information appears on the last page of the book.

⊗ The paper in this book meets the minimum requirements of the American National Standard for Information Sciences—Permanence of Paper for Printed Library Materials, ANSI Z39.48-1984.

To Ruth and Wiki

Contents

Preface

This book had its beginnings in a conversation I had with Bernard Jackson (the Queen Victoria Professor of Law, University of Liverpool) shortly before he delivered his Speaker's Lectures at the University of Oxford in the spring of 1985 on the *Mishpatim* (the laws of the Book of the Covenant, Exod 21:2–23:19). He asked if my theory in which I explain the laws in the book of Deuteronomy by assuming a certain kind of link with the narrative literature also applied to the *Mishpatim*. I was quite sure then that it did not. I had been anxious to demonstrate to myself and to others that my novel views about one body of biblical material did not necessarily extend to other legal material such as the *Mishpatim*, which had been analyzed by the long-standing historical-critical method and found to be (as I accepted) the earliest codification of law in the Bible.

Some months later, in looking again at three of the rules in the *Mishpatim* (seduction, witchcraft, and bestiality, Exod 22:16–19), I changed my mind. Whereas at the time Bernard delivered his Oxford lectures I had been sympathetic to his analysis of the *Mishpatim*, by the time he sent me a draft of his manuscript, however stimulating and innovative I found it to be, I had gone in another direction. Every rule in the *Mishpatim* had indeed the character of those in the book of Deuteronomy and in the decalogues of Exodus 20 and 34 and Deuteronomy 5, its content having a basis in an issue that the lawgiver locates in some of the best-known stories in the Bible (for example, Jacob and his wives, Joseph and his brothers, and the Israelites in Egypt). These stories themselves had already been refined to express legal and ethical judgments. The lawgiver in turn sets down judgments for analogous, hypothetical situations in his own setting in a manner that resembles the academic activity that produced other law codes in the ancient Near East. A rule's bias, the peculiarities of its language, the details of its formulation, and its place in an often puzzling sequence—such particularities could be illumined. So too could the larger, long-standing puzzle: why does the Pentateuch consist of bodies of law embedded in narrative contexts?

I acknowledge my indebtedness to the National Endowment for the Humanities for the award of a research fellowship during 1989–90. I also owe debts of gratitude to the University of Melbourne, Australia, where I spent a semester in 1989 as a Visiting Research Fellow, and in particular to Takamitsu Muraoka of the Department of Classical and Near Eastern Studies (now at the University of Leiden, Holland). I am grateful as well to Lawrence McIntosh, Librarian of Ormond College, Melbourne; to the President and Fellows of Clare Hall, Cambridge, for their award of a fellowship during the Candlemas and Whit terms, 1990; to Graham Davies of the Faculty of

Divinity, Cambridge University, who kindly read part of my manuscript; and to my wife, Debbie, who cast a critical eye on all that I wrote and made many helpful suggestions.

In quoting biblical texts I have relied on the King James Authorized Version of 1611 but made changes where these were called for. I have used the AV because it is almost always a more literal rendering of the Hebrew original than any other translation.

CALUM M. CARMICHAEL

Ithaca, New York

Abbreviations

ANET	*Ancient Near Eastern Texts Relating to the Old Testament*, ed. J. B. Pritchard. 3d ed. (Princeton: Princeton University Press, 1969)
AOAT	*Alter Orient und Altes Testament*, ed. K. Bergerhof, M. Dietrich, and O. Loretz (Neukirchen-Vluyn: Neukirchener Verlag)
ArOr	*Archiv Orientální*
ASTI	*Annual of the Swedish Theological Institute*
AV	Authorized Version
BA	*Biblical Archaeologist*
BDB	F. Brown, S. R. Driver, and C. A. Briggs, *A Hebrew and English Lexicon of the Old Testament* (Oxford: Clarendon, 1906)
Bib	*Biblica*
CBC	Cambridge Bible Commentary
CBQ	*Catholic Biblical Quarterly*
CBSC	Cambridge Bible for Schools and Colleges
CH	Code of Hammurabi
D	The Deuteronomic literary strand in the Pentateuch
HAR	*Hebrew Annual Review*
HLR	*Harvard Law Review*
HTR	*Harvard Theological Review*
HUCA	*Hebrew Union College Annual*
ICC	International Critical Commentary

Abbreviations

ILR	*Israel Law Review*
JAOS	*Journal of the American Oriental Society*
JBL	*Journal of Biblical Literature*
JE	The Y(J)ahwistic and Elohistic literary strand in the Pentateuch
JJP	*Journal of Juristic Papyrology*
JJS	*Journal of Jewish Studies*
JPS	Jewish Publication Society
JR	*Juridical Review*
JSOT	*Journal for the Study of the Old Testament*
JTS	*Journal of Theological Studies*
LawHR	*Law and History Review*
LE	Laws of Eshnunna
LHR	*Legal History Review*
LXX	The Septuagint
MAL	Middle Assyrian Laws
MT	The Masoretic Text
NCBC	New Century Bible Commentary
NEB	New English Bible
OJLS	*Oxford Journal of Legal Studies*
OTS	*Oudtestamentische Studiën*
P	The Priestly literary strand in the Pentateuch
RJ	*Rechtshistorisches Journal*
RSV	Revised Standard Version
SVT	*Supplement to Vetus Testamentum*
TB	*Tyndale Bulletin*
TBC	Torch Bible Commentary
TDOT	*Theological Dictionary of the Old Testament*, ed. G. J. Botterweck and H. Ringren (Grand Rapids, Mich.: Eerdmans, 1980)
VT	*Vetus Testamentum*
WBC	Word Bible Commentary
WC	Westminster Commentary
ZAW	*Zeitschrift für die alttestamentliche Wissenschaft*
ZSS	*Zeitschrift der Savigny-Stiftung für Rechtsgeschichte*

The Origins
of Biblical Law

Introduction

The problems are solved, not by giving new information, but by arranging what we have always known.

—Ludwig Wittgenstein, *Philosophical Investigations*

I argue here that the rules of the *Mishpatim* can be understood in a new light if we link them to certain narratives (as I have done for all the rules in the book of Deuteronomy[1]). The rules of the *Mishpatim* are not to be seen as a direct product of particular problems in the society of the time of the lawgiver, but are the result of scribal art in formulating rules about problems derived from a scrutiny of national traditions, specifically some of those recorded in the books of Genesis and Exodus.

The care we must take to avoid accepting a code of laws at its face value is illustrated by the earliest codification of Roman law, the Twelve Tables (around 450 B.C.). These rules probably do reflect law in practice, but all sorts of erroneous conclusions would be drawn if the background struggle between the social classes were ignored. The code is one prepared by the patricians for the

---

[1] Calum M. Carmichael, *Law and Narrative in the Bible: The Evidence of the Deuteronomic Laws and the Decalogue* (Ithaca: Cornell University Press, 1985).

plebeians. It includes no rules relating to public officials or to the state religion—fundamental facets of life in ancient Rome that were under the control of the patricians.[2] Influenced by H. S. Maine, who read the code at face value, scholars have misleadingly contrasted the integration of law and religion in biblical legal texts with the lack of such integration in Roman texts.[3] In this book I try to avoid such errors and to look behind the face value of biblical rules for their sources in the narrative traditions.

Hypotheses and the Study of Biblical Law

An elementary point should be stressed. The usual approach to the analysis of the biblical legal material involves a hypothesis: the laws are to be linked to their historical setting, to the economic, ideological, religious, and social issues current in the lawgiver's time, or current in the time that saw the supposed origin of a rule that the lawgiver decided to update. So far as I am aware, only Bernard Jackson, attempting a semiotic analysis, and I have distanced ourselves from the conventional approach. All one can ever ask of a hypothesis is whether or not it works. The fact that so many scholars work with the "historical" hypothesis does not make it the correct one. It has to be pointed out that this particular thesis is protected from critical scrutiny because we lack the means of corroborating the historical reconstruction that suppos-

[2] See Alan Watson, *State, Law, and Religion: Pagan Rome* (Athens: University of Georgia Press, 1991), especially chap. 11, "The Paradox Resolved."

[3] H. S. Maine, *Ancient Law* (London: Routledge, 1905).

edly explains the *ratio legis* underlying each rule.[4]

I am skeptical about the conventional approach not only because its results are beyond the reach of examination. The problem is also that the approach too readily assumes that the texts straightforwardly lend themselves to historical, literary analysis. B. S. Childs's attack on scholars who endlessly divide biblical texts to bring out supposed differences in historical periods of time is welcome.[5] Having attacked them, however, and having paid attention to the importance of the final form of the text, he is largely content with the results achieved by historical and literary analysis. There is little recognition of the problem posed by the exceedingly limited availability of material on which to exercise one's historical imagination. The material available is mainly biblical, and much of it has a sophisticated, pseudo-historical character, a feature that has been constantly undervalued.

The pressure to automatically relate a legal formulation to its historical (in our sense of the term) background is strong. It is remarkable to find, for example, that a scholarly thesis about the priestly code of laws (P) has its basis in a single historical notice.[6] Or that two similar texts about the release of slaves are automatically assumed to reflect different periods in actual history and, consequently, a historical picture is constructed to explain the

[4] The same point is made by Meir Malul, *The Comparative Method in Ancient Near Eastern and Biblical Legal Studies, AOAT* 227 (1990), 58, 73–75.

[5] B. S. Childs, *The Book of Exodus: A Critical, Theological Commentary* (Philadelphia: Westminster, 1974), xiv, xv, 338–39.

[6] Menahem Haran claims that Hezekiah's cultic reform referred to in 2 Kings 18:4 is inspired by the ideology of P; *Temples and Temple-Service in Ancient Israel* (Oxford: Clarendon, 1978), 140–48.

differences.[7] What if the two laws contrast for some quite different reasons, for example, because the fictional Moses, showing consistency of judgment, looks at two different instances of slavery in legendary history?

How narrowly conceived is the approach of a strictly literary-historical reading of texts is well illustrated by the analysis of the law about the forgotten sheaf and the gleanings from olive trees and vines in Deut 24:19–22. It is easy to conclude that the two practical injunctions about harvesting olives and grapes without second gleanings, so that the poor can have them, were added at a later date to the initial, singularly impractical injunction. It requires that if a harvester has collected sheaves of grain and has then remembered that he has forgotten one, he should not return to collect it but should leave it for the poor. The oddness of this injunction—it is so inadequate as a rule about welfare policy—is passed over by critics tied to their literary, historical assumptions. Its very oddness, however, suggests a basis for its formulation quite different from the idea that it responded at some time to a social issue in the life of ancient Israel. The strangeness is well brought out in *Tosephta Peah* 3:8. In the words of C. D. Montefiore and Herbert Loewe, "We can observe it [Deut 24:19] only if we do so unwittingly—if we try to keep it, we cannot, since it is, say the sages, 'ordained only for forgetfulness.'"[8]

[7] Sara Japhet, "The Relationship between the Legal Corpora in the Pentateuch in Light of Manumission Laws," *Studies in Bible, Scripta Hierosolymitana* 31, ed. S. Japhet (Jerusalem: Magnes, 1986), 63–89.

[8] C. D. Montefiore and Herbert Loewe, *A Rabbinic Anthology* (London: Macmillan, 1938), 192. For the rule's provenance, see Carmichael, *Law and Narrative*, 278–88.

One implication of a hypothesis that works with an agenda of historical inquiry is that the legal material found in the Bible is viewed as largely the result of accidental deposit. Some comes from this period of time, some from that, but if not haphazardly deposited, it certainly leaves many a gap. My hypothesis produces different results. Each law, by responding to some "historical" aspect of a narrative composition, is itself a well-integrated composition. In addition, in that the laws are related directly to events and issues presented in particular narratives, my hypothesis can explain why each rule is set down in the first place and why the laws appear in the sequences in which we find them.

The difference between my approach and the conventional one is easily spelled out. I too engage in a historical, literary analysis, but I avoid a burden other critics impose on themselves. When they encounter laws that are ascribed to Moses living at a certain period of time, they feel compelled to reject this ascription because their historical sense makes them skeptical. So far so good—I share their skepticism entirely. How can rules that manifestly reflect matters long after the time of Moses go back to him? A kernel of a rule maybe, but not its overall formulation. So they go off on a historical trail, overly reliant on a subjective sense of how language was used in antiquity, overly dependent on biblical accounts of historical events, and they come up with their theories as to when some laws or parts of laws had their origin, and when other laws, or other parts of them, had theirs.[9] I

[9] In recent years the work of Alexander Rofé markedly illustrates this approach, e.g., "The Strata of the Law about the Centralization of Worship in Deuteronomy and the History of the Deuteronomic

Introduction

deviate from this route. Instead I try to make sense of the fact that the text claims the rules all come from Moses (or, in the case of the decalogue, from God).

I see the clue to the interpretation of the laws as lying in the observation that Moses, like God, knows the past, acts in the present, and uncannily anticipates the future. A sophisticated fiction has been created. I assume that the real author works with all the narrative and "historical" material that he has the figures of Moses and God focus on. I further assume that Moses achieved such an elevated status because in the Israelite national tradition he was known as a great lawgiver whose laws, alas, were not in fact set out in the legends themselves. If these assumptions are in any way accurate, we can proceed to observe, with a much greater degree of precision than has been possible before, how the author works out his rules. The rules embody the author's reflection on all of Israel's narrative history, up until, I presume, the events of his own day. Unfortunately, at the point where it would be appropriate to engage in historical inquiry, namely, the time

---

Movement," *SVT* 22 (1972), 221–26; *Mavo le-sefer Devarim* (Jerusalem: Academia, 1982). In my view all of David Cohen's criticisms of the conventional approach to the study of Greek law apply to the conventional study of biblical law; "Greek Law: Problems and Methods," *ZSS* 106 (1989), 81–105. Cohen criticizes, for example, an antiquated historiographical style that employs a "positivist chronological narrative" (85); a reconstruction of the history of early institutions by reading back from their "fossilized remains," a procedure whose roots lie in nineteenth-century social Darwinism (88); and a philological method that "provides a sense of rigour, creating the impression of historical analysis, of the interpretation of evidence" (89).

when the writer created the fiction, it is too difficult a task (at least for this inquirer) to establish precisely the period in which he worked.[10]

I address myself to the types of questions any legal historian would wish to raise. Why, to give specific examples, are the two rules about seduction and bestiality the only two in the *Mishpatim* concerning sexual matters? Why is the rule that is found between these two, about sorcery, concerned with a female offense? Why do we find this sequence: a rule about the hire of an animal followed by one about seduction, then a rule about sorcery and then one about bestiality? Do these particular rules fit the characterization of early law codes so brilliantly delineated in David Daube's "The Self-Understood in Legal History,"[11] namely, as introducing reforms or settling doubts? Despite some indication of these functions for some rules in the *Mishpatim*, I am not inclined to accept this characterization for most of them.[12]

A larger (and I consider a most important) question concerns not the legal but the literary perspective of the Book of the Covenant: Why are its rules ascribed to Moses in his nomadic setting when a great many of them

[10] See discussion in the Afterword.

[11] David Daube, "The Self-Understood in Legal History," *JR* 18 (1973), 126–34.

[12] I should point out that I do not accept the common view that we should separate the rules in Exod 21:2–22:17 from the subsequent ones in Exod 22:18–23:19. James Barr, singling out Exodus 21–23 as containing a relatively high proportion of short spellings, implies that from this angle the material seems to present a unified feature; *The Variable Spellings of the Hebrew Bible* (Oxford: Oxford University Press, 1989), 110–11.

apply only to a later, settled society? Why are they inserted into a narrative history? The regnant hypothesis views the biblical law collections as indeed having a certain kind of link with the narratives in which they are embedded. Ancient Near Eastern treaties, in which an overlord imposes obligations on a subject people in return for his protection of them, contain—I simplify—an accounting of past events that constitutes a basis for the transaction. Certain examples of such vassal treaties seem to be relevant to the idea of a covenant between the Israelites and their divine ruler. The attempts to draw such a parallel—alas, the working out of the details has produced an impasse[13]—have provided one explanation for the relationship between the legal codes of the Bible and the historical narratives that incorporate them. Walter Beyerlin, for example, states, "We may conclude, therefore, that the traditions of deliverance from Egypt and the events at Sinai were connected at a very early date under the influence of the old covenant form going back to the pre-Mosaic period. This is true of the earliest stages of the growth of Israel's tradition and not simply of the later period of literary fixation, and is the reason for the union of history and law which is characteristic of the Old Testament."[14] G. E. Mendenhall had spoken in the same terms

---

[13] E. W. Nicholson states, "The attempt to relate the Old Testament covenant to suzerainty treaties may be said to represent a dead-end in the social/functional approach; the search for a model that will explain how the covenant functions in the religious and social life of ancient Israel here overreaches itself"; *God and His People: Covenant and Theology in the Old Testament* (Oxford: Clarendon, 1986), 81.

[14] Walter Beyerlin, *Origins and History of the Oldest Sinaitic Traditions* (Oxford: Blackwell, 1965), 169–70.

earlier: "What we now call 'history' and 'law' were bound up into an organic unity from the very beginnings of Israel itself."[15]

Such an explanation for the link between the legal and narrative portions of the Pentateuch is a product of these scholars' agenda of historical inquiry. A most complicated construction of a history of ancient Israel underlies it. Some biblical material is selected and read at face value as if, for example, it originated in the Mosaic period of around 1300 B.C. It is then drawn into the orbit of the larger world of the ancient Near East and linked to Hittite and Mesopotamian conventions known to us, often in fragmented form, from many different periods. In the process we are to assume a transformation of the idea of a sovereign and his vassals into that of a god and his people, a process that some scholars infer to be very early, for example, pre-Mosaic, and others to be much later.[16] However plausible is this view, the problems are, nonetheless, major. For example, the Mosaic period the Bible refers to is hundreds of years removed from the supposedly pertinent Mesopotamian environment of vassal treaties.

I argue that, in Mendenhall's words, "history" and "law" are indeed bound up into an "organic unity." The unity, contrary to Mendenhall's view, is not a product of Israel's "very beginnings," but in Beyerlin's words a

---

[15] G. E. Mendenhall, "Covenant Forms in Israelite Tradition," *BA* 17 (1954), 70; so too Klaus Baltzer, *The Covenant Formulary* (Oxford: Blackwell, 1971), 90–91.

[16] Moshe Weinfeld, e.g., links the book of Deuteronomy to Mesopotamian treaties of the ninth to the seventh centuries B.C. in *Deuteronomy and the Deuteronomic School* (Oxford: Clarendon, 1972), 57–146.

product of "the later period of literary fixation."[17] Most fundamental of all is that whereas Mendenhall and Beyerlin use the term "unity," really in a rather general way, in regard to a body of narrative and its link to a body of law, I use it to refer to what is indeed an organic unity, namely, the linkage of every law with some aspect of the body of narrative. It is the demonstration of this thesis that I shall be intent on.

Laws and Narratives

If we concentrate on the question why such collections of rules as the *Mishpatim*, the versions of the decalogue, and the laws of Deuteronomy are part of a narrative history, we break through to a new understanding of these collections. Consider first of all an observation about the nature of biblical narrative. Little or no specialization is needed for one to notice two characteristic features of the first five books of Moses and the "historical" literature about the institution of kingship. The first feature is the interest in origins, in first-time happenings and developments: the origin of the universe, the origin of shame, the first murder, the first bout of drunkenness, the first fa-

---

[17] That period, I might add, is the period of the creation of the myth about Israel's beginnings. The phenomenon is a universal one. J. J. Sheehan refers to how "the apostles of [German] nationalism were able to create a historical memory of 'liberation' which projected their own enthusiasms on to the nation." He further states, "As is always the case with patriotic myths, the historical memory of liberation took many forms and had many different heroes"; *German History 1770–1866* (Oxford: Clarendon, 1989), 386–87.

thers of the nation, the origin of kingship in Israel, and so on. The second feature is the interest in how what goes on in one generation tends to repeat itself in the next: Abraham has a problem about who is to have the right of the firstborn (Isaac and not Ishmael); this problem recurs for Isaac when Jacob wins out over Esau; and Jacob denies the right to Reuben and confers it upon Joseph, whose firstborn son, Manasseh, is in turn displaced by Ephraim. Or again, Jacob's role as a slave with Laban and with Esau (on meeting up with him Jacob addresses Esau as a servant addressing a master, Gen 32:18, 20; 33:5, 8) has its parallel in Joseph's role as a slave in Egypt, and his experience in turn is repeated in the later lives of all the Israelites in Egypt. Or again, problems of deception in male-female relations recur: Abraham has a problem because his wife is beautiful to behold, and he gives out disinformation that she is his sister; his son Isaac is faced with the identical problem with his wife Rebecca; Jacob, in turn, wants the lovely Rachel as his wife but is duped into marrying her not so beautiful sister Leah; his son Joseph is faced with the problem of the scheming wife of Potiphar. Or again, generation after generation a king is judged according to his religious stance.

The salient features of such laws as are found in the *Mishpatim*, in Deuteronomy, and in the versions of the decalogue are precisely those—and I wish to stress this link—that characterize the narrative portions of, for example, the Pentateuch. The formulators of the laws are only secondarily interested in real-life issues in their own time. Their primary focus is on the history of their own national traditions, the very stories and legends available to us in the books of Genesis, Exodus, Numbers, Joshua, Judges, Samuel, and Kings. *What the laws focus on is the first-time-ever occurrence of a problem and the recurrence of that problem in subsequent generations.* Two examples are instances of idolatry—the first of which in Israelite history, the golden calf in Aaron's time, repeated itself in the reigns of some of the kings of Israel—and instances of slavery, the first occurring in the time of the nation's eponymous ancestor, Israel, and recurring in the immediately succeeding generations. The same double focus that characterizes the narrative literature, this interplay between original developments and patterns of conduct over succeeding generations, is found in the laws. Sometimes a single law will address several historical situations, the first and following ones. For example, the law of the king in Deut 17:14–20 incorporates the interlude of Abimelech's reign as king in the time of the Judges (Judg 9:1–6), the people's request for a king in Samuel's time (1 Sam 8:4–9), and the problems of Solomon's reign (1 Kings 10, 11). Or different formulations of a law will embrace the various developments. For example, the rule about wresting justice in Exod 23:2 has in focus Joseph's brothers' use of evidence to convince their father that Joseph had met a violent end (Genesis 37), while the similar rule in Exod 23:6 has under review Joseph's entrapment of his brothers when they came to buy food in Egypt (Genesis 42).

If I had to think of a parallel to one aspect of the formulation and arrangement of laws that I describe, I would refer to any news story of the day, for example, the spillage of oil in Alaska or the election of a Ku Klux Klan member as a Republican to the Louisiana legislature, and note how editorial comments in newspapers bring out the various issues in question and make judgments, but fall short of setting out these judgments in separate lists of moral rules, legal maxims, and the like. If that were done, the list of pronouncements would have a curious lack of coherence and order to it.

One major problem in working with biblical lists of rules is precisely their lack of apparently logical order. In the decalogue a rule about murder comes after one about honor to parents, which itself comes after a requirement about observing the sabbath; in the *Mishpatim* a rule about partiality to a poor man in his suit is followed by one about an enemy's ox (Exod 23:3–5). In regard to these rules the link is not between the subject matter of one law and the next. Critics have consistently drawn major conclusions by interpreting a rule in light of its context in the code. S. M. Paul, for example, noting that, in contrast to Hammurabi's Code (para. 14), the biblical rule about man-stealing is not found among offenses concerning property, draws conclusions about the notion of a person in each culture.[18] In the juxtaposed rules about the hire of an animal and the seduction of a virgin (Exod 22:14–17), we should not conclude, as is invariably done, that the common element is the notion of property. The subject matter of the narratives on which the rules formulate judgments determines the flow of topics in the rules.

Contemporary Impact of the Laws

My primary focus is on the tantalizing question of how the collections of laws were compiled in the first instance. It is not likely, to confine the question to the *Mishpatim*,

[18] S. M. Paul, *Studies in the Book of the Covenant in the Light of Cuneiform and Biblical Law* (Leiden: Brill, 1970), 65; cp. 82 n.5.

that they were intended for judges, as if the laws had statutory power.[19] That the laws were, however, intended to have some impact on the contemporary way of judicial decision making cannot be discounted. But how do we decide what the contemporary concerns may have been? The author(s) ascribes his legal formulations to a legendary Moses living centuries before the author's own time. He knows about the legendary Moses from the traditions available to him. In various combinations, he has this Moses pick up problems that came up, directly or by implication, in the time of Moses's forefathers (Joseph and Jacob), in Moses's own time (events in Egypt and the exodus), and, we might presume, in the author's own era. The legal problems taken up by the author are ones that recur generation after generation. They may be ones that are explicit or implicit in the traditions, or the author may have translated an ancient problem (again possibly only implied in a story) into terms more reflective of his own time and place. It is when we note the difference between a problem in the tradition and the way it is formulated in the law that we may be in touch with the author's contemporary world. For example, the penalties he lays down in his laws are often different from those found for the comparable offense in the tradition. Presumably the author's penalties reflect practices in his own day.

I emphasize that we can but raise questions about aims the lawgiver may have had in influencing his own world.

---

[19] B. S. Jackson discounts such a possibility in "Ideas of Law and Legal Administration: A Semiotic Approach," in *The World of Ancient Israel: Sociological, Anthropological, and Political Perspectives*, ed. R. E. Clements (Cambridge: Cambridge University Press, 1988), 185–202.

Can we say that the general trend of the code is, like the Roman Twelve Tables, to set limits on power?[20] How do we judge the lawgiver's attitude? Is he, for example, hostile to greedy slavemasters, and does he hope, by requiring a mark to be put on a slave who opts for perpetuity of service, that the slave will think twice before going through with the ceremony?[21] Is it significant that at times he introduces monetary resolutions to disputes when, in the analogous disputes in the traditions, the resolutions do not entail any use of money?[22] At every turn we are on surer, less speculative ground when we observe how the lawgiver constructs his laws by working closely with the problems presented by his reading of the narratives. Detailed answers to a host of legal and linguistic problems can be provided.

Hypothetical Character of Biblical and Near Eastern Laws

It is important to emphasize that the lawgiver often chooses issues that are only *suggested* in a narrative. Examples are those rules formulated on the basis of suppositions such as "What if Jacob's status under Laban *had been* that of a slave?" or "What if Esau *had* murdered Jacob?" or "What if Tamar *had* died at Judah's hands?" It is precisely this hypothetical approach to the traditions on the

---

[20] David Daube's claim in "What Price Equality? Some Historical Reflections," *RJ* 5 (1986), 195.

[21] So again Daube, "What Price," 195.

[22] Raymond Westbrook points to "price-fixing" as a major feature of ancient Near Eastern codes; *Studies in Biblical and Cuneiform Law* (Paris: Gabalda, 1988), 46.

part of the lawgiver that permits us to infer the hypothetical character of the legal constructions. One reason that the links between the laws and the narratives have not been picked up before is that this hypothetical element has not been perceived. The recognition of the nature of the rules takes us to one of the most tantalizing problems in the study of biblical law, namely, what can we say about it in relation to ancient Near Eastern legal material?

The claim that biblical law has to be seen in the larger context of the ancient Near East is readily and rightly made. Yet the attempts to demonstrate in any detailed way the links between the two bodies of material have been singularly unsuccessful. The thesis presented in this book makes some inroads on the problem of their relation to each other. Before any historical questions can be asked about the biblical material, and before any comparisons can be drawn between individual provisions in the biblical and ancient Near Eastern codes, we have to recognize the overwhelming influence of the narrative sources that inspire the presentation of each and every law in the versions of the decalogue, the book of Deuteronomy, and the *Mishpatim*. I would not wish this claim, however, to obscure the fundamental need to know what history lies behind the rules so presented. In particular, what kind of legal thinking can we infer for those who choose to present their laws in a given manner? What are their sources of law?

The level of legal knowledge on the part of both narrators of traditions and compilers of laws was undoubtedly sophisticated to a high degree. On this matter it is sufficient to refer to the pioneering work of David Daube in his *Studies in Biblical Law* (Cambridge: Cambridge University Press, 1947). Much more difficult is the question of how to approach the problem of the relationship between biblical and ancient Near Eastern codes. The groundbreaking work of Benno Landsberger, F. R. Krauss, and J. J. Finkelstein has brought to the fore the hypothetical, ideal character of those laws found in the Near Eastern codes in contrast to the day-to-day laws discovered in legal contracts and the like. The contents of the codes suggest an academic school setting. They constitute a "literarisch-schematische Konstruction," an example of Babylonian academic literature couched in phraseology typical of hypothetical scribal compositions.[23]

My thesis argues for a similar scribal setting for the biblical codes, with this book concentrating on the *Mishpatim*. I distinguish sharply between the biblical *formulations* of rules (for example, their bias, sequence, and wording), about which I have much to say, and the *sources* for these rules, about which I can only speculate. All I can suggest about the author's sources for the rules

---

[23] So F. R. Krauss, "Ein zentrales Problem des altmesopotamischen Rechts: Was ist der Codex Hammurabi," *Genava* 8 (1960), 283–96; see too S. M. Paul, *Studies*, 23–25. The construction of laws on the part of jurists as more an intellectual exercise than a wrestling with practical facts is often underestimated in legal systems. For this aspect in Roman law, see Alan Watson, "Artificiality, Reality, and Roman Contract Law," *LHR* 57 (1989), 154, and H. F. Jolowitz, *Historical Introduction to Roman Law* (Cambridge: Cambridge University Press, 1952), 93, 95. The pursuit of hypothetical legal problems by a learned elite in Babylonia is paralleled in Babylonian mathematical circles. The problem texts in general "sometimes exhibit only very remote connections, if any, with practical questions"; Otto Neugebauer and A. J. Sachs, *Mathematical Cuneiform Texts*, American Oriental Series 29 (New Haven, Conn.: American Oriental Society and American Schools of Oriental Research, 1945), 1.

themselves is that they might come from legal practice of
his own time, or from custom, or from folk and scribal
wisdom—or from knowledge of Near Eastern codes. In
regard to these codes, one motivation of the Israelite lawgiver may have been to construct a set of distinctive, *ancient* laws of his own nation—the distinctiveness deriving
from Israel's national literature—in contrast to the, by his
time, ancient laws of well-known neighboring cultures.
This perspective might explain why biblical laws that
have been compiled about a thousand years *later* than the
corresponding compilations of Near Eastern laws are
nonetheless more "primitive" in character than their Near
Eastern counterparts.[24] The same perspective might also
account for the way topics in the biblical material correspond to, for example, those in Hammurabi's code. On
this view a succession of rules concerning, for example,
the topic of assault (Exod 21:12–22:4; CH 195–214)
would not be a result of similar but quite independent
attempts at systematization of law in two societies that
have much in common. Rather we have to think of an
influence on the Israelite lawgiver of the Near Eastern
material available to him. In it he found the topic of as-

[24] See G. R. Driver and J. C. Miles, *The Babylonian Laws*, vol. 1
(Oxford: Clarendon, 1952), 444; A. Van Selms, "The Goring Ox
in Babylonian and Biblical Law," *ArOr* 18 (1950), 321–25. The
view that the explanation has to do with the more advanced social,
economic, and political conditions in Mesopotamia, in contrast to
those in biblical Israel, is based on the erroneous assumption that
the compilations in question are intended for everyday life. Meir
Malul rightly points out that a code such as Hammurabi's, copies
of which were made down through the centuries into the first millennium, represents a *literary* tradition, not one that had practical
legal application; *Comparative Method*, n. 13, 105–7.

sault and he set himself the task to examine the topic in the formative period of his nation's life.[25]

The work of Raymond Westbrook may provide an important key to an understanding of the *Mishpatim*, the decalogues and the laws of Deuteronomy. He characterizes the cuneiform codes as follows: "The basic building blocks were 'schools problems'—a case that may have begun life as a cause célèbre but then became the object of a theoretical discussion in which all manner of hypothetical variations to the actual circumstances were considered so as to build up a series of precedents grouped around a single theme. These problems were not re-discovered by each legal system but form a canon that was handed on from one system to another through the scientific tradition."[26] Westbrook presses into service all of the cuneiform and biblical codes available to us and assumes that each can be made to illuminate the other because they all are part of a "scientific" tradition. The picture, I think, is much more complex than he sketches. Nonetheless, he may well be right in assuming a common academic stock of legal problems that exercised the learned minds of the different cultures in question. The fundamental feature of

---

[25] I would not go so far as M. David, "The Codex Hammurabi and Its Relation to the Provisions of Law in Exodus," *OTS* 7 (1950), 149–78. For him the *Mishpatim* owe nothing to CH. He claims, for example, that one major difference between CH and the *Mishpatim* is that the latter shows no interest in differences in the societal status of a person. I am not convinced that that difference is as telling as David would have it be. The biblical lawgiver does indeed take stock of changes in Jacob's and Joseph's status. Meir Malul has persuasively argued the opposite point of view from David's in *Comparative Method*, 134–43.

[26] Westbrook, *Cuneiform Law*, 4; note also Malul, *Comparative Method*, 105 n. 13, 129, 138, 149 n. 75.

the biblical legal and ethical material would be that stock problems were explored not in relation to a series of causes célèbres in the form of long-lost, actual cases in law, but in relation to the series of dramatic narratives about the ancient history of the people Israel.

Westbrook accounts for the ancient character of biblical laws by claiming that they are part of a very conservative tradition that stretches over thousands of years. Age-old rules are reformulated but in substance they remain the same.[27] I too think it is likely that the biblical lawgiver was familiar with the academic tradition of Near Eastern law. I take Westbrook's argument further by suggesting that those who set down the rules that eventually became biblical laws deliberately formulated them so they would appear as ancient as the laws found in the "schools" tradition (Hammurabi's code, for example, was known well into the first millennium). In other words, the Israelite lawgiver created for his own nation a distinctive body of "age-old" rules that formed a tradition comparable to the Near Eastern tradition. Where else would he look for topics and issues to make judgments on but in the narrative traditions of his people? Malul stresses that the Near Eastern codes represent a literary tradition and not one that was used to inform the practice of law in the real world.[28] I emphasize in turn that the links between the

[27] Westbrook, *Cuneiform Law*, 7.
[28] See note 26. R. M. Cover ("Foreword: *Nomos* and Narrative," *HLR* 97 [1983], 4–68) claims that all law is grounded in a narrative structure: "In this normative world, law and narrative are inseparably related. Every prescription is insistent in its demand to be located in discourse—to be supplied with history and destiny, beginning and end, explanation and purpose" (5). Cover deals with the relationship between the laws and narratives in the Pentateuch, but

laws and narratives in the Pentateuch represent the equivalent Israelite literary activity to what we find in the broader Near Eastern cultural world. By comparing and contrasting the two traditions, we begin the task of evaluating the distinctiveness of biblical law.

I begin with a study of the three decalogues in Exodus 20 and 34 and Deuteronomy 5, because they demonstrate well the thesis that I apply to the larger study of the *Mishpatim*. Moreover, apart from correcting errors in my previous work on the two versions of the decalogue in Exodus 20 and Deuteronomy 5, I can incorporate important points that had escaped me previously. The interpretation of Exod 34:10–26 as constituting another decalogue also derived from a particular tradition is entirely new.

---

not in the manner in which I link the two. If he did accept my thesis, it would, I presume, constitute a remarkable illustration of his general theory about the nature of law and narrative.

[1]

The Decalogues

The Decalogue of Exodus 20 and Deuteronomy 5

Sources (Genesis 2–4, Exodus 32). The first instance of idolatry by the Israelites that is recounted in the Bible is the creation and worship of the golden calf under the leadership of Aaron. The Israelites' "great sin" was their request to Aaron to "make them gods" (Exod 32:21, 23). The problem of gods and humankind in competition is one that is explored in the Adam and Eve story.

An application of the hypothesis outlined in the Introduction explains in the most straightforward way the origin of the decalogue (Exodus 20 and Deuteronomy 5). I do not mean the origin of the rules themselves. As with the origin of the universe, it is foolish ever to expect an explanation of the first appearance of rules such as the prohibition of murder, adultery, stealing, or even the be-

22

ginnings of an observance such as the sabbath day.[1] What can be demonstrated is how the literary unit that is commonly, but wrongly, called the Ten Commandments came into existence. In other words, what I address is the question why the rules are formulated as they are, and why they come in the sequence that they do.

Laws, like prophecies, anticipate the future. Similar conflicts can be expected to recur and the same rule made to apply in resolving them. The rule itself, however, is not constructed solely in anticipation of what might happen but is typically drawn from the resolution of some dispute in the past. Biblical law not only illustrates this universal phenomenon but reveals an actual link between law and prophecy. As prophet, Moses has, we are to understand, insights into developments long after his time, for example, the crisis of leadership because of the people's request for a king (1 Sam 8:4–9). As lawgiver, Moses sets down laws that anticipate these developments. He does so, to illustrate from the example just cited, by turning to the resolution of the problem of deviant authority in his own time. The people rejected him as leader when they gave their allegiance to Aaron in the matter of the golden calf. In reaction to this deviant development, he elevated the Levites to a position of supreme authority along with himself (Exodus 32). In anticipation of a similar crisis of leadership in the time of Samuel, the prophet like him (Deut 18:15), Moses sets down a law establishing a king over Israel, one whose conduct is to be governed

---

[1] "They are not of yesterday, or to-day, but everlasting, Though where they came from, none of us can tell"; Sophocles, *Antigone*, ll. 445–46, trans. E. F. Watling, *The Theban Plays* (London: Penguin, 1947).

by Levitical direction (Deut 17:14–20).[2] Manifestly, the process of lawmaking in question, hindsight masquerading as foresight, is both contrived and complex. The process is not the one that is suggested by critics, whereby rules are updated over the centuries to meet current needs by means of a mechanism that is in fact quite unknown to us.[3]

The decalogue illustrates a similar process of constructing, in this instance, an artificially unified body of largely, but not solely, ethical/legal material. The supposed author, Yahweh, anticipates later developments. In fact, the real author knows of these developments, because they form part of a pseudo-historical record in which Yahweh as a principal participant acts in ways that can be spelled out by means of rules and statements. This distinction between rules and statements is important. Each of the three decalogues in Exodus 20, Deuteronomy 5, and Ex-

[2] See C. M. Carmichael, *Law and Narrative in the Bible* (Ithaca: Cornell University Press, 1985), 95, 96, 99–101 . Cp. J. R. Porter's thesis that the Pentateuchal traditions convey a picture of Moses in line with later Israelite kings; *Moses and Monarchy* (Oxford: Oxford University Press, 1963).

[3] William Johnstone, openly declaring his assumption, refers to "a law-code, the essence of which is to grow and develop over the centuries" in "The Decalogue and the Redaction of the Sinai Pericope in Exodus," *ZAW* 100 (1988), 373. As a legal historian well versed in ancient Near Eastern codes, Raymond Westbrook takes issue with whatever speculations might underlie such an assumption should it ever be examined for the biblical and cuneiform codes; *Studies in Biblical and Cuneiform Law* (Paris: Gabalda, 1988), 7. S. E. Loewenstamm points out that often the types of amendments and interpolations that are suggested for biblical laws presuppose a technique that is too sophisticated, not just for the biblical material but for any material in the history of law; "Exodus xxi 22–25," *VT* 27 (1977), 355.

odus 34 consists of ten "words" or sayings (Exod 34:28; Deut 4:13, 10:4). Confusion arises when we identify them as rules only, by the misnomer "the Ten Commandments." To be sure, most of the ten "words" consist of commandments, but such an assessment excludes the significance that lies in their Hebrew designation. A saying may consist of more than one commandment, or it may be a commandment with explanatory statements, or it may consist of a statement only as in Exod 20:2: "I am Yahweh thy God which have brought thee out of the land of Egypt, out of the house of bondage." It seems unnecessary to belabor this point about the meaning of the "ten words," but scholars continually make major critical assumptions because of their search for ten commandments.[4]

Religious, legal, and ethical judgments are typically, if often implicitly, incorporated in a narrative, or even a narrative framework.[5] In respect of such judgments bibli-

---

[4] In light of this fundamental distinction between a law and a saying, R. W. L. Moberly's statement can be readily set aside as irrelevant: "Such is the variety of proposed reconstructions of a decalogue in [Exod 34] vv. 11–26 that the whole attempt to find one becomes unconvincing"; *At the Mountain of God: Story and Theology in Exodus 32–34*, *JSOT* Suppl. Series 22 (Sheffield: 1983), 102. Both Moberly and the authors he refers to assume the search is for ten commandments. While he sees the problems they run into, he does not question his own assumptions. If he did, he might see that a decalogue ("ten words") can be discerned. The term *dabar* embraces the sense of utterance, commandment, prophecy. All three of these senses are present in the term as used in the "ten words." Even in those texts (e.g., Exod 24:3, 4, 8; Deut 17:19; 2 Kings 22:11; Ezra 7:11, 9:4) where the notion of command is foremost, the term has a wider meaning.

[5] Think of how the story of Laban's cheating Jacob in the matter

cal narrative overlaps with biblical law. According to biblical history, the first documented confrontation between
Yahweh and Israel's propensity to worship other gods is
in Exodus 32,[6] the incident of the golden calf. Like the
laws, the narratives are complex, highly wrought forms
of writing. Whatever the original nature of a story—forever lost to us—its substance has been modified in all
sorts of subtle ways. Even after internal modifications a
narrative can be further altered in meaning by its placement in a wider context. The story of Judah and Tamar,
placed as it is within the story of Joseph, is an example of
such complex development. Exodus 32 is another classic
example. No mere recital of a religious occasion, it includes the Israelites' request that Aaron make gods that
will go before them in their future journeyings; Aaron's
construction of a bull calf and their declaration, "These be
thy gods, O Israel, which brought thee up out of the land
of Egypt"; and the appointment of a feast day to celebrate
Yahweh at an altar on which the man-made calf is placed.
Yahweh's angry reaction to Moses indicates the way a
narrator interjects his evaluation of the event. This evaluation consists of the words of condemnation put in Yahweh's mouth and also of Moses's reasoned response to
them. The story also becomes a means by which the narrator reflects on the nature of Israel's release from slavery
in Egypt.

of his wives is to be read in relation to Jacob's previous cheating of
his brother, Esau. On the tendency in Mesopotamian law to make
explicit what is implicit in an earlier formulation, see B. S. Jackson,
Theft in Early Jewish Law (Oxford: Clarendon, 1972), 47.

[6] The statements in Josh 24:14 and Ezek 20:7, 8 about Israel's
worship of idols in Egypt receive no support from the Pentateuchal
accounts of Israel in Egypt.

Not only is the past evaluated, the future is anticipated: Yahweh is to visit the sin of the golden calf upon future generations (Exod 32:34). The narrator is manifestly writing from a stance long after the exodus from Egypt and the conquest of the land. Indeed, critics are sure that the Deuteronomist's opposition to the installation of the bull calves at Bethel and Dan in the reign of Jeroboam is anticipated in Exodus 32.[7] The link probably explains why the single calf in Exodus 32 is throughout the narrative referred to in the plural: "These be thy gods, O Israel."[8] As will become clear for some statements in the decalogue, this single narrative encompasses not just the first occurrence of some matter but its future history as well.

I I am Yahweh thy God, which have brought thee out of the land of Egypt, out of the house of bondage. (Exod 20:2; Deut 5:6)

Narratives of the kind in question lend themselves to an interesting exercise. In that Yahweh (standing for—I simplify—later interpretation or moralization) reveals in them, directly or indirectly, his views on certain subjects,

[7] Moses Aberbach and Leivy Smolar list some thirteen parallels in "Aaron, Jeroboam, and the Golden Calves," *JBL* 86 (1967), 129–40.

[8] See, however, R. W. L. Moberly's view (*At the Mountain*, 47, 48) that, in light of certain other texts (Gen 20:13, 35:7; 1 Sam 4:8; 2 Sam 7:23), the plural *'elohim* might signify "god." His comments, plus his view about the independence and precedence of Exodus 32 in relation to 1 Kings 12, are a rationalization of a difficult problem. Neh 9:18, "This is thy god," in quoting from the incident in Exod 32:4, 8, underlines the problem rather than supporting the original sense of "These be thy gods."

The Origins of Biblical Law

these views can be encapsulated in a briefer form to indicate his responses, standards, and requirements. The decalogue is readily explained on this basis. The first part (tablet) of the decalogue is, as I have argued elsewhere, a response to the incident of the golden calf.[9] Its initial statement is a necessary counterresponse to the people's false claim after the creation of the calf: "These be thy gods, O Israel, which have brought thee up out of the land of Egypt."[10] That this counterresponse is given initial attention is wholly understandable because the significance given to the calf is the primary concern of the narrative.[11]

Built into this story of the golden calf in Exodus 32 is an implicit condemnation of the later establishment of golden calves in the religious shrines of Bethel and Dan (1 Kings 12:25–33). They were set up to counter the influence of the temple at Jerusalem in the time of Jeroboam,

[9] Carmichael, *Law and Narrative*, 315–26.

[10] The term ʿalah is used in reference to the calf (Exod 32:4, 8), also when Moses is said to have brought Israel out of Egypt. yaṣaʾ is used in the decalogue and in Exod 32:11, 12 in reference to Yahweh. The decalogue's reference to the house of bondage may be intended to focus on the role of Yahweh during the time of slavery in Egypt as well as during the exodus from Egypt, whereas the people's acclamation of the calf appears to focus on the latter aspect only.

[11] I do not exclude other reasons for the significance of this initial statement, e.g., that it sets forth the event, transaction even, that entitles God to lay down ordinances for the people—so David Daube, *The Exodus Pattern in the Bible* (London: Faber and Faber, 1963), 43. We come across this kind of introduction, declaring the basis of someone's standing, in many ancient codes, Hammurabi's, for instance.

King Solomon's successor in the Northern Kingdom. Indeed, the purpose of such narrative construction as is
found in Exodus 32 about Aaron's creation of the golden
calf is to attack political developments in later Israelite
history. The incident of the calf in Aaron's time is set
down as the first outbreak of idolatry in Israelite history.
That is why the incident is of such enormous significance
for an understanding of the origin of the decalogue. Its
compiler looked back on events of Israelite history and
judged them from his own religious, ideological, and political perspective.

II 3 Thou shalt have no other gods before me. 4 Thou
shalt not make unto thee any graven image, or any likeness of any thing that is in heaven above, or that is in
the earth beneath, or that is in the water under the
earth: 5 thou shalt not bow down thyself to them, nor
serve them: for I Yahweh thy God am a jealous God,
visiting the iniquity of the fathers upon the children
unto the third and fourth generation of them that hate
me; 6 and shewing mercy unto thousands of them that
love me and keep my commandments. (Exod 20:3–6;
cp. Deut 5:7–10)

The second statement of the decalogue in Exodus 20,
prohibitions with explanatory comments, condenses the
spirit of Yahweh's negative reaction in Exodus 32 to the
Israelites' acknowledgment of other gods. There is first
the continuing response to the people's claim about the
golden calf, "These be thy gods, O Israel," namely,

"Thou shalt have no other gods before me." The gods referred to are the golden calves, although other kinds of gods need not be excluded. The Israelites who identified the calves as Yahweh were substituting them for the unseen and unseeable Yahweh portrayed in the account of the exodus from Egypt. That is why the formulation of the prohibition is "Thou shalt have no other gods before me," that is, in Hebrew, ʿal panay, "at the cost of, in preference to me."[12]

The extended prohibition wavers between the singular and the plural. A graven image, such as the golden calf,[13] is not to be made—ʿaśah as in Exod 32:23, "Make us

[12] So BDB, 818b. In a written comment to our joint seminar for college professors, "Biblical Law in Historical Perspective," on behalf of the National Endowment for the Humanities, Berkeley Law School, 1988, David Daube stated, "Not lephanay, toward my face, but ʿal panay, upon. ʿal peney is often hostile (Gen 16:12, Ishmael). ʿal panay is always hostile, although it does not rule out different use in fact. (Exception, of course, where a person is upon his own face; e.g., I fall upon my face to pray.) So far not noticed: this goes for meʿal panay, 'from upon,' always like 1 Kgs 9:7, 'And this house I will cast out from being aggressive to my face.' L. H. Koehler (Lexicon Veteris Testament Libros [Leiden: Brill, 1948], 767) reasonably translates Exod 20:3 and Deut 5:7, 'mir zum Trotz, in defiance.' But doubtless it shades off into another nuance, 'zum Schaden von, to the cost of': Deut 21:16 (a man with a younger wife may not give preference to her son 'upon the face of the firstborn,' ousting the firstborn in favour of the new arrival). Exod 20:3 and Deut 5:7, then, are not just about other gods in general, nor even about defiance in general, but about substitution à la golden calf: 'these are our gods.' By the way, 1 Kgs 9:7 also mentions other gods specifically."

[13] The Hebrew is pesel. In Exod 32:4, 8 the calf is massekah. Isa 30:22 refers to graven images of silver (pesel) and molten images of gold (massekah); Deut 27:15 to "a graven image or a molten one." I suppose pesel is the more inclusive term: melting is the process by which the image is crafted.

gods"—and they, not it, are not to be bowed down to or served. The golden calf in Aaron's time and those in the reigns of later Israelite monarchs are in focus, with the resulting grammatical irregularity.[14] Recall that both the laws and the narratives are interested in first-time developments and how these developments show up over succeeding generations.

The famous and puzzling statement in the decalogue, about how God will visit the iniquity of the fathers upon the sons to the third and fourth generation of those that hate him, illustrates this interest in the history of the generations. That history is already anticipated in Exod 32:34, "In the day when I visit I will visit their sin upon them."[15] The idolatry of the golden calf was a recurring feature in succeeding generations of kings. Sons of King Jehu to the fourth generation are singled out by the Deuteronomic narrator of the book of Kings as wrongly committed to the use of the calves. What is surprising to learn is that God himself, despite the continuing offense against him, guaranteed this history of succession (2 Kings 10:30).[16] The point is that, strange as it may sound,

---

[14] Walther Zimmerli is correct in observing that the language about bowing down and serving is used by the Deuteronomist in reference to "strange gods" and nowhere else in reference to an image; "Das Zweite Gebot," *Gottes Offenbarung, Gesammelte Aufsätze zum Alten Testament* (Munich: Kaiser, 1963), 234–48. The point is, however, that the Deuteronomist interprets the golden calf as a god, concentrates on it in the decalogue, but in his mode of thinking would link it to the history of Israel's later worship of foreign gods.

[15] *ḥaṭṭat* in Exod 32:34; *ʿawon* in Exod 20:5 and Exod 34:7. *ḥaṭṭaʾah* and *ʿawon* are used together in reference to the sin of the calf in Exod 34:9.

[16] The decalogue refers to three or four generations. It is therefore most interesting to observe that while 2 Kings 10:30 refers (Jehu is

the composer of the decalogue attributes to God the ultimate source of such persistent iniquity.[17] That God is the author of evil is, however, so pervasive an idea in biblical literature that we need not dwell on it. Suffice it to say that it is the way biblical writers express the ultimately unfathomable. Insofar as later biblical writers, and Judaism and Christianity, introduced—and it is no advance—the figure of Satan, they are expressing the same idea.[18]

The comment about Yahweh's mercy to thousands who love him and keep his commandments refers to those Levites who were loyal to Yahweh in the incident of the calf. In that they slaughtered some three thousand malefactors, each Levite "slaying every man his brother, and every man his companion, and every man his neighbour," thousands of Levites must have demonstrated their loyalty.

III Thou shalt not take the name of Yahweh thy God in vain; for Yahweh will not hold him guiltless that taketh his name in vain. (Exod 20:7; Deut 5:11)

The first part of the decalogue in Exodus 20 and Deuteronomy 5 is an accurate and detailed response to the

---

being addressed) to sons of the fourth generation, 2 Kings 13:2 (Jehoahaz), 14:24 (Jeroboam), and 15:9 (Zachariah) encompass in fact three generations of Jehu's sons.

[17] Cp. Isa 63:17, "O Yahweh, why hast thou made us to err from thy ways, and hardened our hearts from thy fear."

[18] "While superior power was to the Greeks always a characteristic of the gods in relation to men, superior goodness was attributed to them only at a later stage and as an article of faith, often running counter to what seemed to be the facts of daily experience"; J. W. Jones, *Law and Legal Theory of the Greeks* (Oxford: Clarendon, 1956), 248.

issues explicitly or implicitly raised by Yahweh's reaction to the construction of the calf. Another example of this detailed response is the formulation of the prohibition against the utterance of Yahweh's name in vain. After Aaron had built an altar before the calf he made a proclamation that the next day would be a feast to Yahweh. He meant the calf, Yahweh. Aaron's proclamation is what prompts the prohibition against lifting up, by way of proclamation (*naśaʾ*), Yahweh's name for a vain purpose, using it for something not real (*laššawʾ*), namely, a calf as a god.[19]

The comment in the decalogue that "Yahweh will not hold him guiltless that taketh his name in vain" is a response to Aaron himself. In Exod 32:21 Moses brought up the issue of Aaron's guilt: "What did this people unto thee, that thou has brought so great a sin upon them?" The narrative does not pursue the matter further. In the account of the incident in Deut 9:20 it is, significantly, Yahweh himself who recognizes Aaron's guilt: "And Yahweh was very angry with Aaron to have destroyed him: and I [Moses] prayed for Aaron also the same time."[20]

[19] Cp. Deut 32:21, "They have moved me to jealousy with that which is not God; they have provoked me to anger with their vanities" (*hᵃbalim*). In Ps 31:6 trust in Yahweh is contrasted with vain idols (*hable-šawʾ*); cp. Jer 6:29, 18:15. W. E. Staples, "The Third Commandment," *JBL* 58 (1939), 325–29, interprets the sense of *šawʾ* in terms of idol worship. He translates, "Thou shalt not give the name of Yahweh (thy God) to an idol." The conventional view that interprets this prohibition as condemning the use of God's name in a false oath does not do justice to the language of the prohibition, as B. S. Childs points out in *The Book of Exodus: A Critical, Theological Commentary* (Philadelphia: Westminster, 1974), 410–11. For an analysis of what it might mean to believe that divinity can be ascribed to an object, see Avishai Margalit, "Animism Animated," *S'vara* 1 (1990), 41–49.

[20] The pervasive Deuteronomic language of the decalogue (cited

The Origins of Biblical Law

Clearly, Yahweh did not hold Aaron guiltless for his role
in the incident. (Aaron died because of his offense at Mer-
ibah [Num 20:24].) In Exod 34:6, 7 the same sentiment is
expressed precisely in regard to the sin of the calf and,
equally interesting, in a statement in which Yahweh pro-
claims his name: "And Yahweh passed by before him
[Moses] and proclaimed, Yahweh, Yahweh God . . . for-
giving iniquity and transgression and sin [Aaron's, for ex-
ample], and that will by no means clear the guilty."[21]

> IV 8 Remember the sabbath day, to keep it holy. 9
> Six days shalt thou labour, and do all thy work: 10 but
> the seventh day is the sabbath of Yahweh thy God: in it
> thou shalt not do any work, thou, nor thy son, nor thy
> daughter, thy manservant, nor thy maidservant, nor
> thy cattle, nor thy sojourner that is within thy gates: 11
> For in six days Yahweh made heaven and earth, the sea,
> and all that in them is, and rested the seventh day:
> wherefore Yahweh blessed the sabbath day, and hal-
> lowed it. (Exod 20:8–11)

> 12 Keep the sabbath day to sanctify it, as Yahweh thy
> God hath commanded thee. 13 Six days thou shalt la-
> bour, and do all thy work: 14 But the seventh day is the
> sabbath . . . that thy manservant and thy maidservant

---

by S. R. Driver in *The Book of Exodus*, CBSC [Cambridge: Cambridge University Press, 1911], xviii) points to its origin in Deuteronomic circles.

[21] The use of the infinitive absolute *naqqeh* may well be intended
to emphasize that Aaron's sin, although forgiven, was not regarded
lightly. For a Rabbinic attempt to absolve him of blame, see *Babylonian Sanhedrin* 7a.

may rest as well as thou. 15 And remember that thou
wast a servant in the land of Egypt, and that Yahweh
thy God brought thee out thence through a mighty
hand and by a stretched out arm: therefore Yahweh thy
God commanded thee to keep the sabbath day. (Deut
5:12–15)

Aaron set aside a special day to honor the calf Yahweh.
His proclamation elicits from the lawgiver the formulation of the pronouncement to remember the sabbath day
in honor of the Yahweh who created the world.[22] The
lawgiver is so motivated because he has to counter the
notion implied in the construction of the golden calf,
namely, that humankind can create god.[23] The emphasis
of the commandment is not solely on the sabbath day—
after all there is no suggestion that Aaron's special day
was a sabbath—but also on the uses of a special day to
honor the real god Yahweh as against an idol. The
prophet Hosea's comment about the calf's construction is
"The workman made it: therefore it is not God" (Hos
8:6). Jer 51:15–18 contrasts the emptiness of idols with
Yahweh's powers as creator. The topic of who creates
what and whom is sharply raised by Aaron's workman-

[22] For texts that link the sabbath day to festive activity and hence
provide us with an additional reason why the evocation of the sabbath day was the appropriate response to Aaron's festive day, note
Hos 2:11; Isa 1:13, 58:13. Roland de Vaux goes so far as to claim
that these texts present the sabbath as a joyful feast day; *Ancient
Israel: Its Life and Institutions* (London: Darton, Longman, Todd,
1961), 482.

[23] The initial, similarly positive, pronouncement of the decalogue, "I am Yahweh thy God which have brought thee out of the
land of Egypt," is the same type of counterresponse to a comparable aspect of the narrative.

ship. We shall find that from this point on, reflections on aspects of creation determine the decalogue's content and sequence.

In the Deuteronomic version of the decalogue the pronouncement about the sabbath incorporates the idea of Yahweh as the agent responsible for bringing the people of Israel out of Egypt. This major difference from the Exodus version is readily accounted for. Not only was Aaron having the Israelites celebrate what was in effect a man-made god, but the specific purpose of the celebration was to acknowledge the calf as the agent responsible for bringing them out of Egypt. This notion had to be opposed.

The link between the sabbath command and the narrative of the exodus requires further elucidation. The intent of the command is a rest from work. This fundamental aspect has its parallel in a development in Egypt. When the Israelites requested to go on a pilgrimage to the wilderness in celebration of their god, the pharaoh interpreted the request as a desire to rest (šabat) from work (Exod 5:5). He consequently chose to increase their tasks. The lawgiver, opposing such an attitude, recognizes the need for a rest from labor in Israelite working life, a need served by the institution of the sabbath.

When the Israelites eventually left Egypt they never in fact held a festivity in honor of their god, Yahweh. What is most interesting to observe, however, is that Aaron's festive occasion involving the golden calf constituted something of a parallel to that much-anticipated event in the wilderness. In sum, the Israelites' pilgrimage (ḥag) to honor their god, Yahweh—which, as the pharaoh rightly saw, would have constituted a rest from their work—eventually occurred in a corrupt form when Aaron proclaimed a feast (*ḥag*) in the wilderness. The sabbath command in the decalogue has to be read against this background of the exodus story and its aftermath.

V   Honour thy father and thy mother: that thy days may be long upon the land which Yahweh thy God giveth thee. (Exod 20:12; cp. Deut 5:16)

The issue of apostasy dominates the first part of the decalogue. Apostasy is fundamentally an intellectual concern about right ways of thinking and about the nature and limits of human aspiration and creativity. If the judgment of both the narrator of the golden calf story and the like-minded author of the decalogue is that human beings cannot create gods, the question remains whether there is any sense in which human beings approach the level of creativity attributed to a god who creates the world and all forms of life. The answer is only in regard to their participation in procreation, in the generation of new life. The story that addresses itself to this topic is the creation myth about Adam and Eve, the first parents, who with the help of Yahweh produced the first children, the brothers Cain and Abel. The reason there are two tablets of the decalogue is that judgments are formulated first from a scrutiny of the story of the golden calf, and then from the story of Adam and Eve, Cain and Abel.

The commandment to honor a father and mother has as its justification, we can infer, the fact that it is they who have created, in this instance, a son (it is a son who is addressed in the decalogue). The lawgiver has in focus the first son ever, Cain. It was he, moreover, not Moses's brother Aaron, who was the first being ever directly to offend against creation. He destroyed what God and his parents created, namely, his brother Abel. In a quite fundamental sense, because of the notion that what one creates redounds to one's honor, Cain dishonored his father and his mother.[24] Just as the brothers had sought to give vegetables and animal offerings by way of honoring the god who had created all forms of life, so honor is due to parents who had given them life.[25] It is worth pointing out that the first action of the deity after his completion of creation—whether it be his work on six days with a rest on the seventh or his interaction with Adam and Eve—is his participation in human procreation (Gen 4:1). The name Cain (*qanah*) is intended to indicate this participation. Cain's punishment was that as a tiller of the ground he was no longer able to live on the land ("ground" in Hebrew) that God had given to him. The totally puzzling reference in the decalogue, that one should honor a father and a mother so that one should live long upon the land (ground) that God has given, becomes immediately intelligible once we realize that the focus is on Cain's misdeed.

VI   Thou shalt not murder. (Exod 20:13; Deut 5:17)

What also becomes intelligible once we keep the focus on Cain is the solution to a puzzle seen before New Testament times, namely, why does a rule about murder follow immediately after a rule about honor to parents? The

[24] In Isa 43:7 we have the idea expressed that Yahweh creates someone for his honor.
[25] Texts such as Isa 43:23 and 1 Sam 29:30 bring out well the notion of honoring God with sacrifices.

answer lies in Cain's history. The answer is not simply that he committed the first murder, but even more important because of the process of rule making we are observing, that God himself put a mark on Cain to ensure that he was not murdered when he became a fugitive and wanderer upon the earth. From this action the lawgiver infers that Yahweh is opposed to unregulated killing. It is not that Cain himself was in turn murdered. The deity's anticipation of the future problem of violence among human beings allowed the lawgiver to make explicit the deity's implicit rule against murder. In regard to the preceding rule about honor to parents there was likewise no explicit indication in the Adam and Eve story that honor was due to them because they had procreated.

VII Thou shalt not commit adultery. (Exod 20:14; Deut 5:18)

The prohibition against adultery that follows the prohibition against murder is a rule that the lawgiver derives, not from any offense as such by Cain, but from the fact that Cain was the first person ever to be married in the sense that was ordained at the creation of his parents. When they were created the future institution of marriage was anticipated. Because the first man and woman were originally one flesh their unity symbolizes the marital state. So too a son of every future generation, when he marries, leaves his father and his mother and cleaves to a wife, becoming one flesh with her. Implicit in this description of marital union, as later Rabbinical interpreters also saw, was that it should not be violated.[26]

Cain had offended against his parents' procreative act

---

[26] *Babylonian Sanhedrin* 58a.

that had produced Abel. It was consequently an understandable step for the lawgiver to contemplate a violation of the marital bond itself. We can observe with some precision the way the decalogue's author works with the Genesis story. The birth of Cain is introduced with the words, "And Adam knew Eve his wife." These words are a prelude to Cain's offense against his brother, his punishment, and God's protection of him from being murdered himself. The Genesis narrator, consistent with so much of biblical narrative, next switches to the history of Cain's own generation, namely, the birth of his son, Enoch. That account is itself introduced with the words, "And Cain knew his wife."

In contemplating Cain's procreative act, the decalogue's author must have noted what we immediately note: how could Cain have known his wife when there was none for him to know? Like the Genesis author, the lawgiver would not have been caught up in the apparent absurdity of Cain's marriage. (These authors were living exponents, not of historical narrative as we have come to know it, but of etiological myth, a sophisticated attempt to account for current reality by inventing a mythical past.) Focus on Cain's procreative act leads not to questions about who his wife was and where she came from, but to thoughts on the nature of male-female union. The idea of Cain's marriage has to be linked back to God's creation of the first human beings and the institution of marriage, which, it might be noted, focuses on a son's leaving his father and mother to marry. Cain was the first such son, not Adam. The decalogue's author in particular, having in mind from the Adam and Eve story the etiological myth about marriage, and presupposing the institution of marriage, could turn his attention to the offense against that institution, namely, adultery.

It is worth pointing out that we could not have expected, instead of a prohibition against adultery, an injunction that a man should marry. Such an injunction
comes into focus only in a much later (the Tannaitic) period of Jewish life in the context of the duty to procreate.
Ben Azzai (in the first third of the second century A.D.)
stated that he preferred to remain unmarried in order to
devote all his time to the study of the Torah. As David
Daube points out, he could not have spoken this way
about matrimony if there had been a binding duty to produce children.[27]

What invites particular attention in the Genesis description of marriage is the language about a man's cleaving to
his wife and their becoming one flesh. Both in Rabbinic
and New Testament literature the statement was understood to point to the notion that the first man, Adam,
was an androgynous being, male and female in one.
When a man married he again exemplified the state of
androgyny characteristic of the original order of creation.[28]
While this interpretation of the verse reflects views current around the beginnings of the Christian era, we are
not off base in seeing some such notion in the biblical
period itself. The reference to one flesh is not just a metaphor for sexual union but appears to be related back to
the notion of Eve's origin from Adam's body, and consequently to the original male-female oneness that was
Adam. Viewed in this light, marriage was a reflection of

[27] David Daube, *The New Testament and Rabbinic Judaism* (London: Athlone, 1956), 78. For Daube's fuller discussion of when the
duty to procreate came into Judaism and Christianity, and of the
misunderstanding of the blessing (not the duty) "Be fruitful and
multiply" (Gen 1:28), see *The Duty of Procreation* (Edinburgh: Edinburgh University Press, 1977).

[28] See Daube, *The New Testament and Rabbinic Judaism*, 71–86.

41

the created order; adultery, like the killing of someone's offspring, would be seen as an offense against that order.

VIII   Thou shalt not steal. (Exod 20:15; Deut 5:19)

The Adam and Eve story proceeds from the description of marriage to its chief concern, namely, to explain how the origin of shame is bound up with the awareness of the distinction between the sexes. God does not wish Adam and Eve to acquire this profound awareness, but he is, fortunately from the point of view of the ancient author, but not of later Judaism and Christianity, unsuccessful.[29] Having commanded that the fruit of the tree of the knowledge of good and evil should not be consumed, he finds that first Eve and then Adam take of it. It is the first act of stealing, a wrongful taking of something openly declared to be denied to them. The lawgiver infers from the incident that a prohibition against stealing went back to the very beginning of things.[30]

IX   Thou shalt not bear false witness against thy neighbour. (Exod 20:16; cp. Deut 5:20)

[29] See C. M. Carmichael, "The Paradise Myth: Interpreting without Jewish and Christian Spectacles," in *The Garden of Eden*, ed. Deborah Sawyer and Paul Morris (Sheffield: Academic Press, 1992).

[30] The reason why the prohibition against stealing follows the prohibition against adultery is not, as is commonly claimed, because adultery is a form of stealing. Adultery is hardly theft of a woman, because she participates willingly. The sequence is owing to the fact that in the Adam and Eve story reflection on the nature of sexual union as involving nakedness without shame is followed by an account of how the male and the female acquired a sense of shame. The theft of the fruit is the key development.

When God learned from their awareness of nakedness that they had eaten the forbidden fruit, he questioned them in the manner of a judge cross-examining an accused person. Adam was questioned first, and he tried to lay the blame on Eve. She, in turn, tried to evade the responsibility by placing it on the serpent. The decalogue (in the version in Deut 5:20) next has the rule "Thou shalt not respond as a misleading witness in regard to thy neighbour." The quasi-legal tenor of God's interrogation of Adam and Eve explains why this pronouncement is not a blanket condemnation of lying but instead betrays a legal bias.[31] The bias is oriented precisely to the specific events that occurred at this point in the garden.

X   Thou shalt not covet thy neighbour's house, thou shalt not covet thy neighbour's wife, nor his manservant, nor his maidservant, nor his ox, nor his ass, nor any thing that is thy neighbour's. (Exod 20:17; cp. Deut 5:21)

The climax to the Adam and Eve story is God's successful attempt to ensure that what happened with the tree of the knowledge of good and evil would not happen with the tree of life. It was understood that Adam and Eve would find the tree of life similarly desirable, something to be coveted—the two terms "to desire" and "to covet" are used to describe their desires for the fruit of the tree of the knowledge of good and evil. That fruit had

---

[31] This observation runs counter to a common view that claims a general character for each item of the decalogue. G. Henton Davies, e.g., states, "The brief but basic stipulations are so comprehensive . . ."; *Exodus*, TBC (London: Student Christian Movement, 1967), 168.

not only been coveted, it had also been appropriated. With regard to the tree of life God was able to prevent its appropriation by expelling the couple from the garden and, consequently, causing them to live the life known to all future human beings.

Note that God could not prevent their coveting the life of the gods, represented by the tree of life, only its appropriation. To be sure, the life in question was of a kind known only to the gods. It is understood, however, that the coveting of life in a form similarly enviable would be a feature of future human life (cp. Prov 13:12, "Hope deferred maketh the heart sick, But desire fulfilled is a tree of life"). Indeed, there may be the notion that the problem of desire and envy is linked to the failure to attain unending life. The very first development after Adam and Eve's expulsion from the garden was the problem of desire confronting Cain ("And unto thee shall be his [sin's] desire," Gen 4:7) when his brother's offering to God proved to be preferable to his. Even before the expulsion from the garden, God had sought to minimize the future problem of wrongful sexual desire by putting clothes on the first human couple.

The author of the decalogue derives from the climax of the Adam and Eve story his final rule against coveting. He cannot prohibit coveting life in the sense of the unending life of the gods. He has to focus on notions of enhanced life that prevail among mortals. But even these notions can be related to the substance of the Adam and Eve story. Adam's future was to be a life of hardship in obtaining food from the ground, in contrast to the ready abundance of food in the garden. Unable to return to the garden, he would be confronted with those whose living conditions might be preferable to his: enviable houses, fields, servants, and work animals. Wrongful sexual desire would also be a problem as God had anticipated when he clothed the first couple. There is consequently a prohibition against coveting someone else's wife, as well as against coveting another's house, field, servant, and work animals.[32]

The Genesis (1:1–2:3) Creation Story and the Sabbath Command

A marked feature of the *Mishpatim*, the book of Deuteronomy, and the decalogues is that if a rule contains an explicit reference to a historical period, only an event in the lifetime of Moses is cited. There is one apparent exception. In the sabbath command in Exod 20:8–11 the "event" of the world's creation is invoked to justify why the sabbath should be observed. Is this link between the rule and the creation story in Genesis 1 on a par with the kind of link that is claimed for all the other rules? I think not. In other words, the formulation of the sabbath command in Exod 20:8–11 is not prompted by some aspect (God's rest on the seventh day) of the creation story. Rather, both the rule itself, as its Deuteronomic version reveals, *and* the story of creation in Genesis 1 are re-

---

[32] The common view that the emphasis on the deity in the first part of the decalogue distinguishes it from the second part is without warrant. The deity's action prompts the formulation of each of the statements in the second tablet: (1) Yahweh's involvement with Eve in creating Cain (whose name *qanah* supposedly indicates this involvement) and Abel: honor to parents; (2) Yahweh's protective mark on Cain: murder; (3) Yahweh's creation of the male and the female: adultery; (4) Yahweh's prohibiting the fruit: stealing; (5) Yahweh's cross-examination of Adam and Eve: false witness; and (6) Yahweh's denial of the tree of life: coveting.

sponses to Aaron's special day in celebration of the golden calf (Exod 32:5). How then do we account for the link between the sabbath command and the creation of the world, and how do we explain why this particular link is different from the typical Deuteronomic way of setting out rules? The answer lies in the role of the Priestly writer (P).

In Exodus 32 the calf is affirmed as the divine power that brought the Israelites out of Egypt (vv. 4, 8). Objection to the notion that a human being can create a god is not explicitly raised, even though the actions of Aaron and his followers are judged negatively in the story. That such an objection did at some point in time attain overt expression is illustrated in Hos 8:6, "The workman made it: therefore it [the golden calf] is not god," and in Ps 106:20, "They made a calf in Horeb, and worshipped the molten image. Thus they changed their glory into the similitude of an ox that eateth grass." The formulation of the sabbath commandment in Exod 20:8–11 represents the same kind of condemnatory reaction to the incident of the golden calf. Its formulation, representing as it does a modification of the Deuteronomic version of the sabbath command, is owing to the Priestly writer.

While the Deuteronomic version concentrates on affirming that Yahweh, not the calf, brought the Israelites out of Egypt, the Exodus version concentrates on the Yahweh who created the world. It might be suggested that at the same time as the Priestly writer reformulated the command, he composed the story of creation in Genesis 1 in reaction to the incident of the golden calf. Moreover, he also placed his account of creation before the other (JE) story of creation about Adam and Eve, because, in line with the opposition to the ideas that underlay the creation of the calf, he noted that the story of Adam and Eve recognized the same problem of human aspiration to godlike capacity.

If we assume this view of the various texts in question, one in line with the JEDP hypothesis, we can make better sense of some long-standing puzzles. First, the two stories of creation are not reconcilable, and on the above view we can comprehend why. While on the one hand the Adam and Eve story could be used to uncover the deity's rules about the future governance of human conduct, on the other hand it needed a counterweight story to emphasize the transcendent character of the deity in relation to humankind. The tension between the two stories contains a contrast that permits each story to communicate different matters. The first story is, if only secondarily, composed by way of undoing problems that arise in the second because in it the deity's involvement with Adam and Eve inevitably introduced an undesirable anthropomorphic character to the deity's role. The problem with such anthropomorphizing is precisely that human beings create gods according to their own conceptions, and this tendency is but a short step from the creation of physical images representative of divinity.

Second, the original (Deuteronomic) decalogue is a composition inspired by the lawgiver's reaction to, initially, the story of the calf and then to the story of Adam and Eve. The puzzling sequence of the two stories of creation can be explained by the fact that the first is itself primarily a reaction to the incident of the calf. It was set down alongside the story of Adam and Eve, but given priority of position, and the result was a thematic sequence parallel to the one found in the decalogue. There is, for example, the obvious contrast between the condemnation in the first part of the decalogue of the creation of anything that resembles what is "in heaven above, or that is in the earth beneath, or that is in the water under the earth" (Exod 20:4), and the affirmation in the first story of creation that God created the heaven, the earth, and the seas (Gen 1:1–10). There is the contrast too between the condemnation of the human use of the divine name, again in the decalogue's first tablet, for something judged to be unreal (Exod 20:7), and the affirmation in the first story of creation that God named the various entities that he had created and that were manifestly real. Again too, the first part of the decalogue and the first story of creation share a focus on the sabbath.

Third, we can understand why the climax to the Priestly account of creation is God's sabbath. It is the climax because the setting aside of a special day to honor a man-made god is precisely what prompts the need for a true account of who creates whom and what. In a way, the day of celebration for the golden calf constituted a climax on that occasion as the goal of the exodus from Egypt (Exod 32:5, 6), in line with the pharaoh's fear that the Israelites would let up on their labors in order to honor their god in the wilderness (Exod 5:5).

Fourth, another puzzling feature of the Priestly creation story is its assumption of a plurality of gods: "And God said, Let us make man in our image, after our likeness" (Gen 1:26). Conceivably, the resort to a plural designation is a counter-assertion to the gods that were proclaimed by the people to be the ones who exercised divine power in bringing Israel out of Egypt (Exod 32:4, 8; 1 Kings 12:28). In Gen 1:26 the gods make man after the likeness (dᵉmuth) of them. The prophet Isaiah, in an attack on the making of the kind of image that Aaron had fashioned, states, "To whom then will ye liken God? or what likeness [*d*ᵉ*muth*] will ye compare unto him?" He then describes the making of a graven image and discounts its significance by invoking the perspective of all creation and its Creator (Isa 40:18–31). This perspective and this contrast are, I am suggesting, what determine the presentation of the Priestly account of creation. An anti-idolatrous bias in this account has been detected in the omission of the specific names for the sun and the moon in Gen 1:16, because of the worship of these named entities in foreign religions.[33]

Fifth, contrary to what I have argued elsewhere,[34] the reason there are ten pronouncements of the decalogue (Exod 34:28; Deut 4:13, 10:4) is not that this feature is a deliberate parallel to the ten pronouncements of God at the creation of the world. It is the other way around. A characteristic of the Priestly writer is his interest in numbers and schemes of numbers, for example, the enumeration of the seven days of creation in Gen 1:1–2:3. It was he who took stock of the fact that the decalogue had ten pronouncements. When composing his account of creation he took over the feature of a pronouncement by God and sought to parallel the fact that there were ten such. After all, we might have expected him to have had seven pronouncements of creation, because of the scheme of the seven days of creation.

The view that there were ten pronouncements at creation is found as early as *Pirqe Aboth* 5:1, "By ten sayings

---

[33] So Gerhard von Rad, *Genesis* (Philadelphia: Westminster, 1972), 53, 54; Robert Davidson, *Genesis 1–11*, CBC (Cambridge: Cambridge University Press, 1973), 21.

[34] Carmichael, *Law and Narrative*, 337–38.

was the world created." The observation is presumably derived from the use ten times of "And God said," for example, "Let there be light." That the tenfold use of "And God said" in Genesis 1 is a borrowing from the decalogue, and not the other way around, might be indicated by the fact that no internal or external feature of the decalogue suggests why there should be ten pronouncements. There just happen to be ten. It was the Priestly writer who chose to make something of the fact that there were ten pronouncements of the decalogue by duplicating this number in the attribution of ten words of creation to God.

It may be interesting to note that in regard to the creatures of sea and air in Gen 1:22 ("And God blessed them, saying, Be fruitful, and multiply"), we might have expected the formula to be used as it is in regard to human beings in Gen 1:28 ("And God blessed them, and God said unto them, Be fruitful, and multiply"). The reason for the avoidance of the formula "And God said" in Gen 1:22 is, it might be suggested, that the Priestly writer wanted to have ten sayings, not eleven, to correspond to the ten sayings of the decalogue.[35]

---

[35] Curiously, there is no corresponding blessing to be fruitful and to multiply for the land animals. No doubt it has to be inferred. Its omission means that no attention is focused on their capacity to reproduce. It is probably unlikely, however, that the intention was to downplay the land animals because so much power was ascribed to the replica of one (the golden calf) in Israelite religion. Unlike the Adam and Eve story in which man is formed from the ground before the animals (Gen 2:7, 19), the Priestly account of creation has the animals created before man. It follows that the idea that a man could create god in the form of an animal is all the more impossible in that living animals were created before he was. In

The Decalogue of Exod 34:10–26

Sources (Exodus 32; 1 Kings 12:25–33). The worship of
the golden calves began in Aaron's time and extended
through the period of the monarchy. In this latter period the main development occurred in the reign of
King Jeroboam, who set up the calves in the sanctuaries
at Bethel and Dan in order to have the people worship
these gods as the ones who brought the people of Israel
out of Egypt. His political aim, overriding his religious
one, was to encourage people to worship Yahweh at
these sanctuaries rather than at the temple of Jerusalem
where King Rehoboam had his political base.

The first tablet of the decalogue in Exodus 20 (and
Deuteronomy 5) anticipated the problems that would
arise with the worship of the calf in Exodus 32. The decalogue in Exodus 34 is spoken in the aftermath of this idolatry. Its contents are again determined by the incident,[36]
but also, as in the decalogue in Exodus 20 and, indeed, in
the write-up of this incident itself (Exod 32:34), by the
anticipation of similar problems in the future, particularly
the worship of the calves in the reign of King Jeroboam.

---

other words, we should not view, as is common, the creation of
humankind as the climax of creation—hardly convincing because
the sabbath patently enjoys this distinction—but view man's creation by God in light of the author's intention to downplay man's
creative abilities as compared to the deity's.

[36] For a parallel to such a dual response to a single incident, we
might recall how frequently and sometimes on a large scale—for
example, Chronicles and the books of Samuel and Kings—different
biblical narratives take up the same incident. The feature constitutes
a major characteristic of the construction of the laws in both Deuteronomy and the *Mishpatim.*

The narrative in which the decalogue in Exodus 34 is embedded is almost entirely taken up with the event of the calf. Moses makes two new tablets and ascends Mount Sinai. Yahweh appears and "proclaimed the name of Yahweh" (Exod 34:5). This concern with the name is much emphasized: "And Yahweh passed by before him [Moses] and proclaimed, Yahweh, Yahweh God" (Exod 34:6). The concern is to be related back to the distorted understanding of the name Yahweh when Aaron associated it with the calf.[37] The proclamation proceeds to refer to Yahweh's mercy to thousands, his awareness of those guilty of iniquity, and his visitation of the iniquity of the fathers upon the sons to the third and fourth generation. These references hark back to the incident of the calf but they also anticipate further, comparable Israelite idolatry.

I Behold, I make a covenant: before all thy people I will do marvels, such as have not been done in all the earth, nor in any nation: and all the people among which thou art shall see the work of Yahweh: for it is a terrible thing that I will do with thee. (Exod 34:10)

[37] The meaning of the name Yahweh, "I am that I am," or some other comparable sense of the verb "to be," refers to something that cannot be defined. It is surely interesting, in light of the pervasive influence of the story of the calf, that the meaning of the name stands in sharp contrast to the specific identification of Yahweh with a calf. The possibility presents itself that the name was indeed coined to oppose the perceived idolatry bound up in the creation of the calf. For the linguistic form *yahweh* as a causative, "He causes to be," see W. F. Albright, *From the Stone Age to Christianity* (Baltimore: Johns Hopkins University Press, 1940), 197–99.

The first statement of the decalogue in Exodus 20 was Yahweh's claim that it was he who brought Israel out of Egypt. What prompted this assertion was the people's claim about the significance they attached to the calf. The evidence that this deliverance was the triumph of the imageless Yahweh, and not the Yahweh associated with the calf, is seen to lie in the signs and wonders that occurred in Egypt (Exod 32:11; Deut 4:34, 6:21–23, 7:18, 19).[38] The opening statement of the decalogue in Exodus 20 could be expanded to "I am Yahweh thy God which have brought thee out of the land of Egypt by my signs and wonders, with great power and a mighty hand." In Jer 16:21, to know such a hand and such might is to know that the name is Yahweh. The contrast is with those gods made by a man (v. 20).

Similarly embodying a historical reference, the opening statement of the decalogue in Exodus 34 is analogous to the one in Exodus 20. It refers to a comparable time of signs and wonders to be performed by Yahweh during the conquest of the land, the next stage after the deliverance from Egypt. The term *nipla'ot*, in reference to the wonderful acts of Yahweh, was also used to describe the marvels performed in Egypt (Exod 3:20; cp. too Ps

---

[38] The Deuteronomic references to the signs and wonders are in their context intended to contrast Yahweh with other gods, including the first of these in Israelite experience, the graven image of the calf (Deut 4:23). Critics view Exod 34:11–16 as Deuteronomic. See Martin Noth, *Exodus* (Philadelphia: Westminster, 1962), 262; B. S. Childs, *Exodus*, 608, 613. In my view all three decalogues (Exodus 20 and 34 and Deuteronomy 5) are Deuteronomic constructions, except that there is evidence of a Priestly redaction (P) for the one in Exodus 20.

106:22, where both *nipla'ot* and *nora'ot* are used as in Exod 34:10). The assertion that the people will see the work of Yahweh may be intended to oppose the people's desire to view Yahweh himself in tangible form. As in Exod 20:2, Yahweh speaks in the first person. Moreover, his commitment to rid Israel of certain enemies and take Israel as his inheritance (Exod 34:9) is the equivalent of his defeat of the Egyptians and his protection of Israel as his first-born son.

> II 11 Observe thou that which I command thee this day: behold, I drive out before thee the Amorite and the Canaanite, and the Hittite, and the Perizzite, and the Hivite, and the Jebusite. 12 Take heed to thyself, lest thou make a covenant with the inhabitants of the land whither thou goest, lest it be for a snare in the midst of thee: 13 But ye shall destroy their altars, break their images, and cut down their Asherim: 14 For thou shall worship no other god: for Yahweh whose name is Jealous is a jealous God: 15 Lest thou make a covenant with the inhabitants of the land and they go a whoring after their gods, and do sacrifice unto their gods, and one call thee, and thou eat of his sacrifice; 16 And thou take of their daughters unto thy sons, and their daughters go a whoring after their gods, and make thy sons go a whoring after their gods. (Exod 34:11–16)

The second statement of each decalogue is a prohibition against the worship of other gods: in Exod 20:3–6, against gods acknowledged in the incident of the calf; in Exod 34:11–16, against the gods of the lands to be conquered. While each prohibition is focused on a different period of time,[39] the same point about Yahweh's jealousy is made.[40] Both also acknowledge how idolatry is passed from one generation to the next, from fathers to sons.[41] Each also contains references to god(s) in both the plural and singular numbers.

III Thou shalt make thee no molten gods. (Exod 34:17)

The third statement of the decalogue is obviously similar to the rule against making a graven image of any kind (Exod 20:4). This latter rule is part of the second statement of the decalogue in Exodus 20, because it is intimately related to the prohibition against the gods identified by the people when the calf was constructed. In Exodus 34 the specific prohibition against molten gods is separate from its preceding injunction against the gods of other cultures, because the molten gods represent an internal Israelite development, not one under foreign influ-

[39] The listing of nations in Exod 34:11 is in the same order as in 1 Kings 9:20 except the latter omits the Canaanites.
[40] Umberto Cassuto, *A Commentary on the Book of Exodus* (Jerusalem: Magnes, 1967), 444, argues that this reference is a deliberate echo of the phrasing of the decalogue in Exod 20:5. B. S. Childs, *Exodus*, 613, views the language in general as a reminder of the episode of the calf: "not worship, nor sacrifice, nor eat, nor play the harlot (cf 32.6ff.)." R. W. L. Moberly suggests that the unique use of the singular, "another god," is a reference back to the specific sin of the calf; *At the Mountain*, 97. If this observation is accurate, we have the characteristic interest in what recurs in succeeding generations.
[41] The female contribution to idolatry in Exod 34:16 has its counterpart in the donation of jewelry by wives and daughters in Exod 32:2.

The Origins of Biblical Law

ence.[42] The lawgiver in Exodus 34 has in mind not so much Aaron's single molten calf,[43] but, in keeping with the future orientation of the preceding utterances, the Israelite use of molten calves in the period of the monarchy (for example, 1 Kings 14:9, "For thou [Jeroboam] hast gone and made thee other gods, and molten images"; cp. 2 Kings 17:16).[44]

IV   The feast of unleavened bread shalt thou keep. Seven days thou shalt eat unleavened bread, as I commanded thee, at the time appointed in the month Abib: for in the month of Abib thou camest out from Egypt. (Exod 34:18)

The sequence of statements in both decalogues is tied to the sequence of events concerning the calf in Exodus 32, or to later developments in Israelite history that are perceived to parallel what took place in Exodus 32. After

[42] Martin Noth, *Exodus*, 263, makes the same point.
[43] Other scholars have readily linked this prohibition to the story of the calf, for example, H. Kosmala, "The So-Called Ritual Decalogue," *ASTI* (1962), 33; R. W. L. Moberly, *At the Mountain*, 133–35. Only the latter, however, takes seriously the implications of such a link. Indeed, in many ways, his thesis is the one I am arguing for. He comments on how little discussion there has been about the close relation of Exod 34:11–26 to its narrative context. My approach differs from his in that, because I work with a theory about an integral link between law and legend, I claim a more fundamental and detailed link between the two than he sets out.
[44] G. H. Jones states, in reference to the words "other gods," "This typical deuteronomic phrase refers to the golden calves of [1 Kings] 12:28–30, and to the molten images that were made of them"; *1 and 2 Kings*, vol. 1, NCBC (Grand Rapids: Eerdmans, 1984), 272.

Aaron made the golden calf he declared the following day
to be a feast to Yahweh. Jeroboam proceeded similarly in
his time to institute a special feast (1 Kings 12:32). Such a
climactic occasion inevitably invites attention and consequently, because it was a wrongful development, requires
a correspondingly significant response. Indeed, as we
shall see, this response dominates the decalogue in Exodus 34.

There is no corresponding prohibition in Exodus 34 to
Exod 20:7 against using Yahweh's name in vain. The latter prohibition was prompted by Aaron's declaration that
there would be a feast to Yahweh, that is, to the bull calf.
What is most interesting, and may well account for the
lack of some comparable prohibition in the decalogue of
Exodus 34 (whose narrative context after all [vv. 5, 6]
contains an explicit concern about the name Yahweh), is
that in Jeroboam's special feast the reference is simply to a
feast for the people of Israel (1 Kings 12:33).

In the decalogue in Exodus 20, the injunction to remember the sabbath day (vv. 8–11), because Yahweh created the world in six days and rested on the seventh,
counters Aaron's special feast day for Yahweh. Likewise,
the injunction in Deut 5:12–15 to keep the sabbath, because the Israelites should recall Yahweh's rescue of them
from slavery in Egypt, counters the association the people
were making on their feast day between the calf and the
gods that rescued them from Egypt.[45] The compiler of the

[45] Note how in Exod 31:12–18 an injunction about the sabbath
follows immediately upon directions about worship at Yahweh's
altar. This same combination, I am claiming, is revealed in the
presentation of the rule about the sabbath because of the context of
Aaron's worship of the calf at his altar. I can think of no other

decalogue in Exodus 34 focuses initially not on Yahweh's special day as such, but equally to the point on an appropriate type of feast for Yahweh. In that Israel's future existence is anticipated, Jeroboam's wrongful feast may account for this focus. Although Jeroboam's institution is on a set day, the emphasis, if one can put it so strongly, is the reverse of Exodus 32—less on the day, more on the feast itself: "He ordained a feast unto the children of Israel" (1 Kings 12:33). At that feast the people presumably celebrated the calves as the gods that had brought them out of Egypt (1 Kings 12:28). The first of the feasts the lawgiver turns to is indeed one that is linked to the rescue from Egypt, namely, the feast of unleavened bread.

> V 19 All that openeth the womb is mine; and all thy cattle that is male, the firstlings of ox and sheep. 20 And the firstling of an ass thou shalt redeem with a lamb: and if thou wilt not redeem it, then thou shalt break its neck. All the firstborn of thy sons thou shalt redeem. And none shall appear before me empty. (Exod 34:19, 20)

---

inherent connection at this stage of development between the sabbath rest and the world of worship. Moshe Weinfeld, however, adds an important, larger dimension when he argues for a link, in the Mesopotamian world in general, between the divine sanctuary and notions of the divinity at rest. This perspective focuses on the gods. The biblical material's focus is on human conduct and is consequently only indirectly indicative of the ideas Weinfeld draws attention to. See "Sabbath, Temple, and the Enthronement of the Lord—The Problem of the Sitz im Leben of Genesis 1:1–2:3," *Festschrift Cazelles*, AOAT 33 (1981), 501–12. I am indebted to Moshe Greenberg, Hebrew University, Jerusalem, for drawing my attention to this article.

In reaction to Aaron's and Jeroboam's wrongful feasts, rules concerning other appropriate feasts are about to be set down, but a rule about firstlings and a rule about the sabbath, constituting the fifth and sixth statements respectively, intervene. From statement five to statement ten of this decalogue the focus will be on these feasts. The sabbath, strictly speaking, is not a feast day in the sense in which the others are, although Roland de Vaux claims that it is.[46] Like them, however, it is a day set apart. Moreover, this particular rule about the sabbath concerns the agricultural processes that lead to the presentation of offerings on the feast days proper. The festive character of the sabbath should be emphasized, as many texts illustrate, for example, Hos 2:11, "And I will put an end to all her mirth, her feasts, her new moons, her sabbaths, and all her appointed feasts" (cp. Isa 58:13).

The reasons for this decalogue's focus on festive occasions can be detected. First and foremost is the need to respond to Aaron's and, more to the point because of the future orientation of the rules, to Jeroboam's unacceptable institution which, it is important to note, incorporated a reference to the exodus from Egypt (1 Kings 12:28). At the same time it should be noted that the reason Yahweh brought the Israelites out of Egypt was to have them serve him at sacred feasts. Throughout the story of the exodus there is the recurring statement about how the Israelites are obliged to go and serve their god (Exod 3:18; 4:23; 5:1, 3; 8:1, 8, 20, 25–29; 9:1, 13; 10:3, 7–9, 24–26; 12:25, 26, 31).

If we assume a link between the various statements

---

[46] Roland de Vaux, *Ancient Israel: Its Life and Institutions* (London: Darton, Longman, Todd, 1961), 482.

about feasting and sacrificing and Aaron's and Jeroboam's feasts, we can infer what in particular the lawgiver finds objectionable in them. He objects to the idea that an inert, man-made object could be the source of life. His aim is to reinforce the view that it is Yahweh who is the source of all life. The implicitly negative assessment of the man-made god is comparable to the one expressed in Hos 8:6, "The workman made it [the calf of Samaria]: therefore it is not God," or in Ps 106:20: "They made a calf in Horeb, and worshipped the molten image. Thus they changed their glory into the similitude of an ox that eateth grass." This contrast between Yahweh's glory and Yahweh in the shape of an ox is precisely the one underlying the lawgiver's perspective. Yahweh's glory is what was experienced in Egypt, as a text in Num 14:22 brings out: "Because all these men which have seen my glory, and my miracles, which I did in Egypt and in the wilderness. . . ." The revelation of Yahweh's glory to Moses in Exod 33:18, 22, which was accompanied by the proclamation of his name (v. 19), affirms the divine Yahweh as against the calf Yahweh. By way of countering the false notion that a religious image can represent the kind of divine power that creates life, the remaining statements of the decalogue in Exodus 34 attribute to the imageless Yahweh the power to give, and take, life. It follows that, just as the topic of creation is central to the decalogue of Exodus 20 (and Deuteronomy 5), so it will dominate the remaining statements of the decalogue in Exodus 34.

The rule about Yahweh's claim to all that opens the womb follows the rule about the feast of unleavened bread on account of the reference in Exod 32:4 to that part of the exodus story about Israel's actual removal from Egypt (cp. Exod 13:11–16). The juxtaposition of

the two rules illustrates well how narrative history determines their formulation and placement. Unleavened
bread is a symbolic reminder that, on the last night of
Israel's stay in Egypt, Yahweh redeemed the life of the
Israelites at the time when he inflicted death upon the
Egyptian human and animal firstborn. Underlying both
this aspect of the exodus story and the law is the view
that Yahweh gives life, but that he also takes it away. A
concern with redemption is found also in both narrative
(God redeems his firstborn son, Israel) and law (a firstling
ass is to be redeemed with a lamb; a firstborn son is to be
redeemed).

The rule that a male firstborn animal issuing from the
womb belongs to Yahweh, because his creative power
contributes to its birth, serves also to devalue the meaning attributed to the artificial production of a bull calf.
The fact that the rule devotes attention first to animals
and then to human offspring may support this conten-
tion.

The final part of this fifth statement is that no (male)
Israelite should appear empty-handed before Yahweh.
This requirement also ties into the exodus story. When
the pharaoh relented and said that the Israelites could go
and serve their god, he stated that their flocks and herds
should remain behind. Moses countered that they had to
accompany them because offerings had to be given to
Yahweh their god (Exod 10:24–26).[47] It is some such
background issue that would explain an injunction that,
on the face of it, seems unnecessary.

The injunction is understandably set down alongside
the requirement about offering the male firstborn of ani-

---

[47] Whose firstborn son Israel was (Exod 4:22).

mals. Indeed its placement is all the more appropriate in that there appears, in the same context as Moses's discussion with the pharaoh about the people being required to offer something to Yahweh, the latter's decision to strike down the Egyptian firstborn (Exod 11:1).

Equally noteworthy is the issue that arose between the pharaoh and Moses about who among the Israelites could go and serve Yahweh. Pharaoh had wanted the adult males only to participate in the religious rites (Exod 10:11). The lawgiver Moses affirms in his rule at this point (Exod 34:20), and more explicitly in v. 23, that this restriction, unacceptable to him in the context of his dealings with the pharaoh in Egypt, is nonetheless in order for the Israelites in their own land. Conceivably, the restriction may also owe something to the fact that none such was observed on the occasion of the feast for the golden calf (Exod 32:6).

VI Six days thou shalt work, but on the seventh day thou shalt rest: in plowing time and in harvest thou shalt rest. (Exod 34:21)

Preceding a pronouncement about the two other feasts to Yahweh is the sixth declaration of the decalogue in Exodus 34, one concerning the sabbath. Its placement can again be linked to the exodus story. The unending work of the Israelite slaves in Egypt is an appropriate background for raising the issue of a rest from work on the seventh day. After all, the pharaoh himself raised the issue of rest when he reacted negatively to the Israelites' request to worship their god in the wilderness (Exod 5:5). However, just as the two feasts, the firstfruits of wheat harvest and the ingathering at the year's end, point to the future life in the new land, so the particular formulation of this sabbath injunction likewise anticipates this future. Since the injunction mentions plowing and harvesting, it understandably precedes the pronouncement about the feasts of the early wheat harvest and the ingathering of crops.

A major reason for the placement of the sabbath rule at this point—after the feast of unleavened bread and the related rules about the final days in Egypt—is the focus on Aaron's and Jeroboam's setting aside a special day for a feast to Yahweh the bull calf in acclamation of his bringing Israel out of Egypt. To counteract this development the lawgiver in his decalogue of Exodus 34 responds doubly, first with a pronouncement about the proper feast, that of unleavened bread, for the Yahweh of the exodus story, and then with the proper day, the sabbath, to recognize Yahweh in his role as provider of the fruits of the earth. The lawgiver's response is similar to the response of the sabbath rules in Deut 5:14, 15 and Exod 20:8–11 if these are considered together: emphasis on the Yahweh of the exodus story in one and on the creator Yahweh in the other. The difference is that the lawgiver in Exodus 34, in choosing to set down two pronouncements, addresses the problem by giving attention to the fact that Aaron's and Jeroboam's occasions were both festivals and special days.

The sabbath rule in Exod 34:21 is that, work having been done in six days, a rest should be observed on the seventh and (the main point of the rule) this rest should be observed during the time of plowing and harvest. In the decalogue in Exodus 20 the sabbath functions as a day to acknowledge Yahweh as the creator of the world and

The Origins of Biblical Law

so to oppose the special day assigned by Aaron to Yahweh in the form of a human creation. This same perspective prevails in the sabbath rule in Exod 34:21. Only, in line with the focus on the fruit of the womb in the preceding rule, the emphasis is on the particular manifestation of Yahweh's creative activity, namely, the yield of the earth. The rule's bias is not that work should cease on the seventh day even during plowing time and harvest,[48] but that precisely during these times the Israelite can, or should, be alert to Yahweh's role in nature, a role that could not possibly be ascribed to Aaron's bull calf.

Already in this decalogue there is reference to Yahweh's creative activity. In Exod 34:10 the verb *bara'*, "to create," is surprisingly used in reference to the marvels that Yahweh will accomplish in putting down Israel's enemies. The implication is that the powers to be exhibited will be on a par with those manifested in creation.[49] As I have already argued, in the decalogue in Exodus 20 the rule about honoring parents follows the rule about the sabbath observance of Yahweh's creation because of the view that human participation in the creative process is to be found only in procreation. In that the method underlying the composition of each decalogue is the same, and in that similar views are likely to surface, the juxtaposition of a rule about animal and human firstborn and a rule about resting on the seventh day during plowing and har-

[48] According to S. R. Driver, the Israelites must rest "even at times when the need of working continuously might seem most urgent," *Exodus*, CBSC, 372–73. This observation might apply to harvest time (although surely less to harvests in an oriental climate), but hardly to plowing time.
[49] B. S. Childs observes the puzzling use of *bara'* and comments, "He will perform marvels never before created"; *Exodus*, 613.

64

vest time is also explained by the underlying focus on creation. To rest at the times of plowing and harvest is to acknowledge that, as with animals and human beings, it is Yahweh who mysteriously causes increase. This acknowledgment further devalues any role that might be ascribed to some magically endowed imitation of nature like the bull calf.

> VII   And thou shalt observe the feast of weeks, even of the firstfruits of wheat harvest, and the feast of ingathering at the year's end. Three times in the year shall all thy males appear before the Lord God, the God of Israel. For I will cast out nations before thee, and enlarge thy borders: neither shall any man desire thy land, when thou goest up to appear before Yahweh thy God three times in the year. (Exod 34:22–24)

The seventh declaration of the decalogue in Exodus 34 lists the two other feasts for celebrating the authentic Yahweh: the firstfruits of wheat harvest and the ingathering of crops at the year's end. As already indicated, these two feasts along with the feast of unleavened bread counter Aaron's and Jeroboam's false feast in celebration of Yahweh the bull calf. Yahweh proceeds to refer to the three feasts when he reminds the male Israelites that they must appear before him three times a year.[50] When they

---

[50] This statement is closely allied to the preceding commandment about the two feasts and hence both together constitute a single utterance. Its summarizing character is owing to the separation of the injunction about the feast of unleavened bread from the injunction about the two other feasts.

so appear, he further reminds them, he will protect their land whose borders he has enlarged.[51] Like the growth of the earth's crops, the enlargement of borders constitutes a sign of Yahweh's activity on behalf of the Israelites. The enlargement is also an indication of how the lawgiver anticipates the future. The people had expected the golden calf to exercise power for them in their future existence (Exod 32:17). But such a man-made sign of divine power is unnecessary, we can infer, because the visible sight of crops and extended borders is a sufficient sign of the invisible Yahweh's influence.

In regard to the reference to the place where the pilgrims are to go, I agree with Martin Noth that we are dealing with a Deuteronomic outlook and should probably assume the sole sanctuary in Jerusalem.[52] The pilgrims will have traveled far from their land to this sanctuary. The use of the term 'adon, "Lord," in the context of Exod 34:23, the requirement to appear three times a year before the Lord Yahweh, is similar to its use in Exod 15:17: Moses anticipates the settlement in Canaan and the sanctuary that the Lord will establish.

The concern in the rule with the protection of the pilgrims' land while they are away from home may be a quite specific response to the development in Jeroboam's reign. His establishment of the sanctuaries at Bethel and Dan was, he reasoned to himself (1 Kings 12:26, 27), to prevent the people from turning back again to the Jerusa-

---

[51] Contrast the pharaoh's concern: he feared that the Israelites would willingly quit their territory in Egypt, and consequently he wanted only the males to go and celebrate a feast to Yahweh (Exod 10:8–11).

[52] Noth, *Exodus*, 264.

lem leadership. In appealing to them to worship the calves at the sanctuaries distant from Jerusalem, he spoke of how it was too much for them to go up to Jerusalem. Presumably he was referring to problems of inconvenience, even the problem of protection of their homes while they were away. The lawgiver may well be addressing himself to the truth in this particular aspect of Jeroboam's concern.

> VIII   Thou shalt not offer the blood of my sacrifice with leavened bread; neither shall the sacrifice of the feast of the passover be left unto the morning. (Exod 34:25)

At Aaron's feast extolling the golden calf, burnt offerings and peace offerings were presented. Jeroboam's feast similarly involved the presentation of sacrifices. In the decalogue of Exodus 34, after the listing of the proper feasts for Yahweh, the final three statements concern offerings. Each of these statements can be viewed against the background of the offerings made to the calf. The intention of the lawgiver is again to embody in rules signs that recall the character of the authentic Yahweh as against the Yahweh signified by the calf.

It should be emphasized that context is crucial to an understanding of the significance of these rules. The meaning of some, perhaps all of them, has undergone a transformation. We have already observed how the context of the exodus story determines the bias of the rule about animal and human firstborn. We might note too that this latter rule is about offerings but is placed, not with the three under discussion, but after the one concerning the feast of unleavened bread and before the injunction about the sabbath. It is one indication of the process of transformation in question, a process in fact long familiar to critics studying the development of the passover laws. The unleavened bread and the firstborn were, it is commonly assumed, originally bound up with notions of fertility that were prevalent throughout the society but that went unrecorded, even unrecognized. At some point in time the unwritten rules and practices were brought into association with an incident in history, the exodus from Egypt, so that this history displaced their original significance and gave them new meaning. Perhaps once this process was underway it took on a momentum of its own so that a hitherto nonexistent rule could be forged solely by way of comment on the history. A possible example is the rule prohibiting leaven to be offered with the blood of the passover sacrifice.

The incompatibility of leaven with the blood of Yahweh's sacrifice can be read as being derived from the night of departure from Egypt. The presence of blood from the slaughtered animals on the Israelites' houses saved their lives. The absence of leaven in the bread or dough that night similarly signified a rapid departure for the Israelites from Egypt and avoidance of the destruction that befell the Egyptian firstborn. The rule would constitute historical commentary, indeed a prime illustration of the integration of law and legend. Specifically, a rule prohibiting leaven in the presence of blood would serve to remind the Israelites how they were brought out of Egypt by the god Yahweh.

The fact that animal offerings such as the passover sacrifice were made in commemoration of historical events highlights another aspect of the use of the bull calf. All indications are that the development is an internal Israelite

one. In that both the people in Exod 32:4 and Jeroboam
in 1 Kings 12:28 relate the calf's significance to Israel's
deliverance from Egypt, there emerges the same tendency
to link an animal to a historical event. However that may
be, the observation lends additional support to the attempt to view the rules about animal offerings in the
decalogue of Exodus 34 as competing against the significance attributed to the bull calf.

The meaning (in the present context) of the rule against
leaving overnight the sacrificial offering of the feast of
passover can also be derived from the events in Egypt, in
particular, Yahweh's saving the lives of the Israelites
when he inflicted death at midnight upon the Egyptian
firstborn of men and cattle. The contrast that informs the
rule is again between life and death, in particular, the hid-
den Yahweh's power to distinguish them as against the bull
calf's incapacity. The passover sacrifice has the opposite
significance—life for the Israelites—from the subsequent
slaughter of the Egyptian firstborn. The recognition
that the two rules about leaven and about the pre-midnight consumption of the sacrifice share a similar historical content explains why the lawgiver would include them
in a single statement of his decalogue.[53]

IX The first of the firstfruits of thy ground thou shalt
bring unto the house of Yahweh thy God. (Exod
34:26a)

[53] Note how they are linked with the conjunctive *waw*, unlike,
for example, the two rules in Exod 34:26 which constitute two
separate utterances. The difference in language between the formulation of this rule in Exod 34:25 and its formulation in Exod 23:18
may testify to its made-up character in relation to the history of the
exodus.

The next and ninth statement, about bringing the first of the firstfruits of the land into the house of Yahweh, can also, in part, be related to the same occasion of the death of the Egyptian firstborn. Hebrew *bikkurim*, "firstfruits," is cognate with *bᵉkor*, "firstborn." The unleavened dough that symbolized death for the Egyptian firstborn but life for the Israelites has a parallel in the very first produce of the land. By bringing this produce into the house of Yahweh the Israelites acknowledge that the imageless Yahweh not only brought them out of Egypt but also led them into the land.[54] Like the unleavened dough, the agricultural produce constitutes a visible sign of Yahweh's activity on behalf of the Israelites. The man-made bull calf enjoys no such significance.

The rule's focus, consistent with the trend in other statements of this decalogue, is on future developments, as the reference to the land's fertility indicates. Specifically, it may be intended to counter Jeroboam's wrongdoing: "If this people go up to do sacrifice in the house of Yahweh at Jerusalem, then shall the heart of this people turn again unto their lord, even unto Rehoboam king of Judah" (1 Kings 12:27). Jeroboam proceeded to have the two bull calves made and installed in Bethel and Dan. In particular, he built a "house of high places" for the worship of the bull calf. The specific injunction in the rule

[54] H. Kosmala argues persuasively that these particular "first of the firstfruits" are to be connected with the feast of Passover-Mazzot. The juxtaposition of these two occasions in the listing of feasts in Lev 23:4–14 is important evidence. See "The So-Called Ritual Decalogue," *ASTI* (1962), 45–49. Other texts about the significance of the first of the earth's yield, e.g., Deut 26:1–10, make explicit the link between the exodus from Egypt and the entry into the land.

that the first of the firstfruits be brought to the "house of
Yahweh thy God" may have the particular intention of
countering Jeroboam's policy. I do not mean that the injunction represents actual historical legislation dating
from Jeroboam's time. Rather it constitutes an inference
on the part of the lawgiver as to how Moses would have
responded.

X Thou shalt not seethe a kid in its mother's milk.
(Exod 34:26b)

The final declaration of this decalogue requires that a
dead young animal not be cooked in its mother's milk.
That milk had been its life-giving sustenance when alive.[55]
To boil the dead kid in it is to invite an unacceptable significance to be attributed to the mother's milk in its new
application. The rule constitutes a most appropriate final
response of this decalogue to the unacceptable supernatural significance that was attributed to the bull calf.
The prohibition against cooking a dead young kid in its
mother's milk is a powerful condemnation of the type of
confusion that arose with the calf. If the dead animal were

[55] Modern scholars have revived Maimonides's attempt to see the
prohibition as having an anti-Canaanite bias, but their use of a
Ugaritic text is flawed. That text has no reference to the mother's
milk. See C. M. Carmichael, "On Separating Life and Death: An
Explanation of Some Biblical Laws," *HTR* 69 (1976), 1–7; M. Haran, "Seething a Kid in Its Mother's Milk," *JJS* 30 (1979), 23–35; P.
C. Craigie, "Deuteronomy and Ugaritic Studies," *TB* 28 (1977),
155–69; G. R. Driver, *Canaanite Myths and Legends*, 2d ed. (Edinburgh: Clark, 1978), 29, 30, 123. The Ugaritic text is, however,
interesting in that it illustrates how notions of life are readily applied to such a combination as a dead young animal and milk.

used by way of an offering to the deity, special divine properties might be attributed to the mother's milk, or, more specifically, to the young animal after it had been prepared in this milk, in the same way that these properties were attributed to the calf.[56]

It might be worth reflecting on the fact that the Israelites had made an offering to the calf. What type of offering is not stated, but a kid prepared in its mother's milk could have been viewed by the lawgiver as a possible one. In both the prohibition and the incident of the calf the fundamental confusion lies in the failure to locate the proper origin of life, namely, the invisible Yahweh. No intermediary, a dead kid prepared in its mother's milk or a piece of molten metal crafted into the image of an animal, should come between certain manifestations of life (the mother's milk, the power exhibited in Egypt) and the true source of that life, Yahweh.

I am not suggesting that the prohibition about the mother's milk had its origin because of the development involving the bull calf. Like us, the compiler of this decalogue would have no historical knowledge other than the traditions available to him (which may well be the same ones available to us). The way in which significance is attributed to aspects of nature is the key factor in the lawgiver's assessment of certain practices known to him, be they from the world of sacrificial offerings or from customary habits such as, possibly originally, cooking a kid in the mother's milk. These offerings and habits were reassessed in light of the attempt to specialize religious

[56] In this light the Canaanite ritual cited in the preceding note offers something of a parallel.

knowledge by associating them with historical events rather than with the world of nature.

All three decalogues are products of didactic, reflective activity. Their placement in a flow of historical narratives is part of the same didactic aim that underlies the presentation of these narratives. In regard to the decalogue in Exodus 34 the link with Wisdom circles might be seen in the dominant role of the distinction between life and death. I have already drawn attention to the fact that there are quite specific links between the two decalogues in Exodus 20 and Deuteronomy 5 and the Wisdom story of Adam and Eve.[57]

[57] The individual pronouncements of the decalogue, not surprisingly, link up with Wisdom's concerns as expressed, for example, in the book of Proverbs. Note, for example, Prov 2:21, 22 (dwelling upon the land or ejection from it); Prov 3:19, 8:22-31 (Wisdom's role at creation); Prov 1:8, 15:5, 17:21, 19:26, 20:20, 23:22, 30:17 (cp. 11) (honor owing to parents; cp. Sir 3:1-16); Prov 6:29, 32 (adultery); Prov 6:19, 14:25, 19:5, 24:28, 25:18 (testimony's effect upon others); Prov 30:9 (use of Yahweh's name); Prov 6:25 (lusting after a woman).

[2]

Jacob's Problems
(Part One)

A study of the *Mishpatim* has to be preceded by an examination of the rules in Exod 20:23–26 if we are to understand why Moses presents rules about slavery as the opening ones of the *Mishpatim*.

Rules about Worship (Exod 20:23–26)

23 Ye shall not make with me gods of silver, or gods of gold, ye shall not make unto you. 24 An altar of earth thou shalt make unto me, and shalt sacrifice thereon thy burnt offerings, and thy peace offerings, thy sheep, and thine oxen: in every place where I record my name I will come unto thee and I will bless thee. 25 And if thou make me an altar of stone, thou shalt not build it of hewn stone: for if thou lift up thy tool upon it, thou hast polluted it. 26 Neither shalt thou go up by steps unto mine altar, that thy nakedness be not discovered thereon.

Sources (Gen 2:4–3:24; Exodus 32). The incident of the

golden calf and the related story of Adam and Eve, both of which are concerned with the preservation of the distinction between Yahweh and humankind.

Much discussion focuses on the placement of these rules about worship.[1] They are set down after the decalogue but before the rules of the Book of the Covenant. If we bear in mind the manner in which the decalogue was produced, in relation to the narratives about the golden calf and creation, we can evaluate anew both the significance and placement of the rules in Exod 20:23–26.

We have to ask why these rules are focused on altars. In the creation story, after Adam and Eve acquired the knowledge of good and evil and became aware of their nakedness they were excluded from the garden. The result was that they would no longer experience the divine presence directly as they had done. In similar fashion, the later incident of the golden calf ended the Israelites' direct experience of the divine presence: "For I will not go up in the midst of thee" (Exod 33:3).

In both these narratives the deity removes himself from direct contact with humankind. Therefore the question arises how people might be permitted to encounter God, albeit in less direct ways. The issue arises in the Genesis material when Cain and Abel offer sacrifices to God, presumably with a view to bridging the gap, brought about by their parents' action, between humankind and divinity. Later, after Seth was born to Eve and a son was born to him, men began to call upon the name of Yahweh (Gen 4:26).

Altars and sacrificial systems provide a means by which

[1] S. M. Paul, *Studies in the Book of the Covenant in the Light of Cuneiform and Biblical Law* (Leiden: Brill, 1970), 28, 34.

humans can experience some kind of encounter with their gods. Immediately after giving the decalogue God communicated some rules about such matters to Moses (Exod 20:23–26). Indeed the context is one in which the people had recognized how dangerous it would be to encounter the deity directly and had asked Moses to intervene (Exod 20:19). The rules about altars that follow immediately after this request address the problem of how men can continue to encounter God indirectly when Moses is no longer around.

The feature common to the rules about the construction of places of worship is the opposition to human aspiration to godlike powers of creativity and knowledge. This is precisely the stance found in the decalogue's judgment on the incident of the golden calf and in the story about Adam and Eve and their acquisition of knowledge. The rules in Exod 20:23–26 forbid people to exercise their creativity by fashioning images of gods in silver and gold and setting them up alongside Yahweh. The reference to "gods of gold" is found only in the rule about images (Exod 20:23) and in the story of the golden calf (Exod 32:31).[2] In the construction of an altar only earth and stone in their natural state can be used. It is expressly forbidden for man to change the stone by hewing it. The puzzling final rule prohibits ascent by steps to an altar. The reason given, "that thy nakedness not be discovered thereon" (Exod 20:26), suggests that care must be taken to prevent the exposure of nakedness in the place of worship. It is tempting to see this rule as harking back to God's response to Adam and Eve's awareness of their na-

---

[2] Graham Davies drew my attention to this fact.

kedness when he ensured that in the future they would be clothed (Gen 3:21). After Adam and Eve ate the fruit of the tree of the knowledge of good and evil, they became aware of their nakedness and experienced shame. The deity interpreted their experience as their becoming godlike: "Behold, the man is become as one of us, to know good and evil" (Gen 3:22). In light of these events in the garden, the concern with nakedness in the rule about ascending an altar lines up with the preceding ones in opposing human beings' usurpation of divine prerogatives. The rule should be read as a symbolic reminder. Human beings had provoked the deity by their awareness of nakedness in their first encounter ever with God in the garden. Therefore, at times when man attempts to approach God at an altar, he should take measures to keep himself from becoming aware of nakedness in order to avoid repeating Adam and Eve's provocation.

The *Mishpatim*

A long-standing puzzle is why the *Mishpatim* begins with the topic of slavery (Exod 21:2–6). A common view is that the larger context of the account of Israel's enslavement to the Egyptians is the reason—a view, incidentally, that assumes some link between law and narrative. The problem is a different one if, as some critics argue, the preceding rules about worship (Exod 20:23–26) are to be viewed as, in some sense, the introductory rules to the *Mishpatim*.[3] I have just noted, however, that they are to be

---

[3] S. M. Paul, *Studies*, 28, 34. Anthony Phillips argues that the

viewed precisely in the context in which we find them, that is, as a response to the issue of the avoidance of any direct communication between the people and the deity. The term "introductory" is consequently misleading. Whatever critical assessment is made—the statement in Exod 21:1 ("Now these are the judgments which thou shalt set before them") is also awkward if the rules in Exod 20:23–26 are claimed to constitute the introduction—the question remains whether there is any reason why laws about slavery should follow these laws about worship.

The answer lies in the task that Moses sets himself in presenting the *Mishpatim*. He will scrutinize the history of his people, the sons of Israel, by looking back over matters in the lives of the father of the nation, Jacob (Israel); of the next generation, Joseph and his brothers; and of the next generation, the one to which he belongs, and which with him has experienced the enslavement in Egypt. He does not begin with this latter experience of slavery, but with the form of slavery encountered by his immediate forebears, Jacob and Joseph, especially the former because his enslavement was the first in the nation's history. Why is this particular experience of Jacob's selected as the first to have rules set down about it? The reason appears to be that the issue of Jacob's form of slavery came up immediately after Jacob's encounter with God at Bethel. After

---

focus of the law on slavery is on the Israelite nationality of the male debt slave. Consequently the emphasis is on his freedom and participation in the legal life of the nation. For this reason, he thinks, a law about him had to come first before any other rules were set down; "The Laws of Slavery: Exodus 21.2–11," *JSOT* 30 (1984), 51–66.

he built an altar of stone there and received the deity's assurance of future protection for himself and his seed (Gen 28:16–22), he ran into the problem of his service to Laban (Genesis 29). Presumably, because Jacob duly acknowledged the supremacy of the deity, the latter's protection of him in all future matters, including those of succeeding generations, would be spelled out in the form of rules. This is precisely the task that Moses was given by the deity at Sinai. It is the same process we saw at work in the construction of the decalogue: the deity's actions, whether of protection or judgment, are translated into rules appropriate for humankind to observe.[4]

In the *Mishpatim*, the antagonism toward Jacob on the part of Laban, Esau, and a divine attacker provides the issues that are judged in the rules relating to Hebrew slaves, concubines, homicide, and striking a parent.

Hebrew Slaves (Exod 21:2–6)

> 2 If thou buy an Hebrew servant, six years he shall serve: and in the seventh he shall go out free for nothing. 3 If he came in by himself, he shall go out by himself: if he were married, then his wife shall go out with him. 4 If his master have given him a wife, and she have born him sons or daughters; the wife and her chil-

[4] Jacob's acknowledgment of the deity at Bethel was followed by his time of service under Laban. Moses's acknowledgment of the deity at Sinai came after Israel's experience of slavery in Egypt. As David Daube points out, an Israelite, having been freed from slavery in Egypt, became a servant to God, the service being expressed at altars; *The Exodus Pattern in the Bible* (London: Faber and Faber, 1963), 42–46.

dren shall be her master's, and he shall go out by himself. 5 And if the servant shall plainly say, I love my master, my wife, and my children; I will not go out free: 6 Then his master shall bring him unto the gods; he shall also bring him to the door, or unto the door post; and his master shall bore his ear through with an aul; and he shall serve him for ever.

Source (Gen 27:41–31:55). Jacob fled from his murderously disposed brother, Esau, and, after his encounter with the deity at Bethel, traveled to Aram, to Laban, his mother's brother. Laban, cunning and exploitative, ostensibly not wishing Jacob to serve him without wages, but intent on maximizing his own well-being, manages to get fourteen instead of seven years of service from Jacob, in return for Laban's daughter Rachel. Jacob ends up with two wives, one of whom, Leah, he was tricked into having. He serves yet another six years in order to obtain, through trickery, wages in the form of cattle. Laban has no intention of releasing Jacob from service, but God, representing a community or universal standard, has him release himself without Laban's knowledge. When Laban finds out he pursues Jacob and his entourage but is prevented from doing him harm. They part ways after Laban obtains promises about his daughters' future.

A rule about a Hebrew servant is set down against the background of Jacob's service under Laban, even though his service is not, because of all sorts of complex factors, that of a slave to a master.[5] Moses has turned to the first

---

[5] On Jacob's legal position, see Daube's comments, *The Exodus*

example in the history of his ancestors when one of them, Jacob/Israel himself, experienced, if not a regular form of slavery, at least a condition in some respects akin to it. Moses could absorb from Yahweh's response to Jacob's oppression guidelines for the way a Hebrew slave should be treated by an Israelite master. Even though this latter aim is indicated, it is nonetheless illuminating to read the rule as if it were addressed to Laban himself: "If thou [Laban] buy an Hebrew servant . . ." Jacob's father-in-law, like Moses's (Jethro in Exodus 18), can be included in Israel's life as a nation in matters of law and ethics.

Joseph's experience as a slave in Potiphar's house is also pertinent, because the rulemaker, like the narrators of the traditions, is alert to matters that recur over succeeding generations. In the rule the qualifying term "Hebrew" is used. In other contexts the term invariably draws attention to the Hebrew in a foreign setting, for example, Pot-

---

Pattern in the Bible, 62: "Is he [Jacob] a resident alien? A dependent relative? A member of the family of the standing of a brother, or maybe a younger brother? A hired labourer? A shepherd? A slave? A combination of some of these?" He notes that the language is heavily weighted with terms indicating slave's work, even though Jacob is not actually termed a slave. In a later article, Daube comments that Laban and Jacob's relationship, "while not that of master and slave, is not totally unlike it"; "What Price Equality? Some Historical Reflections," *RJ* 5 (1986), 194–95. In commenting on Exod 21:2–6, without reference to any background, J. I. Durham, *Exodus*, WBC 3 (Word Books: Waco, Texas, 1987), 321, states that the Hebrew slave is perhaps best thought of as "less than a full citizen but as more than a full slave." In other words, Daube notes the less than clear-cut status of Jacob with Laban, and Durham similarly analyzes the status of the Hebrew slave in Exod 21:2–6. I am arguing that there are indeed overlapping features and that these are not coincidental.

iphar's wife in Egypt refers to Joseph as the Hebrew servant (Gen 39:17; cp. Exod 2:11; 1 Sam 4:6, 9; 14:11, 21; 29:3). Rather than explaining, as is common, the use of the term in the rule by suggesting that the background contrast is with a foreign captive—a Hebrew, not a foreign slave[6]—we can understand its use in light of the treatment of the first Hebrew servant in a foreign setting—that is, the one before Joseph—by Laban, the Aramean.[7]

If a Hebrew slave is bought, he should not be treated as the Aramean Laban treated Jacob. There should not be the confusion, deception, and crookedness that prevailed in Laban's treatment of him, for example, when Jacob served fourteen years in order to acquire Rachel, the first seven years constituting, from his viewpoint no doubt, service for nothing. Initially, because they were kin, Laban said that Jacob should not serve him for nothing (ḥinnam) but should name his wages (Gen 29:15). There began the long struggle between the two, with Jacob being ill-treated by Laban but despite the ill-treatment prospering because of providential assistance. Eventually Jacob fled from his oppressive service because not just Laban himself but his sons also were hostile toward him (Gen 31:1, 2). Twenty years he had served: fourteen years

[6] See, e.g., Umberto Cassuto, *A Commentary on the Book of Exodus* (Jerusalem: Magnes, 1967), 265; J. P. Hyatt, *Exodus*, NCBC (London: Oliphants, 1971), 228.

[7] Although Moses lays down rules for the nation Israel, his perspective is global and consistent with the Deuteronomic one expressed, for example, in Deut 4:6: "For this is your wisdom and your understanding in the sight of the nations, which shall hear all these statutes, and say, Surely this great nation is a wise and understanding people."

for Laban's two daughters and six years for his cattle. His wages had been changed ten times and, Jacob further complained, if Laban had released him from service he would have sent him away empty (Gen 31:41, 42), that is, according to the status of a slave, not of a kinsman.

The rule takes up from Laban's remark that Jacob should not serve him for nothing (*ḥinnam*)[8] and lays down the conditions when someone should serve for nothing, that is, have indeed the status of a slave. The rule pursues the hypothetical issue of a Hebrew slave by borrowing as many features as possible from Jacob's experience with Laban. There is first considered a Hebrew slave who, like Jacob, comes into service as a single male.[9] Without the complication of marriage he has to serve six years and go out free for nothing (*ḥinnam*), that is, without wages and sent away empty.[10] Jacob, if he had not married and served fourteen years for his two wives, would presumably have served six years before Yahweh would have di-

---

[8] On the semantic development of the term *ḥinnam*, "gratuitously," derived, as it is, from *ḥen*, "grace, graciousness," see David Daube, *Roman Law, Linguistic, Social, and Philosophical Aspects* (Edinburgh: Edinburgh University Press, 1969), 118–19.

[9] The peculiar expression *bᵉgappo*, "by himself," literally, "with his back [or body]," is found only in this rule. The sense appears to be that that is all he comes with—surely an apt depiction of Jacob's state in the aftermath of his flight from Esau. At one point he had prayed that he might have bread to eat and raiment to put on (Gen 28:20). Cassuto, *Exodus*, 266, compares the meaning to Jacob's statement in Gen 32:10, "For with only my staff I crossed this Jordan."

[10] Raymond Westbrook is correct in stating that it means the slave about to be released will not have to repay the debt for which he was enslaved. This meaning, however, can surely be taken for granted. See *Studies in Biblical and Cuneiform Law* (Paris: Gabalda, 1988), 91.

rected him to release himself (Gen 31:3). Moses deduces the rule in light of the tradition. The deity's intervention, for example, constitutes the basis for his laying down a six-year period of service.[11]

Next is the contrasting situation in which a Hebrew slave comes into service married. The preceding rule, not the tradition, prompts consideration of this case. We should nonetheless recall that the question of Jacob's marriage before departing for Laban's country came up. Isaac did not wish his son Jacob to marry locally among the Canaanites as his brother Esau had done (Gen 28:1, 2). If not for his parents' attitude (cp. Gen 26:34, 35), Jacob might have come to Laban married. Recall that, although his father sent him for the purpose of marrying Laban's daughter (Gen 28:1, 2), his mother sent him with a view to avoiding Esau's wrath. In any event, the rulemaker puts aside special features of the tradition and lays out hypothetical developments. The rule is that the slave's wife goes out with him. It is no surprise to find that consideration of contrasting cases is a natural and typical feature of the construction of biblical rules,[12] a feature that is also characteristic of the narrators of Israelite tradition when they recount its subject matter.

---

[11] Such a period reflects an attempt to construct a model and will not reflect a living reality. As in Rome, the situation would be a fluid one. Cicero, for example, thought that even six years was too long for any careful, hardworking slave who, we might note, had been captured in war; Alan Watson, *Roman Slave Law* (Baltimore: Johns Hopkins, 1977), 23. In CH 117, the one comparable prescription (it concerns a debt-slave), emancipation is granted in the fourth year.

[12] See C. M. Carmichael, *Law and Narrative in the Bible* (Ithaca: Cornell University Press, 1985), 213, 297 n.18, 298, 301 n.21.

Jacob's service under Laban accounts for the presentation of the rules about a slave who is given a wife by his master and who, like Jacob, has children by her. He goes out by himself and they remain the master's. The rule acknowledges in what circumstances a claim that was made by Laban is in fact a valid one, just as the preceding rule about the unmarried bondman considered Laban's actual but unavowed aim to treat Jacob as a slave instead of a kinsman. When Jacob left his service, Laban claimed, "These daughters [Jacob's wives] are my daughters, and these children are my children" (Gen 31:43). The rule follows on the lawgiver's choosing to assume (not because it may accurately reflect the tradition but because it serves his instructional purposes) that Jacob's relation to Laban was in some respects that of slave to master.

Laban did not wish to have Jacob leave his service when the latter requested, "Send me away, that I may go unto mine own place, and to my country. Give me my wives and my children, for whom I have served thee, and let me go: for thou knowest my service which I have done thee" (Gen 30:25, 26). The rule, formulated for relations among Israelites, would not recognize Jacob's claim if his status had been that of slave.[13] And it is on the basis of such a status that the issue is raised: in what circumstances might a slave remain attached to his wife and chil-

[13] Gerhard von Rad, *Genesis*, OTL (Philadelphia: Westminster, 1972), 294–95, mentions together, without suggesting any specific link, Jacob's request to dissolve his servant status and the requirements of this rule. He speaks of "the rather obscure legal situation" in the Genesis story. In fact, this obscurity is tied up with Laban's cunning. One instance of a tangled issue is Jacob's service for his two wives. He willingly served for Rachel, but Leah was "given" to him.

dren? Observing the bad feeling that prevailed between Jacob and Laban, the lawgiver perceives that the slave's relationship with his master—for whom, unlike Jacob with Laban, he must have love—is the crucial consideration.[14] This recognition explains why, puzzlingly, the love of the master is cited first before love of wife and children.[15]

If the slave opts for permanent attachment to his master's household, he is to be brought to *ha^{ʾe}lohim*, "the gods," and a special ceremony undertaken at the door of his master's household. Possibly, the mark to be put on the slave's ear, visible for all to see, is manifest indication that the slave is indeed a slave—and thus without the ambiguity surrounding Jacob's status with Laban.[16] The reference to "the gods" is a very old crux.[17] The solution

[14] Regardless of the issue of permanent servitude, the need for the slave to assert love of his master is surely such an unusual aspect of the rule that it reflects less a matter of legal development and more a peculiar feature in a specific background such as we find in Jacob's contrary position with Laban. S. M. Paul's comparative linguistic evidence to suggest that *ʾahab*, "to love," has legal overtones is forced; *Studies*, 49 n.2.

[15] On the heart-rending dilemma facing the slave, see Daube, "What Price Equality?" 194–99. His comment on the slave's affirming love of his master reveals puzzlement about the reference: "The master, I guess, appears chiefly for appearances' sake though, as he supplied the wife, a modicum of substance may be conceded," 194. But why, if this consideration be the sum of the matter, is the master cited first?

[16] This possibility would not exclude the other one that the ear is peculiarly associated with the slave because of his required obedience; H. J. Boecker, *Law and the Administration of Justice in the Old Testament and Ancient East* (Minneapolis: Augsburg, 1980), 159.

[17] See S. R. Driver, *The Book of Exodus*, CBSC (Cambridge: Cambridge University Press, 1911), 211. Martin Noth assumes that

appears to be that the lawgiver, working with the Jacob-Laban model, has Laban's household gods, or some analogue, under consideration (Gen 31:30).

Concubines (Exod 21:7–11)

> 7 And if a man sell his daughter to be a maidservant, she shall not go out as the menservants do. 8 If she please not her master, who hath not designated her for himself, then shall he let her be redeemed: to sell her unto a strange nation he shall have no power, seeing he hath dealt deceitfully with her. 9 And if he designate her for his son, he shall deal with her after the manner of daughters. 10 If he take him another wife; her food, her raiment, and her conjugal right, shall he not diminish. 11 And if he do not these three unto her, then shall she go out free without money.

---

the reference is to a domestic deity who had his place at the door of the house. He further assumes, like most other scholars, that the rule is a very old one; *Exodus*, (Philadephia: Westminster, 1962), 178. This attribution of the rule to an early historical period I cannot accept, because I attribute an intended archaic quality to the formulated rules. Moses looks back on a development in patriarchal history. In this sense we are meant to tune into ancient history, but biblical history is not the kind of history Noth, for example, is discussing. The law dates from that period of time when it was attributed to Moses, probably the time of the Deuteronomist(s). Determining if there are genuinely old elements in their construction, as is reasonable to inquire, is, alas, a virtually impossible task. Z. W. Falk's observations from comparative sources about the role of the gods in Exod 21:6 seem much more pertinent to Jacob's position with Laban than to the rule itself; "Exodus xxi 6," *VT* 9 (1959), 86–88. Presumably the Aramean Laban, brother of Isaac's wife, had a religious orientation that was judged to be compatible with that of the patriarchs.

Source (Gen 27:41–31:55). As for the preceding law, the source is Jacob's dealings with Laban, specifically this time in regard to Laban's giving his two daughters to Jacob by way of paying for his services.

The less than obvious switch from the topic of a man's acquisition of a Hebrew slave to the topic of a man's sale of his daughter as a concubine can be accounted for by the lawgiver's taking stock of the position of Laban's daughters.[18] At one point they claimed that their father no longer regarded them as daughters but as strangers, for he had sold them (Gen 31:15). It is a curious claim and one implication is that he had in his dealings with Jacob treated them as something akin to slave-girls and not as daughters. The rule states initially that the girl should not be released in the way in which the menservants (of v. 2) are.[19] Moreover, it becomes clear that the rule contem-

---

[18] There is no reference in the rule to a *Hebrew* daughter, possibly because it is set against the background of Laban's daughters who are Arameans. Jacob in relation to Laban was a Hebrew; that is, the term is only used when there is a contrast in the background between a Hebrew and someone of another group. B. S. Jackson gives two different reasons why the topics, male slaves and concubines, are juxtaposed. One, he assumes that the first topic is about a Hebrew debt-slave, the second about a debtor who has to sell his daughter to a creditor. Two, the first topic is about how the status of a debt-slave is not affected by his master's use of him for breeding purposes, the second about the alteration in status of a woman because of her sexual services. It seems to me that what he thinks is a reason for the rule is but an interesting observation from a perspective that plays no part for the lawgiver. See "Ideas of Law and Legal Administration," in *The World of Ancient Israel*, ed. R. E. Clements (Cambridge: Cambridge University Press, 1989), 198.

[19] There is no justification for the common claim that this provision is set aside in Deut 15:12. We are simply not comparing like

plates women in the role, not of domestic maidservants, but of wives or concubines. Even more to the point as regards the influence of the story, the intent of the rule is to preserve their status as commensurate with that of daughtership. The arrangement whereby Laban sold Leah and Rachel to Jacob by way of wages for his service again prompts the formulation of the specific rules. The rules about slavery in Exod 21:2–6 are set down from the angle of Laban's attempt to treat Jacob as a slave, those about concubines in Exod 21:7–11 from the angle of Laban's contract with Jacob for his daughters.

This background solves the long-standing puzzle why there is consideration of the woman who does not please her master, "who hath not designated her for himself."[20]

---

with like. The Hebrew maidservant in Deut 15:12 is not like the concubine of Exod 21:7. The latter verse is making this very distinction. B. S. Jackson, *The Mishpatim* (forthcoming), draws attention to the fact that Exod 21:7 constitutes what is uncommon in biblical law, a cross-reference to Exod 21:2 about the release of the male slave. The reason can be attributed to the fact that, for hypothetical purposes, the situation of Jacob, Rachel, and Leah is under scrutiny. The differing rules about the male and female slaves are linked insofar as the situation in Genesis is the basis for the lawgiver's judgments.

[20] The reading of the MT (*ketibh*) is typically changed to "Who hath designated her for himself" (*qere*). The *ketibh* represents the *lectio difficilior* and the *qere* indicates just how ancient (as far back as the LXX, e.g.) are the attempts to avoid the problem of the *ketibh*. There are at least three problems with the emendation. First, it is just that, an emendation. Second, if accepted, it is an unnecessary statement. The description of the transaction between the father and the husband/master and the reference to the girl's being disagreeable in the eyes of her acquirer indicate that such a designation is understood and need not be spelled out. Third, if her purchaser had understood that she was his designated concubine and then

The rule leaves us puzzled as to why he might be in this position in the first place. It plainly means—if we read the Hebrew text as it stands and do not adopt the commonly accepted emendation, "who hath designated her for himself"—that the father has sold his daughter to a husband-master, who finds her "unpleasing in his eyes," but who in fact, bewilderingly, has not designated her as his concubine. How can that be? In focus is Jacob's arrangement to acquire Rachel by way of wages for seven years' service to her father. Laban cleverly chose to interpret the arrangement by granting Rachel to him but making him understand that he was obliged to take the elder daughter, Leah, first. Jacob only learned of the obligation after Leah had been slipped into the bridal tent in place of Rachel.[21] From Laban's point of view—a deliberately narrow one, *au pied de la lettre* in order to marry her off for the same price as Rachel[22]—he acted according to his country's custom that dictated that Jacob from the outset had desig-

---

changed his mind—the view of those who accept the emendation— why does such a change constitute treacherous treatment of her? Why can he not change his intent without incurring such harsh judgment? The verb *bagad*, "to deal treacherously," in other contexts presupposes much more serious infractions than critics postulate for the one they speculate about in Exod 21:8 as emended.

[21] The term *ya'ad* "to designate" (as concubine) is used more in the sense of appointment to meet at a certain time or place. We could translate, "Who had not appointed her to meet him [on the nuptial night]," and the link to Jacob's problem on his wedding night would be a direct one.

[22] See David Daube's analysis in *Studies in Biblical Law* (Cambridge: Cambridge University Press, 1947), 190–92. The use of the term "sale" in reference to the acquisition of a woman by a man should not be understood in our modern, commercial sense. See the comments of A. S. Diamond, *Primitive Law, Past and Present* (London: Methuen, 1971), 248; and Phillip Grierson, *The Origins of Money* (London: Athlone, 1977), 15.

nated the elder daughter, Leah, as his wife. But Leah did not please Jacob (Gen 29:31). Yet here he was with a woman whom he had not designated as wife but who had in effect been acquired by purchase from her father—exactly the situation assumed by the Hebrew text. Laban was rightly concerned about how Jacob might treat her in the future once Jacob had moved to his own country (and its customs). For Laban knew perfectly well that he had duped Jacob into taking a wife he had not designated.

The rule borrows from the facts of this situation and legislates for some hypothetical, no doubt less idiosyncratic, one in the future. The unwanted woman has to be redeemed, presumably by her father or relative, and her husband-master cannot sell her to a "strange people," because he has dealt treacherously, deceitfully, with her. From Leah's point of view, she had been dealt with in just this fashion. If the custom was what her father claimed it was, she would have understood that Jacob had entered into the union with her in good faith. She would not have been party to her father's chicanery.[23] Moreover, Jacob did consummate the marriage with her. His presumed failure to recognize who she was on the occasion—no doubt because there had been a banquet, he was drunk, and it was dark—was hardly an excuse for his not preventing a marriage he did not want.

The rule, contemplating the conduct of a future Israelite (son of Jacob), transfers the features in the story to him. The focus would be on the Israelite's intentions, not on the father's duplicity, because the latter would require another type of rule not relevant to the topic of a wom-

[23] Contrary to David Daube's assessment in *Appeasement and Resistance and Other Essays on New Testament Judaism* (Berkeley: University of California Press, 1987), 35, 36.

an's release from concubinage. It should be pointed out, however, that the rule's formulation of the problem accurately describes Leah's position with Jacob so that we do not need to raise the issue of the male's intentions. In some way, for example, because of custom, or even through careless negotiation at the time of the arrangement—biblical law appears not to know of written agreements in this area[24]—the woman thinks that she is to become the man's wife or concubine, but in the event that has not been his intent at all. He must let her be redeemed, but he cannot sell her to a "strange people," that is, to a foreign nation. A large part of Laban's distress at Jacob's departure with his daughters was that he was going to lose them to a foreign country. He was likely never to see them again.[25] The rule, concerned with the woman, reveals the same sensitivity.

The lawgiver focuses on the issue of the woman's treatment at the point in the story when Jacob found out that Leah was the wife assigned to him. Jacob took the matter to Laban, who negotiated a deal whereby Jacob would retain Leah but acquire the wife he assumed he had designated, Rachel. It turned out, from Leah's side of things, to be a loveless, humiliating marriage. Observing Leah's position, the lawgiver judges that in the negotiation with Laban the latter should have bought her back and then made the arrangement for Jacob's marriage to Rachel.

---

[24] So Z. W. Falk, *Hebrew Law in Biblical Times* (Jerusalem: Wahrmann, 1964), 152–53.

[25] J. P. Hyatt, *Exodus*, NCBC, 230, is skeptical about the reference to a foreign nation, and like Cassuto, *Exodus*, 268, and S. M. Paul, *Studies*, 54, weakens the sense to mean a family or clan other than her own. Again, however, the background in the Genesis narrative proves illuminating.

Leah should not have continued with Jacob because the prospect of his treating her badly was a real one—as Laban himself saw when Jacob was leaving with her for foreign parts.

Observing Jacob's retention of Leah, the lawgiver contemplates a hypothetical situation in which the master designates the woman for his son. His judgment is that he should treat her, as S. R. Driver puts it, as a daughter of his own household.[26] The reason for the rule would be that the lawgiver, thinking of a less idiosyncratic development than the one involving Jacob with Leah,[27] understandably considers the situation where the master decides to give her to his son because she does not please him. In other words, observing that Jacob did retain Leah when her return to her family might have or should have been expected, the lawgiver formulates a rule in which the woman is brought into a family but not retained by her acquirer. Instead she is given to his son.[28]

It is just conceivable that a different, later feature of the tradition may be pertinent. Jacob's eldest son, Reuben, lay with one of Jacob's concubines, Bilhah, who was supplied originally by Laban (Gen 35:22). This unacceptable development in the next generation can readily raise the

[26] S. R. Driver, *Exodus*, CBSC, 213.

[27] Jacob had little alternative but to remain bound to Leah despite his antagonism to her and her father. See C. M. Carmichael, *Women, Law, and the Genesis Traditions* (Edinburgh: Edinburgh University Press, 1979), 41.

[28] We may have to reckon with a stock legal issue that is known to the lawgiver from his acquaintance with Near Eastern laws. See, e.g., Isaac Mendelsohn, "The Conditional Sale into Slavery of Free Born Daughters in Nuzi and the Law of Ex. 21:7–11," *JAOS* 55 (1935), 190–95.

issue as to the circumstances in which a father might in fact provide a concubine for a son. The situation contemplated in the rule would be one such circumstance and would revolve around the *hypothetical* reflection of how someone in Leah's position might be passed on to a son. She is to be treated according to the "rights of daughters." The rule suggests that, like Reuben with Bilhah, the son and concubine will live in the father's household. It is important to emphasize that we are necessarily less sure of a rule's formulation whenever the lawgiver pursues the topic in the narrative beyond the circumstances found there. In that these are frequently peculiar, he will understandably turn to less strange ones that require on our part more speculation as to why he formulates as he does.

The final part of the rule deals with the man's acquisition of a second wife, to the detriment of the rights of the first. The major problem has long been noted that this statement clashes with the preceding one about his in fact having dismissed the first wife.[29] How then can the rule speak about a second wife who is around at the same time as the first? Relating the formulation of the rules, not to each other, but to aspects of Jacob's relationship with Leah, we can again resolve the problem. Indeed, the contradiction illustrates well how the narratives pose hypothetical problems that are then given resolution in the rules.

Jacob had to take Leah even though for him (but not for Laban) she was not the appointed wife. Laban had

[29] Driver, *Exodus*, CBSC, 213, 214, lays out the problem and the various solutions—inevitably involving emendations of the text—that have been proposed to resolve the contradictions.

94

power over him and if Jacob had not treated Leah as the designated wife to be maintained by him, Laban would not have given him Rachel. In more ordinary circumstances, someone in Jacob's position would have dismissed the woman as soon as he realized he had been duped. The preceding rule in v. 8 about a dismissal explores this possibility even though the narrative takes a different turn. It is the development in the narrative—in which Jacob retains the disliked wife, Leah—that the lawgiver lays out in the final part of his rule about the rights of a first wife when a second is acquired. He considers a case similar to Jacob's relationship with first Leah and then Rachel. His concern is precisely the one attributed to Yahweh's protection of Leah in the story.

The rule requires that the husband not curtail the first wife's food, clothing, or conjugal rights. The term *'onah*, "cohabitation," is only found in this rule, and the sense seems to be the times when the first wife has access to her husband, precisely a prominent aspect of Leah's position with Jacob. Only when she obtained mandrakes from her son Reuben, and her sister and co-wife desired them, was she able to make an arrangement with Rachel to lie with Jacob that night (Gen 30:14–17). Manifestly, her conjugal rights had been diminished.[30]

---

[30] S. M. Paul's attempt (*Studies*, 56–61) to translate *'onah* as "oil" by linking the listing of the three commodities, food, oil, and clothing, in a number of Mesopotamian legal texts—they have nothing to do with the rights of concubines—with the three items cited in Exod 21:10 lacks a proper basis for analysis. He notes what appears to be a stereotyped formulaic triad of commodities and uncritically comments, "This, then, has a direct bearing upon Ex. 21:10" (p. 59). In what sense is there a direct bearing? In appealing to biblical texts as well, he cites Eccles 9:7–9, "Up, eat your *bread*

The term for food, *š'er*, refers to animal meat, and it is
rightly observed that its sense should not be weakened to
mean bread and vegetables.[31] It is possible that the lawgiver draws the inference that the rootlike plants given to
Leah by Reuben constituted typical fare and that Jacob's
dislike of her (Gen 29:31) extended to his curtailing provision of food. Or simply that this one reference to what
Leah ate when she was the disregarded wife of Jacob suggests to the lawmaker the need to pay attention, not just
to her food in general but to its particular variety. There
is no reference to Leah's need for clothing. Presumably, a
husband who dislikes a wife feels no wish to make her
look attractive. We might recall that Jacob had found
fault with Leah's looks (Gen 29:17). There is, however,
no need to strain after such links between the rule and the
tradition, because the relationship between the two is not
that of a one-to-one correspondence in every detail. On
philological grounds Robert North argues that the rule,

with joy, and drink your wine with a glad heart. . . . At all times
let your *clothes* be sparkling clean, and *oil* on your head not be
lacking. Enjoy life with the woman you love" (Paul's italics). He
could have equally well underlined wine and woman, but he is set
on a triadic formula. He does not note that the reference to the
enjoyment of a wife is close to the meaning long accorded to *'onah*.
If *'onah* does mean a wife's conjugal access to her husband and the
term is etymologically related to *'anah*, "to respond," Jacob's lack
of sexual response to Leah is possibly illuminating. Paul is skeptical, perhaps rightly so, that there would be a requirement in the
ancient Near East for a wife to be given such a conjugal right. I am
again claiming that the specific background of Leah's sexual initiative with Jacob is what is in focus, not some general concern about
the position of co-wives.

[31] Driver, *Exodus*, CBSC, 214.

which he translates as "He shall not diminish her flesh, covering, and response," signifies "He shall not curtail her physical [sexual] satisfaction, her honorable standing in the harem, or her right of parenthood." The sense comes remarkably close to Leah's problems with Jacob.[32]

The sensitivity in the story to Leah's shabby treatment as a wife shows up in the rule in the judgment that, should the husband fail to provide for her needs, she must be let go without payment of money to him. It is noteworthy that Laban himself sought, with God as a witness, an agreement with Jacob that when he took his daughters off to his country, he would accord them fair treatment, particularly if he took additional wives. This concern about the consequences of a man's acquisition of an additional wife is the one pursued by the lawgiver. He hypothesizes, however, about the known, prior example of Jacob's acquisition of Rachel by way of judging such issues. It might be better to focus on Laban's concern as the one that provides the initial impetus for the topic in the rule. We have noted how the lawgiver in some of his preceding rules has viewed matters from Laban's perspective. Laban's concern about Jacob's acquisition of a wife in addition to Leah and Rachel is readily prompted by the problem between Jacob and Leah.

To summarize: the rules about the release of a wife acquired through purchase from her father are shaped first by reflection on Leah's initial acquisition by Jacob when he did not want her, and then by reflection on her established position as a wife when he treated her shabbily.

[32] Robert North, "Flesh, Covering, and Response, Ex. xxi 10," *VT* 5 (1955), 204–6.

The Origins of Biblical Law

Homicide (Exod 21:12–14)

12 He that smiteth a man, so that he die, shall surely be put to death. 13 And he who does not lie in wait, but God deliver into his hand; then I will appoint thee a place whither he shall flee. 14 But if a man come presumptuously upon his neighbour to slay him with guile; thou shalt take him from mine altar, that he may die.

Source (Gen 27:41–45; 32:1–33:16). Jacob's life was at risk on two linked occasions. He had become a member of Laban's household because, having cheated Esau out of his birthright, he had to flee on account of Esau's intention to slay him. Providentially, after Jacob quit Laban's household and he faced again the prospect of a murderous encounter with Esau, Esau's attitude changed and he spared his brother's life. This change was paralleled at a supramundane level: just after his departure from Laban, and anticipating his hostile encounter with Esau, Jacob was confronted with an angel of God. The terrifying event, however, passed without Jacob's succumbing to his power.

From Jacob's disputes with Laban, Moses turns to the dispute that led to Jacob's departure from his own family to the family of his mother's brother, Laban. Esau was set on killing his brother because Jacob, with their mother's assistance, had cheated Esau out of their father's blessing (Gen 27:41). Esau's hatred for his brother, and, in the next generation, the hatred that resulted in the theft of Joseph by his brothers—the hatred each time involving a parent's preference for one sibling over another—accounts for the succession of rules: homicide, striking a parent, stealing a man, and cursing a parent.[33] The odd order of the rules does not reflect a historical process, whereby a rule has been badly inserted into an existing set of rules, but is determined by the lawgiver's following through on events in the Genesis narratives.

It is perhaps worth noting in passing that the lawgiver's initial, explicit focus on slavery is sustained in his scrutiny of the Genesis material. When Jacob eventually confronts his murderously disposed brother he approaches him as a slave, and addresses him as master (Gen 32:4, 18; 33:5, 14).[34]

The initial, general prohibition against homicide is set down against the backdrop of Esau's intention to slay Jacob. Esau's hostility is precisely the subject matter following Laban's agreement with Jacob about the latter's acquisition of his daughters (Gen 31:43–55), the subject matter of the preceding rule. What also takes the lawgiver to the topic of homicide is the fact that the preceding rule was prompted by the concluding episode of Jacob's stay with Laban when the threat of harm, even death, to Jacob was avoided only by divine intervention (Gen 31:29). Equally noteworthy is Gen 32:28. It links three attacks on

---

[33] That these four rules stand apart, in the sense that each begins with the use of a participial clause and the ones subsequent to the first are linked by *vav* "and," becomes intelligible in light of this *particular* shared background. Those who note the formal feature of the four rules, e.g., B. S. Childs, *Exodus, The Book of Exodus; A Critical, Theological Commentary* (Philadelphia: Westminster, 1974), 469–70, make the largest (and most dubious) of claims: it represents "a redactional effort to break down the sharp distinction within Israel between civil and religious law."

[34] The incident is the springboard for the rule about the fugitive slave in Deut 23:15, 16. See C. M. Carmichael, *The Laws of Deuteronomy* (Ithaca: Cornell University Press, 1974), 186, 187.

Jacob—Laban's, Esau's, and God's (Genesis 32): "For thou hast fought with God and with men, and hast prevailed." The reference to men is specifically to Laban and Esau.

Perhaps the most significant reason why Moses turns at precisely this point to Jacob's encounter with Esau is that just prior to it Jacob encountered the angels of God at Mahanaim (Gen 32:1). We noted how the lawgiver had Moses translate Jacob's first encounter with God at Bethel into rules that gave substance to the deity's promise to protect Jacob in his subsequent journeyings, in particular, his service under Laban. Or rather, in keeping with the promise at Bethel, Moses laid down rules governing slaves and concubines that would serve the well-being of future generations of Israelites. The encounter at Mahanaim with the angels is a prelude to the deity's protection of Jacob's life itself. Such protection again requires Moses to communicate rules, this time concerning homicide.

Esau's original intention to slay Jacob in the end slipped away and was replaced by an apparently benign attitude. This change probably provides the motivation for the general statement of the rule about homicide: it is thought necessary to state the consequence if the deed had taken place. A parallel to this hypothetical approach to biblical events is furnished by the example of Joseph's brothers, who did not receive capital punishment for kidnapping their brother. The lawgiver responds (in his rule in Exod 21:16) by setting down a death penalty for such an offense. Esau did *not* murder Jacob. The rule sets down the penalty should he have done so. The lawgiver brings out issues that are but suggested by developments in the tradition, or that call for different answers should similar circumstances be imagined to present themselves in the lives of later Israelites.

Instead of Jacob's meeting death at the hands of a murderous Esau, he was confronted with the threat of death from God. The two confrontations are intimately linked. The same sequence of topics—human killer, divine killer—turns up in Exod 21:12, 13.

The reason why Jacob at this time avoids death at Esau's hands illumines the rule in Exod 21:13, with its strange formulation about God's delivering the victim into the hand of his killer who has not lain in wait for him. The deity's active role stands out. After Jacob fled from Laban he feared death at the hands of Esau and prayed to God: "Deliver me, I pray thee, from the hand of my brother, from the hand of Esau: for I fear him, lest he will come and smite [*nakah*] me, and the mother with the children" (Gen 32:11). There follows instead the encounter with God's messenger (recognized as an angel in Gen 32:1, a man in Gen 32:24), whose hand, it might be noted, is very much involved in grappling with Jacob. Such an encounter threatens death to Jacob. He later expresses this view by his remark that he had seen God's face but his life had been delivered (Gen 32:30).[35] His relieved response when Esau is found not to be hostile is similar: "For therefore I have seen thy face, as though I had seen the face of God" (Gen 33:10). Each time could have expected death, but just as, remarkably, he had survived seeing God's face, so, remarkably too, he had survived seeing Esau's. The angel is an extension of or substitute for the deity himself, as is made explicit in

---

[35] To see God is to die (Exod 33:20; Judg 6:22, 23; 13:22).

The Origins of Biblical Law

Gen 32:28, where Jacob is said to have fought with God.[36] No motivation for the divine action is given, and once the action is completed the angel disappears to the realm of the sacred. There, although the issue does not arise in the story, he is protected from any human pursuit.

If the man (angel) who wrestled with Jacob had killed him, it would have been an instance of God's delivering Jacob into the man's hand, or alternatively, purposely placing the man into the situation of striking out at Jacob. A strange event accounts for the formulation of the rule that chooses to consider the victim's death (a tacit feature of the narrative) and the fact that God caused the two men to meet.[37] The rule would have the divinely directed killer protected from the consequence of his action and, significantly, just as the strange encounter in the tradition occurred at a sacred place, Peniel, so Yahweh appoints a similar place to which the killer may flee from human vengeance. As in the tradition, so in the law the entire matter—both the "intention" to kill and any consequences—is the deity's sphere of responsibility.[38]

---

[36] For a comparable identification of an angel with God, note Judg 2:1.

[37] Note again the lawgiver's procedure in pursuing the hypothetical issue of Jacob's death. The uncommon 'anah "be opportune, encounter" is found in Prov 12:21, "There shall no evil happen to the just: but the wicked shall be filled with mischief." The deity's role in controlling what occurs is understood. Critics interpret Exod 21:13, "He who does not lie in wait," as tantamount to an expression of lack of intent. But the statement could just as easily refer to the unpredictable appearance of the angel in the Genesis narrative.

[38] S. M. Paul, *Studies*, 64, is struck by the fact that only in this part of what he (on the basis of some modern distinction) calls the legal portion of the Book of the Covenant (Exod 21:2–22:17) do we find that the deity speaks in the first person. The deity's direct

The language of the rule may be another indication of its link to the tradition. A plain reading reveals the following curiosity. The rule states, "He that smiteth a man . . . ," and then, "And he who does not lie in wait, but God deliver into his hand." (Or, as the translations [e.g., AV, JPS] and grammarians [e.g., Gesenius][39] loosely have it, "And if a man lie not in wait.") Why is the formulation of the second part of the rule not "And if he lie not in wait," that is, a reference to the preceding attacker? Interpreters, not alert to the oddity, appear to assume, wrongly, that the two subjects are one and the same.[40] The victim, on the other hand, does indeed appear to be the same in each situation. The problem is solved if we assume that the lawgiver has under consideration two different attackers—Esau and the nameless divine agent[41]—and the one victim, Jacob. In the second part of the rule it is taken for granted that the victim is the same as in the first part because the text reads, "But God deliver [him—understood from the first part] into his hand."

---

role in the narrative is, it might be suggested, the pertinent factor. I consequently see no justification for the common view that the change from the participial form in the initial part of the rule to the different form in the next, with its use of the first person, indicates an interpolation. Martin Noth speaks of "excursuses" that are "clearly secondary additions," and then, less sure, speculates that they constitute insertions after the Book of the Covenant had been compiled; *Exodus*, 180. His "evidence" is again differences in language.

[39] *Gesenius' Hebrew Grammar*, ed. E. Kautzsch (Oxford: Oxford University Press, 1910), 337 para 112ii.

[40] Those who hold that vv. 13 and 14 have been interpolated are in their own way recognizing a discrepancy. See J. P. Hyatt, *Exodus*, NCBC, 231; Noth, *Exodus*, 180.

[41] Referred to in the rule not as "a man" but as "the one who."

The narrative invites the question why the deity proceeded against Jacob with the likelihood that he would die. It seems clear that his comparable, subsequent avoidance of death at the hands of Esau is somehow related to his prior avoidance of death at the hands of the deity. The link suggests that Jacob's culpability in cheating Esau out of his father's blessing by deceiving their father, Isaac, is recognized as deserving punishment. Indeed, there may be an aspect to Jacob's encounter with the divine antagonist that mirrors his action against his father. The latter's blindness was the means by which Jacob took advantage of him. Isaac imagined that he was dealing with his son Esau. In the narrative about the encounter at night with the divine attacker, we have to interpret the incident as belonging to the world of dreams and nightmares, when the eyes are closed and a man, conscience-stricken, thinks that he is under attack. Of further note: just as Jacob's problems began when, to obtain the special blessing, he took advantage of his father's blindness, so he, in obtaining the divine blessing, ended up with a disability too, his halting gait (Gen 32:31, 32).

Jacob deserved to die for his cavalier treatment of his father, but he was let off. Disrespect for a father is a capital offense in the following rule in Exod 21:17. If we had to speculate about the lawgiver's view in his homicide rule that there are occasions when a man has to die at the hands of heaven, we might think along the lines of the views underlying the narrative in Genesis, namely, that the person (Jacob) has indeed committed an offense for which he had avoided death at the mundane, human level.[42]

---

[42] In fact, this is Philo's view of the rule, *De specialibus legibus*

The third and final part of the rule pronounces capital punishment for the human killer who acts with cunning in slaying his victim. Again the language of the rule may be revealing. It is "But if a man come presumptuously upon his neighbour" and not "But if he come [namely, the same person as in the preceding rule whom God caused to kill]." The formulation is perhaps further evidence that the rule focuses on different developments in the Genesis account of Jacob's precarious situation.

In the rule the human killer is to receive no protection at Yahweh's altar. This part of the rule is read as setting down a situation contrasting to the preceding supramundane development. It may, however, be owing to Jacob's response to Esau's surprisingly benign reception of him. Despite Esau's avowed intention to kill his brother (attested by his actions, such as taking four hundred men with him), Esau not only welcomed Jacob but wanted to accompany him on his journey, or at least to leave some of his men to help Jacob.[43] Jacob declined both offers and said that he would make his own way to Esau's country of Seir, an event that no account confirms.[44] If Jacob chose

---

3.21.120. I can understand why almost all commentators instinctively, but without allowing for the full force of the language, introduce the notion of accidental killing in their discussion of this homicide rule. If, however, the influence of the story is paramount, the idea of accident is not relevant. On the lack of interest in the topic of accident in antiquity, see Daube, *Roman Law*, 149–50, 174–75.

[43] In a way they were now neighbors. The rule speaks of the man's attack upon his neighbor.

[44] Note Franz Delitzsch's curious statement, "Jacob's destination is Hebron, thence he seems to purpose visiting his brother in Seir: he deceives him by deceiving himself"; *New Commentary on Genesis*, vol. 2 (Edinburgh: Clark, 1889), 211.

to remain detached from Esau out of fear that Esau might slay him by an underhanded approach this time—mirroring his own guile in cheating Esau—we would have reason to think that this feature of the tradition evoked the rule. The tradition, however, gives little or no clue for Jacob's refusal of assistance.[45] It does refer to Jacob's safe (*šalem*) arrival at the city of Shechem. The implication is that he has survived any attempt on his life, including such as involved human plotting. Gerhard von Rad defines the term *šalem* as meaning "guileless, loyal, the contrary of everything crafty."[46] The rule, as formulated, would reflect both the hypothetical consideration that can be derived from the narrative and, by way of contrast, the preceding rule's consideration of the "sacred" killer protected for all time from execution.

Striking a Parent (Exod 21:15)

> And he that smiteth his father, or his mother, shall surely be put to death.

> *Source* (Gen 26:34–27:46). The hostility between Jacob and Esau had its origin in conflicting parental attitudes toward them.

The troubles within Jacob's family would account for the appearance at this point of the topic of striking a par-

---

[45] Von Rad, *Genesis*, 323, infers Jacob's suspicion. August Knobel before him had raised the issue; *Genesis* (Leipzig: Hirgel, 1882), 236.
[46] Von Rad, *Genesis*, 323. Curiously, he thinks that it has a forward reference to the Shechem incident in Genesis.

ent. The specific interest in a physical assault is carried over by the lawgiver not just from the preceding rule but, as is easily observed, because the topic of assault is indeed his main focus in a succession of rules.[47] The tradition that is related immediately after Jacob's meeting with Esau includes a conflict between violent sons—Simeon and Levi, who slaughter the Hivites—and their disapproving father, Jacob (Genesis 34). The traditions about Jacob and Esau, whose parents' actions created the enmity between them, also suggest the problem of intergenerational violence. These narratives furnish the first examples in the (Israelite) nation's history of antagonism between parents and offspring from which the lawgiver draws out the topic of assault against a parent.[48]

If Jacob's refusal to let Esau accompany him was motivated by fear that Esau might kill him by stealth, it is of passing interest, in light of the switch in the rules from the topic of murder by stealth to striking a parent, that the two brothers next met when burying their father (Gen 35:29). Esau's murderous intent against Jacob resulted from Jacob's tricking him out of their father's blessing. That trickery had been inspired by the mother's favoring Jacob over Esau. When Jacob expressed a fear that his deception might be found out and that a curse, not a blessing, would come upon him, Rebekah re-

[47] This focus may owe something to Moses's role in the tradition in Exod 2:11–14, when a fellow Hebrew, involved in a fight that Moses intervened in, complained, "Who made thee to be a prince and a judge over us?" This consideration need not exclude the further one that the lawgiver sets down the Israelite equivalent to Near Eastern rules about assault.

[48] Ham's offense against his father, Noah, belongs to pre-Jacob/Israel "history."

sponded by saying that the curse could fall upon her (Gen 27:13). She referred presumably to her husband's cursing her. The narrative brings out how in this instance a husband might react angrily against a spouse. The lawgiver has in focus Esau's potentially explosive reaction against a parent.

Nothing is expressed in the tradition about whether or not Esau knew of his mother's scheming. The lawgiver, however, hypothetically takes up the issue of violence within a family and, because the topic of striking a person in the preceding rule is one he is going to pursue, he sets down the dire warning against striking a parent. After all, if Esau could show murderous intent against his brother for cheating him, and that brother was under the control of his mother, it is natural to reflect on how Esau might have reacted to his mother's role in the deception. Again, too, Esau's despair when his father informed him about the loss of the blessing reminds us how such intensity of emotion could result in a son's potentially dangerous response to a parent. It is a typical procedure of the lawgiver to note the explicit aspect of a narrative, in this instance, parental attitudes toward sons, and, in Wisdom fashion, to look at the matter from the reverse angle, namely, sons' attitudes toward parents.

The other feature of the tradition that could have contributed to the lawgiver's focus is the grief that Esau brought to both his parents because of his choice of wives (Gen 26:35). It is but a short step to the lawgiver's contemplating what a son's foolish reaction might be to such parental objection. I repeat, however, that the generational conflict in the story invited attention and that the exploration of the topic of assault has determined why the rule particularly concerns violence against a parent.

[3]

Joseph's Problems
(Part One)

The aggression against Joseph by his brothers, the violence Jacob was led to believe had been done to Joseph by a wild animal, and the retribution visited upon Judah for his role in disposing of Joseph generate the topics covered in the rules: theft of person; contempt for a parent; assault on a free person, on a slave, on a pregnant woman; mutilation of a slave; a goring ox; and pits.

Theft of Person (Exod 21:16)

And he that stealeth a man, and is selling him, and he be found in his hand, he shall surely be put to death.

Source (Genesis 37). The brothers of Joseph turned against him because their father favored him. A consequence was that they set in motion the means to sell him abroad.

The history of Jacob's family again accounts for this rule at precisely this point in the material. From the strife, amounting to a desire to kill, between the brothers Jacob and Esau, Moses turns to the strife, similarly involving an intent to kill, between brothers of the succeeding generation, namely, the antagonism toward Joseph on the part of his brothers. Jacob's favoring this son of his old age brought in its wake his other sons' hatred of Joseph, just as Esau's hatred of Jacob was a consequence of their mother's favoritism.

The lawgiver's focus on assault (verb *nakah*) is again dominant. The brothers refrained from killing Joseph because of Reuben's intervention: he did not wish them "to strike [*nakah*] to the life" (Gen 37:21). Instead, they threw him into a pit, and when they saw a company of Ishmaelites approach, decided to sell him. In the event, if we keep to the story as it is related, a group of Midianites came by and took Joseph out of the pit, and he was sold eventually to the Egyptians.

In regard to the rule in Exod 21:16, David Daube points out that it appears illogical: if the victim has been sold he can no longer be in the thief's possession. Daube sees the rule as over time incorporating an insertion that reflected an advance in legal development. At one point theft of a man was proved only if the person was sold, but eventually theft could be proved even if the person was still in the thief's possession.[1]

If the rule is linked to the Genesis narrative, however, it accurately conveys the situation of Joseph about to be sold abroad by his brothers.[2] They intended to sell him

---

[1] David Daube, *Studies in Biblical Law* (Cambridge: Cambridge University Press, 1947), 95.

[2] S. R. Driver, *The Book of Exodus*, CBSC (Cambridge: Cambridge University Press, 1911), 216, thinks, on other grounds, that sale to a foreign country must be meant.

but did not do so because in the meantime another group had taken hold of Joseph. The brothers' offense, the law-giver judges, still remains. They had not yet sold him, but they had him in their possession and that fact too constituted the offense of stealing. The issue of stealing a man as expressed in the rule is just how it presents itself in the tradition.

What is interesting in the rule's formulation is that *vav*, "and," and not *'o*, "or," is used in "And he that steals a man and is selling him and he is found in his hand." To be sure, *vav* can express an alternative, but if we accept its usual signification, the formulation accurately conveys what the position is regarding the treatment of Joseph. Indeed, the formulation is a necessary one in view of the fact that, if we assume that the story existed in its present form in the lawgiver's time, in the end the brothers did not actually sell Joseph to the Egyptians. In other words, there was a time when the brothers were selling Joseph but he was still in their hands.[3] The rule's appearance in the *Mishpatim* can be accounted for by its close tie to Joseph's treatment by his brothers. The rule's possible legal application is more difficult to assess.[4]

---

[3] Raymond Westbrook also takes the literal translation of the Hebrew seriously. However, claiming that the formulation is confusingly terse, he introduces a change of subject: "He that steals a man and sells him and he in whose possession he is found shall be put to death"; *Studies in Biblical and Cuneiform Law* (Paris: Gabalda, 1988), 119. I have difficulty with his objection about the rule's terseness, but note that the Joseph story does work with the original kidnapper (the brothers) and a second possessor (the Ishmaelites, Gen 37:27).

[4] To apply strictly legal criteria to most biblical rules is probably inappropriate. A rule such as Deut 22:1–4 about taking in a straying animal should the owner not be around, or even known, can-

Joseph's brothers were punished in a subtle, complex fashion for their offense, but they were not put to death. We can speculate that one reason for formulating the rules in the Book of the Covenant was the need to clarify what the judgment should be in later Israelite life in contrast to how comparable matters were handled in the narrative traditions.[5]

Contempt for a Parent (Exod 21:17)

And he that treateth contemptibly his father, or his mother, shall surely be put to death.

Source (Gen 37:31–35). After the brothers' involvement in the sale of Joseph, they sought to conceal their offense against him by devising evidence to deceive their father.

The verb *qalal* means to treat a person in a light, contemptible way. Interpreters naturally wonder why the rule was not appended to the one before the theft of a

---

not be examined along legal lines. To do so is to bring in the problem of theft and thereby confuse matters immeasurably. The legal historian Alan Watson finds no comparable rule in ancient or modern legal systems; "Artificiality, Reality and Roman Contract Law," *LHR* 57 (1989), 147. This example serves well as a warning for many other rules. For a recent example where modern legal notions obscure an understanding of the rule about straying animals, see Alan Cooper, "The Plain Sense of Exodus 23:5," *HUCA* 59 (1988), 16.

[5] Umberto Cassuto also links the rule concerning theft of a man to the brothers' offense. He does not lay out the assumptions underlying his view; *A Commentary on the Book of Exodus* (Jerusalem: Magnes, 1967), 271.

man, namely, to the rule against striking a parent.[6] Again, however, the narrative story line has determined the sequence of the rules. After Joseph's sale, the brothers tried to cover up their offense against him by concocting a scheme to deceive their father. They killed an animal, dipped Joseph's coat in its blood, and let their father draw the conclusion that a wild beast had devoured Joseph. Their action represents a classic instance of treating a parent in a contemptible way, an action worse than uttering a curse against the parent. As S. R. Driver points out, the verb in the rule is stronger than the "maketh light, dishonoureth" (*qalah*) of the similar rule in Deut 27:16.[7]

We should also link the Exod 21:17 rule to Jacob's comparable deception of his father when he let him think that Esau stood before him. Jacob at the time feared that a curse (*qᵉlalah*) would come upon him for his deception (Gen 27:12, 13). As already noted, the lawgiver, like those responsible for compiling the narratives in the Pentateuch, is alert to similar developments over the generations.

The lawgiver sets down his rule on contempt after his rule about the sale of a person, and not immediately after the one about assaulting a parent. The reason appears to be that the contemptible treatment of Jacob by his sons is so closely linked to their assault on Joseph and intended sale of him.

---

[6] The LXX had already changed the sequence of the rules in this way. Critics commonly interpret these two rules about parents as violations of the commandment in the decalogue to honor them. The latter rule, however, is concerned with honor to parents because of their role as progenitors.

[7] Driver, *Exodus*, CBSC, 217.

Assault (Exod 21:18)

> And if men strive together, and one smite another with a stone or with his fist, and if he die not, but keepeth his bed [literally, fall into a place of lying]: If he rise again, and walk abroad upon his staff, then shall he that smote him be quit: only he shall pay for the loss of his time [or, his sitting], and shall cause him to be thoroughly healed.

Source (Gen 37:18–24). Joseph was set upon by his brothers, who stopped short of slaying him.

A number of rules about assault are set down. They are prompted by the continuing interest in the topic, but in particular at this point by the content of Reuben's successful appeal to his brothers after they had decided to kill Joseph: *lo' nakkennu napeš*, "Let us not strike to the life" (Gen 37:21). They might assault Joseph, the implication is, but should not kill him. The topic, as one worthy of legal scrutiny, is explored, with other elements in the tradition also playing a role, in the following four rules (Exod 21:18–27). These rules concern an assault that does not cause death but has other consequences; blows to a slave that do cause immediate death and those that do not; blows to a pregnant woman that cause death only to the fetus in her womb, and those that cause her to die also; and blows to a slave that cause disfigurement.

At first glance it might appear that, when we assess the rules about assault that precede Exod 21:18 and the three that follow, we should judge that the two rules not involving assault (stealing a man, treating a parent with contempt) are out of place. The reason, however, for the appearance of these two rules is the fact that the topics in question are very much tied to the context of the physical abuse experienced by Joseph.

Joseph was presumably first struck, at least forcibly taken in some sense, by his brothers, because Reuben had to deliver him from their hands (Gen 37:21).[8] He was then stripped of the coat that symbolized for them his superior stance and thrown into a pit. The rule deals with a dispute between men that ends with one receiving a blow that does not kill him but at some point causes him to "fall into a place of lying." Initially the dispute in the rule, "And if men strive," is probably not physical but about words and feelings,[9] as is the problem to begin with between Joseph and his brothers. After being struck, the victim, we should possibly interpret, has to take to his bed because of the injuries received. The Hebrew *napal l*^e*miškab* is generally viewed to have the meaning of taking to bed in the rule, but it is noteworthy that it can literally refer to Joseph's lying in the pit.

Should the victim be able to rise and walk with the aid of his staff, the attacker is not held culpable should his foe die when he venture forth. It is again noteworthy that

[8] The law refers to striking with a stone or the fist. Umberto Cassuto translates "stone" as meaning a weapon because he thinks it is probably an archaic term that reflects the fact that weapons were made of flint; *Exodus*, 272. The plain meaning is the more likely and might have regard to the brothers' situation in the wilderness. For this reason too the term "fist" should not be given the meaning "spade, hoe." S. R. Driver also rejects the latter sense, *Exodus*, CBSC, 217.

[9] So Driver, *Exodus*, CBSC, 217; also S. M. Paul, *Studies in the Book of the Covenant in the Light of Cuneiform and Biblical Law* (Leiden: Brill, 1970), 67. The verb is *rib*, "to contend."

Joseph was placed in a life-threatening situation and that Jacob's sons, being shepherds, would have had staffs. In other words, although the rule should perhaps be given a sense close to the usual translations, its language evokes the circumstances surrounding Joseph's situation.

The one who struck the blow has to pay for the injured person's *šebet*. The translation usually given—I suspect because it fits interpreters' assumptions that biblical rules must have been practical in character—is "loss of time [from work]," because the verb "to desist, rest" may be behind the form *šebet*. Or the sense may derive from *yašab*, "to sit," again presumably with a reference to his incapacity. This link between money and, if we opt for the meaning, "his sitting" is interesting in light of the observation that his brothers compounded their offense against him when they sat down (*yašab*) and came up with the plan to obtain money for him (Gen 37:25–27). As their sitting down led to the nefarious anticipation of money for them, so they in turn, a lawgiver might judge, should be faced with the prospect of paying money to Joseph for his enforced sitting in the pit. A punishment that mirrors the offense is a major feature of the narratives themselves; for example, Joseph eventually traps his brothers into enslavement to him in Egypt by the use of money (Genesis 42). In the rule the guilty party must also attend to the victim's restoration to health. We do not learn of Joseph's injuries—there may have been none—but Reuben's desire to have him restored unharmed to their father could have prompted the analogous consideration in the rule. I repeat, however, that all we can be sure about is why the topic in the rule presents itself. How the lawgiver reasons about the offense in question is more open to speculation.

Assault on a Slave (Exod 21:20, 21)

> 20 And if a man smite his servant, or his maid, with a rod, and he die under his hand; he shall be surely avenged. 21 Notwithstanding, if he continue a day or two, he shall not be avenged: for he is his money.

Source (Gen 37:18–27). Instead of killing Joseph, his brothers decided to treat him as a bondman.

We have to ask why at this point in the code a slave comes into the lawgiver's reckoning and a rule is presented which reveals concerns similar to those underlying the preceding rule. The explanation appears to be the change in Joseph's status. When Judah stated to his brothers that there was no profit in killing Joseph, he was already treating Joseph as a slave. In other words, Judah's view was that it was not profitable to beat this bondman to death—precisely the issue in the rule. The development in the narrative is behind the switch in the legal material from the assault on a free person to the beating of a slave, who is, in the words of the rule, his master's money.

The distinction in status between a free person and a slave accounts for the difference in the lawgiver's response to the results of a beating. If the master does strike a slave "to the life," punishment for the master is in order.[10] If the slave survives a day or two but then dies, the

---

[10] On the face of it this rule, as Cassuto is eager to point out (*Exodus*, 273), confers upon a slave a human status that comparable Near Eastern codes do not approach. More likely, however, we have to focus on the fact that it is the brothers' treatment of Joseph

master loses the possession he either once paid money for or, in line with the story, might have obtained money for by selling him.

The rule cites the example of beating the slave with a rod (*šebeṭ*). No such occurrence is mentioned for Joseph, although his state of imposed bondage suggests an example of a slave who might need to be kept down by beatings. Presumably in less dramatic circumstances a master's use of a rod against a slave was common enough and would account for the rod's mention. It might also be noted, however, that a rod is a shepherd's implement (Lev 27:32; Ezek 20:37; Mic 7:14; Ps 23:4 where *šebeṭ* is parallel to *mišʿenet*, the term for staff in the preceding rule), so that again the example of Joseph's shepherding brothers in their hostility to him may have suggested the specific example of injuries owing to a beating with a rod.

Raymond Westbrook rightly insists on an explanation as to why the term *naqam* ("to avenge") and not *mot yumat* ("to die") is used. He notes that *naqam* is often used of revenge that is visited not upon the wrongdoer himself but upon, for example, his children.[11] I would observe that in the Joseph story two of the brothers, in taking responsibility for Benjamin's trip to Egypt to meet Joseph, invite a penalty upon themselves—should Benjamin like Joseph not return to his father—along the lines of the use of *naqam*. Reuben tells his father to slay two of his sons should he fail to bring Benjamin back (Gen 42:37).

---

that influences the lawgiver's attitude: for the purposes of legal instruction, hypothetically Joseph can be considered a slave, but remove the hypothetical perspective and he is a son of Jacob (Israel).

[11] Westbrook, *Cuneiform Law*, 94.

Judah, in turn, says to his father that he will be a surety for Benjamin: "Of my hand shalt thou require him . . . let me bear the blame for ever" (Gen 43:9). From the narrator's perspective the brothers are unwittingly bringing punishment on themselves because of what they did to Joseph. The fact that the focus is on the distress they are causing their father over a son suggests that they in turn will experience grief because of what will happen to their sons.

Assault on a Pregnant Woman
(Exod 21:22–25)

> 22 If men strive, and hurt a pregnant woman, so that her children come out, but death does not ensue: he shall be surely fined, according as the woman's husband will lay upon him; or[12] he shall pay as the judges determine. 23 And if death ensue, then thou shalt give life for life, 24 eye for eye, tooth for tooth, hand for hand, foot for foot, 25 burning for burning, wound for wound, stripe for stripe.

> *Source* (Genesis 37, 38). Judah was the ringleader of the brothers in making their father think that he, Jacob, had lost a son to the savagery of a wild animal. Judah's initiative had its nemesis when he lost two sons, and almost another two, because of Tamar's central role in his family life.

The inspiration for this rule is the story of Judah and the pregnant Tamar. The lawgiver's exploration of first

---

[12] The *waw* expresses an alternative case (as in Exod 20:10, 17).

the example of a blow and then of death to a pregnant woman is attributable to the role the story plays in relation to the brothers' treatment of Joseph, in particular, Judah's role in Joseph's ending up as a slave in Egypt. From this viewpoint the rule about the pregnant woman fits into the preceding sequence of rules. We recall that Judah's substitution of the sale of Joseph for his being beaten to death inspired the immediately preceding rule about the slave beaten to death.

Judah emerged as the leader among the brothers in disposing of Joseph. As their father later commented sarcastically, he was the wild beast, a lion, that had preyed upon his son Joseph (Gen 49:9).[13] His destiny in turn was to experience the loss of sons. Indeed, he almost destroyed his own children conceived by Tamar. Judah's story is told as part of Joseph's—indeed the Judah-Tamar story is embedded within the Joseph story—because of the narrator's belief in an inexorable law of retribution that requires that wrongdoing be visited with its appropriate penalty. Judah (with his brothers) let their father think that a wild beast had torn Joseph to pieces (Gen 37:33). In turn, Judah lost his two sons, Er and Onan, in their bonding with Tamar, and he almost lost another two when he ordered the pregnant Tamar to be burned for what he took to be her harlotry. Only when she had him identified as their father did she, and his twin sons, avoid a fate that would have left all three of them dead. His punishment for the fate he brought upon Joseph is talionic in character: deceiving Jacob about the death of

___

[13] "From the prey of my son"—in Hebrew grammar a construct state. See E. M. Good, "The 'Blessing' on Judah, Gen 49:8–12," *JBL* 82 (1963), 429; C. M. Carmichael, *Women, Law, and the Genesis Traditions* (Edinburgh: Edinburgh University Press, 1979), 60, 61.

his son Joseph and the mutilation of his corpse, Judah in turn nearly caused the death of Tamar's and his sons, and the mutilation of their corpses (had they been burnt).

The rule is about a physical struggle: equivalent, not equal, to the highly idiosyncratic struggle between Tamar's husband, who is dead but who through her tenacity claims his right to a child, and his brothers and father, who by failing to do their duty by him, act against him. Like Tamar the woman in the rule has more than one child in her womb. This reference to children has rightly puzzled interpreters.[14]

The lawgiver, in line with his preceding interest in Reuben's distinction as applied to Joseph, namely, striking a person but not "to the life," applies it to the woman.[15] The consequence of the assault, the presumed loss of the fetuses, may well be owing to the general thrust of the narrative in Genesis 38—Judah has to experience what it is like to lose sons. We might recall how Esau's relationship to his parents raised the issue of a son's assault on a parent even though that kind of aggression is also not actually present in the tradition. If the pregnant woman in the rule is struck deliberately by one of the disputants, a certain kind of penalty follows.[16] Unlike Onan and Shelah

---

[14] Not a generic plural—so Driver, *Exodus*, CBSC, 219, and Cassuto, *Exodus*, 275—but twins, as Julian Morgenstern sensed; "The Book of the Covenant," *HUCA* 7 (1930), 67.

[15] Again I would not exclude the possibility that the lawgiver was acquainted with comparable rules about an assault on a pregnant woman, e.g., CH 209, 210. S. M. Paul states, "The fact that so many of the legal corpora specifically refer to such a case, which apparently was not too common, may be due to the literary dependence of one corpus upon another" (*Studies*, 71 n.1).

[16] See Daube, *Studies in Biblical Law*, 107–8, who points out that whenever *nagap* is used with the accusative it refers to a deliberate

who acted against Tamar by omission, Judah fully intended to strike out at her physically.[17] In an extreme reaction to her harlotry he ordered that she be subject to burning. A beating would have been more appropriate.[18] Although Judah thought that he acted properly in moving to punish Tamar, he in fact proceeded improperly—as he himself came to realize (Gen 38:26). His action constituted an offense against the pregnant Tamar and her husband—as well as, in the broader perspective, his own (unwitting) punishment for his offense against Jacob. The fact that neither Joseph nor Tamar ended up dead, that the fate of each was different from what was intended, would have encouraged the lawgiver to explore the possibilities as to what might have happened. The distinction, as observed, between striking the person and killing him or her is what determines his hypothetical procedure.

There is, however, another powerful factor at work in his procedure. The lawgiver reacts negatively to the vi-

---

act. Many interpreters have spoken of an inadvertent assault upon the woman (e.g., J. I. Durham, *Exodus*, WBC 3 (Word Books: Waco, Texas, 1987), 323). Presumably, they find it too puzzling that she has been struck deliberately. Other interpreters, however, approach the correct meaning when they suggest, on the basis of what occurred in Deut 25:11, that she may have intervened in the affray (so, e.g., Driver, *Exodus*, CBSC, 219). The implication is that at that point she was deliberately struck.

[17] Only one of the disputants is singled out for punishment, even though an unspecified number is stated in the rule. Thus the protasis of Exod 21:22 is "If men strive together," while the apodosis is "He shall surely be fined." Again what the lawgiver carries over from the narrative, namely, Judah's potential action against Tamar, would resolve the problem. B. S. Jackson discusses it in "The Problem of Exod xxi 22–5 (*Jus Talionis*)," *VT* 23 (1973), 287–88.

[18] See note 28.

carious type of talionic penalty he finds in the tradition. Judah would not have been directly punished for his offense against Joseph. Rather Tamar and the children within her womb would have been heaven's instrument in punishing him. The lawgiver chooses to have the individual who is responsible for an offense punished directly for it. This reaction to the kind of punishment found in the tradition is well illustrated in the second rule after the one about the pregnant woman. It requires that if a man has acted irresponsibly in controlling his ox and it kills another man's son or daughter, the owner—not his son or daughter—should be punished for the offense (Exod 21:31). The unnecessary clause about the son or daughter is rightly read as opposing vicarious punishment.

In the rule the penalty for forcibly causing the woman to expel the children from her womb is that her husband claims a certain amount of money from the attacker. Just as in the preceding rule but one, in which Joseph's beating is in focus, the penalty consists of a monetary payment. Moses rules for some case in the future in which, unlike Tamar's case, the husband would be alive and he would define the compensation. But even Tamar's more unusual situation is considered by Moses, and this fact explains the puzzling statement that the judges, not the husband, will fine the culprit. In this part of the rule the husband is assumed to be dead and judges determine the compensation owing. The rule lays out both the unremarkable and the remarkable situations.[19]

[19] The rule about concubines in Exod 21:7–9 is comparable: first the remarkable situation, where the man acquires a woman whom he had not designated, and then the unremarkable, where she is retained by him for his son.

The Origins of Biblical Law

The rule next deals with the pregnant mother as victim too. The term 'ason has caused much difficulty and has been translated "mischief" (AV), "harm" (RSV), and "death" (Mekhilta).[20] The Mekhilta's "death" is the correct translation. What has misled interpreters is their sense that the talionic formula, used in regard to what happens to the woman, refers to various possible injuries, and that these must be included in the range of the term. Needless to say, they have had to separate the part about "life for life" from the rest of the formula and then argue that the text is hopelessly conflated. They have misunderstood the nature of this formula.[21] It does not refer to various injuries in the absence of death, but to the mutilation of a corpse after execution.[22] Its meaning is: "life for life [to be followed by] eye for eye, tooth for tooth," etc. At least two factors should have made interpreters more cautious. First is the major problem that if injuries without death are meant there is a conflict with the preceding rule in

[20] An early, probably pre-second century A.D., Rabbinic commentary on the book of Exodus.

[21] No text has been subject to so much reshaping because of this misunderstanding. B. S. Jackson lays out one such reshaping and, to illustrate just how much disarray supposedly exists, states, "The real trouble began when the rest of the talionic formula, attracted by *nefesh tahat nefesh*, was inserted. That altered the context. Verse 23 was now taken to refer to the woman, not the child, and verse 22 came to be understood as meaning that the woman survived but—by implication—the child did not"; *The Mishpatim* (forthcoming).

[22] Examples of the practice are found at different times and places, e.g., during the Spanish Inquisition. See H. C. Lea, *History of the Inquisition of the Middle Ages* (New York: Macmillan, 1906), vol. 1, Appendix on the persons sentenced in Saragossa between 1484 and 1502. My friend Hein Brouwer of the Spaans Seminarium of the University of Amsterdam, Holland, drew my attention to this reference.

124

Exod 21:18, 19. It requires not a matching injury for someone who has injured someone else, but monetary compensation and restoration of the victim's health.[23]

Second is the use of the term *'ason* elsewhere. It occurs only in the context of the Joseph story—a notable fact in light of my theory about the construction of these rules—in reference to Jacob's fear of disaster overtaking his child Benjamin (Gen 42:4, 38; 44:29). He means death (or just possibly, its equivalent—never seeing him again).[24] The basis of Jacob's fear is his memory of what happened to Joseph. When Judah conveys the father's fear to the disguised Joseph we are meant to recall Judah's own wrongdoing in regard to Joseph. Benjamin is in Egypt at this point and Judah pleads with Joseph to let him replace Benjamin, who has been detained for the theft of Joseph's cup. When Judah further requests that he, Judah, become

[23] Attempts such as S. M. Paul's (*Studies*, 74) to get rid of the discrepancy by introducing distinctions based on notions of original intent fail to understand how intent was dealt with in ancient legal sources. See David Daube's devastating criticism of modern attempts to handle the topic in ancient law codes in *Roman Law: Linguistic, Social, and Philosophical Aspects* (Edinburgh: Edinburgh University Press, 1969), 163–75.

[24] Note how enslavement abroad is equated with death in Gen 44:9, 10: Joseph's brothers refer to a death sentence as appropriate for whoever has stolen Joseph's divining cup. Joseph's steward concurs but mentions enslavement, not death. The equation is a common one in antiquity; see Daube, *Studies in Biblical Law*, 241, but note Westbrook's discussion in *Cuneiform Law*, 128–31. Westbrook, noting that the term *'ason* only occurs elsewhere in the Joseph story, suggests that, because in the contexts in question the offender cannot be identified, this in fact is what it must mean. He consequently attributes this meaning ("If it is a case of perpetrator unknown"), and not the death of the woman, to the rule in Exod 21:23 (*Cuneiform Law*, 69). His observation about the contexts is fine, but not the conclusion he draws from it.

Joseph's slave (Gen 44:33), he is unwittingly suggesting for himself a punishment that mirrors his offense against Joseph, namely, his instigating the sale of Joseph as a slave.[25] The lawgiver takes over the term 'ason from this background because it is precisely the context in which he formulates a rule that reflects the larger significance of Judah's threat to the life of the pregnant Tamar. In each context, the threat to Benjamin and the threat to his own sons in Tamar's womb, the term signifies a potential and not an actual outcome.

In his rule the lawgiver considers first the blow to the pregnant woman that causes her to miscarry. As noted, the monetary penalty compares with the compensation given to someone struck during a fight (Exod 21:18, 19). The lawgiver next considers a blow that causes death. Instead of the penalty being expressed as *mot yumat*, "dying, he shall die," as in preceding rules, it is communicated by the formula "life for life, eye for eye, tooth for tooth, hand for hand, foot for foot, burning for burning, wound for wound, stripe for stripe."[26] The difference is remarkable and demands a thorough explanation.

The talionic penalty is formulated on the basis of Moses's judgment about what should have been done to Judah if he had gone ahead and put Tamar to death. Al-

[25] Just as the lawgiver explores the same offense from different angles with the consequence that similar rules are set down, so the narratives themselves explore someone's offense from different angles. Thus retribution for Judah's role in the offense against Joseph is worked out in his relationship with Tamar and in his relationship with the disguised Joseph in Egypt.

[26] For a discussion of this formula in Deut 19:21 and Lev 24:18–20, see C. M. Carmichael, *Biblical Laws of Talion* (Oxford: Oxford Centre for Postgraduate Hebrew Studies, 1986), 21–39.

ready in the narrative Judah was made to realize that her resort to harlotry in order to obtain a child for her dead husband should not be condemned, but rather he should realize his own culpability in not doing his duty by his dead son, her husband. He in effect was responsible for her resort to harlotry. The rule contemplates the hypothetical situation in which Tamar would have died if Judah had proceeded with the sentence he had pronounced on her. Many of the rules are of this kind; for example, the homicide rules in Exod 21:12–14 work with the hypothetical idea of Esau's and the divine messenger's killing of Jacob.

Judah presumably reckoned that the use of fire was the appropriate means of disposing of Tamar on the basis that one who arouses burning sexual desire deserves such a mirroring punishment. Other biblical texts reveal this proverbial view. "Can a man [indulging his sexual appetite] take fire in his bosom, and his clothes not be burned? Can one go upon hot coals, and his feet not be burned?" (Prov 6:27, 28). Harlots should have branding, not beauty (Isa 3:24). Judah himself in his role as domestic judge responded to Tamar's presumed offense by postulating a mirroring penalty. Ironically, in applying a talionic punishment to Tamar, he was unwittingly visiting upon himself a talionic punishment for his offense against Jacob that required him to act in a mirroring fashion against his own sons in Tamar's womb. This larger context explains why his reaction to Tamar's sexual sin is so extreme.[27]

[27] Contrast the view of M. C. Astour, "Tamar the Hierodule," *JBL* 85 (1966), 185–96, who argues that there is a vestigial motif at work in the story. The designation of Tamar as a *qᵉdešah*, "sacred prostitute," is a motif that has been preserved from a Babylonian

Should Tamar have died at Judah's hands, he would
have deserved to be punished not just for causing her to
resort to harlotry but, because it was his initial offense
against Joseph that brought in its wake Tamar's grim situation, at the same time he deserved punishment for the
original offense. In sum, Judah deserved to be "torn,
torn" like Joseph (Gen 37:33) and, concurrently, his body
visited with the penalties that ordinarily harlots received.
We should recall that this lawgiver reacts against vicarious
punishment and, consequently, he concentrates on Judah's offenses and what punishments they should entail.
While divine justice works in its inscrutable and inexorable way, which involves others as its instruments,
Moses adheres strictly to the principle of individual responsibility. If both Joseph and Tamar had died, Judah
would have deserved death followed by mutilation, that
is, "life for life, eye for eye, tooth for tooth, hand for
hand, and foot for foot." In addition, his corpse would
have been subject to the penalties associated with harlotry, namely, "burning for burning, wound for wound,
and stripe for stripe."

The terms used in the final three members of the talionic formula point to the offense of harlotry. An uncommon word in the law, *kᵉwiyah*, "burning," appears in
Prov 6:28 (the scorching of the adulterer's feet) in the verbal form *kawah* as a parallel to *śarap* in Prov 6:27 (the
burning of his clothes). The narrative uses *śarap* in reference to the harlot Tamar's punishment. In Isa 3:24 the
harlots, the daughters of Jerusalem, will experience burn-

---

background, through a Canaanite one, into an Israelite context.
The appropriate penalty, he argues, for a sacred person who committed an offense was death by burning.

ing (*ki*) instead of beauty. Also, *pesaʿ*, "wound," is not a common word either. It is used of the troubles, such as enticement by harlots, that befall those who imbibe drink (Prov 24:29, 33). In Song of Songs 5:7 the watchmen of the city wound the woman as she searches for her lover, possibly because they regard her as a harlot. The third (also uncommon) term, *haburah*, "stripe," has an interesting use in Isa 1:6 in reference to injuries to the land of Judah under the figure of a human body. Among the offenses that caused such injuries was that of harlotry (Isa 1:21; cp. v. 18).[28] The rule bears a warning that if in reality Judah had had Joseph torn to shreds and Tamar burned, he would eventually have had much the same done to him. Joseph and Tamar had not met such a fate, so the rule itself embodies a made-up case. It is, perhaps, one of the most interesting examples of the lawmaker's construction of a rule incorporating, and extending further, the ethical judgment underlying the story's presentation. Indeed, the two processes probably belong together, namely, the construction of the rules and the fitting together of the various narratives.

Mutilation of a Slave (Exod 21:26, 27)

> 26 And if a man smite the eye of his servant, or the eye of his maid, that it perish; he shall let him go free for his eye's sake. 27 And if he smites out his manservant's tooth, or his maidservant's tooth; he shall let him go free for his tooth's sake.

---

[28] In MAL 40 a harlot who misbehaves receives a severe corporal penalty; see G. R. Driver and J. C. Miles, *The Assyrian Laws* (Oxford: Clarendon, 1935), 129–32.

> *Source* (Gen 37:26–33). The enslaved Joseph was re-
> ported as having been torn to pieces—the dead victim,
> his father thought, of an attack by a wild beast. In fact,
> he had been sold to the Egyptians.

In the preceding rules, including the last one about
Tamar's ordeal, the focus was on Joseph's experience at
the hands of his brothers. Various hypothetical situations
were explored: striking a free person, striking a slave, and
causing injury or death to a pregnant woman. Joseph's
status as a free person, then as a slave came into the reckoning, as did his father's image of him torn to pieces by
some wild beast. We might recall that Jacob's ambivalent
position in Laban's household—slave, hired servant, free
person—served as the lawgiver's focus in his initial rules.

The mutilating injuries inflicted on a slave, in the rule
following the one about a talionic penalty, present a
problem again inspired by a hypothetical exploration of
Joseph's situation. The image of the enslaved Joseph (the
next after Jacob in the history of the nation to experience
some form of enslavement), who also is associated with a
disfigured body, inspires the attempt to imagine a more
realistic situation in which a later Israelite slave might experience disfigurement. The idea of Joseph's disfigurement, it might be noted, is one that was conjured up by
his enslavers. The more conventional example of a slave
beaten by his master readily presents itself.

Joseph as dead, Joseph as alive, is a combination in the
story that is explored in the rules.[29] We recall that Reu-

---

[29] Except that a specific consideration of Joseph's death, independent of its role in the rule about the pregnant woman, is not
necessary at this point because Esau's intention to kill Jacob served
to introduce the topic of homicide in Exod 21:12.

ben's concern that his brothers not strike Joseph so severely as to kill him inspired the construction of rules exploring the distinction between injuries that kill and those
that fall short of killing. The distinction was applied first
to a free person and then to a slave. The rule in Exod
21:20, 21 focuses on the slave's death from a beating, this
rule in Exod 21:26, 27 on a severe beating only, the injuries of which apparently derive from the mutilations cited
in the preceding rule in Exod 21:24, 25. It is probably too
fanciful to imagine that injuries to the eye and the mouth
are discussed because Joseph's brothers were reacting to
the fact that Joseph had come to observe their doings and
report back to their father, as he had done before (Gen
37:2). More likely, Joseph's status as a slave and the image
of his potential disfigurement have been combined in realistic fashion. The slave's obtaining his or her freedom
on account of the mutilating injuries is consistent with
Reuben's aim to restore Joseph to his father as a free person again.[30] It is worth noting that the lawgiver's interest
in slavery, first Jacob's, then Joseph's, is a feature of his
laws from the very first one about the release of slaves.
This feature (including the aspect of the disputes between
Jacob and Laban, Joseph and his brothers) recalls the historical setting given to these rules, namely, just after the
dispute with the pharaoh and the Israelites' release from
slavery.

[30] Commentators are quick to draw attention to the humanitarian
aspect of this rule in contrast to comparable rules in the ancient
Near Eastern collections. I doubt, however, if they are really comparing like with like. If the inspiration for this particular biblical
rule is the treatment of Joseph by his brothers, the elevated attitude
revealed in the rule is more understandable. An apologetic approach to the Bible often underlies claims about its superior stance.

Goring Ox (Exod 21:28–32)

28 If an ox gores a man or a woman, that they die: then the ox shall surely be stoned, and his flesh shall not be eaten; but the owner of the ox shall be quit. 29 But if the ox were wont to push with his horn in time past, and it hath been testified to his owner, and he hath not kept him in, but that he hath killed a man or a woman; the ox shall be stoned, and his owner also shall be put to death. 30 If there be laid on him a sum of money, then he shall give for the ransom of his life whatsoever is laid upon him. 31 Whether he have gored a son, or have gored a daughter, according to this judgment shall it be done unto him. 32 If the ox shall gore a manservant or a maidservant; he shall give unto their master thirty shekels of silver, and the ox shall be stoned.

Source (Gen 37:20, 31–33). In order to conceal their offense against Joseph, the brothers presented evidence that an animal had killed him.

Reflections on Joseph's treatment at the hands of his brothers continue to generate more rules about assault, with animals as culprits this time. From Jacob's point of view an animal had mauled Joseph, but in reality it was his brothers who were acting against him, initially with a view to killing him. The focus on an animal's responsibility, with human culpability for its misdeeds considered too, comes from this background. Joseph's death owing to an animal is only an idea on the part of the brothers, one moreover that they use for legal purposes in order to acquit themselves of any liability for his death.[31]

---

[31] On the legal aspect of the narrative, see Daube, *Studies in Biblical Law*, 4–10.

Like the composer of the narrative, the lawgiver in a succession of rules works with various ideas about animals
and the legal effects arising from their use in a domestic
setting.

The method whereby a tradition's idiosyncratic situation is transformed into a more realistic one in ordinary
life, where a narrative is used to suggest a topic that will
already be familiar to the recipients of the instruction,
again applies in the presentation of this rule. We should
also keep open the possibility that the lawgiver is familiar
with laws from the wider world of Near Eastern culture,
and that the use of his own national tradition is the means
by which he presents the equivalent rule for an Israelite
cultural setting. In any event, his rule first considers a domestic situation equivalent to the notion of Joseph's death
because of a wild beast. The animal that uncharac-
teristically has behaved like a wild one is stoned to death
and its flesh is not to be eaten.[32] The apparent treatment of
the animal as homicidal in some legal sense may reflect
the interplay between human and animal assaults on Joseph. A subsequent rule, Exod 22:31, prohibits eating the
flesh of an animal that has been torn to death by another.
We shall see that that matter too has been raised because
of the Joseph incident.[33] The switch from the human

[32] It is the Genesis narrative, rather than, as S. M. Paul thinks
(*Studies*, 82), some special biblical view (which may still be valid)
about the nature of human beings in contrast to the nature of animals—a human life is valued so highly that it demands retribution
even from an animal—that explains why this rule is found in the
midst of rules about a man's offense against his fellow man.

[33] In light of the principle of first-time developments the juxtaposition of concerns about stoning the animal and prohibiting the
consumption of its flesh could be derived from the similar combination of interests in Genesis 9. B. S. Jackson suggests this link in

world to the animal is in fact an extensive feature in the lawgiver's approach to the incidents in the narratives. In the prohibition against bestiality, for example (Exod 22:18), animals represent humans. It is important to keep in mind the likelihood that the construction of the rules comes from academic, scribal exercises.

The next rule lays out the penalties for the animal and for its owner if the latter has known and been warned about the animal's tendency to be wild. The rule can be seen as an understandable extension of the topic of an assault by a domestic animal. It can again be noted, however, that the alleged killing of Joseph by a wild beast was in fact an attack by his brothers. Consequently one could derive for instructional purposes the hypothetical topic of an animal's killing a person[34] but the blame lying with the human being who has control of a domestic animal that is known for its wild tendencies.

In the rule the person guilty of the offense has a death sentence laid upon him, but if he pays a ransom he goes free. It is understandable to argue that this rule is based on some notion of reasonableness. We might consider, however, that the penalty reflects a response to the brothers' treatment of Joseph. They substituted payment of money for killing of Joseph. An appropriate penalty for their offense might then be a capital sentence that can be changed to a payment of money. The validity of this consideration depends on how much practical jurisprudence has gone into the construction of these rules: was

---

The Mishpatim (forthcoming). If P is responsible for this section in Gen 9:1–7, however, the matter is otherwise.

[34] The use of the conditional form "If a man . . . " in the language of the rules can be viewed as suitable for constructing hypothetical cases.

there, in other words, in ancient Israelite practice such commutation of capital sentences? We simply do not know, nor do we have any way of finding out.

The interpretation of the, on the face of it, unnecessary clause about the penalty should the ox kill a son or daughter may have to do with notions of vicarious punishment. It is not so much that the biblical rule reacts against the kind of penalty found in Near Eastern legal material, where an owner's son or daughter might be put to death instead of the owner himself.[35] Rather the lawgiver thinks of how divine retribution caused Judah's sons to lose their lives because of their father's offense against Jacob in the matter of the disposing of his son, Joseph. The lawgiver's opposition to the kind of vicarious penalties suffered by Judah's sons prompts him to hold the owner of the animal, not his son or daughter, responsible should a son or daughter be gored. Notions of retributive justice have come under review both in the present law under discussion (the wild beast that attacked Joseph) and in the two preceding ones (Joseph's treatment at the hands of his brothers and Judah's punishment because of his role as ringleader). We should bear in mind the role of wisdom in the construction of the rules, in this instance, the capacity to observe the unfortunate consequences of divine retribution and the desire to affirm the principle of individual responsibility.[36]

---

[35] For example, CH 229, 230. B. S. Jackson is skeptical of this common view; "The Goring Ox Again," *JJP* 18 (1974), 90–92. Cassuto expressed it (*Exodus*, 280), as did D. H. Müller, *Die Gesetze Hammurabis und ihr Verhältnis zur Mosäischen Gesetzgebung sowie zu den XII Tafeln* (Vienna: Hölder, 1903) 166–67.

[36] I agree with David Daube that often such divine retribution is based on notions of individual responsibility, or in his words, "ruler punishment." One person is held responsible for an offense,

The Origins of Biblical Law

Culpability for Pits (Exod 21:33, 34)

> 33 And if a man shall open a pit, or if a man shall dig a pit and not cover it, and an ox or an ass fall therein; 34 the owner of the pit shall make it good, and give money unto the owner of them; and the dead beast shall be his.

Source (Gen 37:20–24). The brothers refrained from killing Joseph. Instead they cast him into a pit.

Again it can be suggested that the topic of an animal's falling into a pit because of someone's work on it is inspired by the pit episode in Joseph's story. After the brothers decided not to kill Joseph and make it appear as if an animal had gored him to death, they responded to Reuben's appeal and cast him into a pit (Gen 37:20–24). The example of their casting him into an already existing pit inspires, we might conjecture, the no doubt unintended but nonetheless dangerous example where someone in a domestic setting, in contrast to a wilderness setting,[37] leaves an already existing or newly created pit uncovered so that an animal kills itself by falling into it. To cite the example of the animal's fall into the pit and not a person's is realistic. The person is not likely to die, and if it is a question of injury only to him the rule in Exod 21:19 would presumably apply: payment for any loss of his time or for medical expenses. The example of

---

but he is punished by harm done to his subjects (*Studies in Biblical Law*, 160–89).

[37] Pits may have been dug for the purpose of capturing wild animals; Driver, *Exodus*, CBSC, 222.

the animal's fall is all the more realistic in that the brothers' occupation was with animals, especially guarding them against such hazards as open pits.

Again it has to be stressed that the lawgiver's aim is to note certain features of the narrative and to incorporate them into a rule that (1) furnishes the likeliest parallel problem in ordinary life and (2) continues a topic in line with what he sets out in his preceding rules. Above all, we must keep in mind the lawgiver's focus on the notion, derived from the Joseph incident, that something in nature is responsible for a mishap, but in fact human agency is the underlying cause. We should not underestimate the difficulty in ancient legal development of how to deal with such a tort. The merit of a dramatic story like the tale of Joseph is that it makes the subject alive because it revolves around the use of deception and the hiddenness of human responsibility. The tale is a stimulus to reflection on the nature of dramatic happenings in ordinary life.

Ox Killing Ox (Exod 21:35, 36)

> 35 And if one man's ox hurt another's, that he die; then they shall sell the live ox and divide the money of it; and the dead ox also they shall divide. 36 Or if it be known that the ox hath used to push in times past, and his owner hath not kept him in; he shall surely pay ox for ox; and the dead shall be his own.

> *Source* (Gen 37:31–33). As in the preceding rules, the source is the brothers' lie about the damage done by a beast.

This rule continues the lawgiver's exploration of the issue that was prompted by the incident in the narrative about Joseph. The rule is an extension of the preceding rule in Exod 21:28, 29: the ox that kills a person. It is not set down immediately after that rule. The reason may be that its formulation owes more to the substance of a preceding rule than to the substance of the narrative about Joseph. In other words, the momentum of an aspect of a narrative, in this instance the physical assault on Joseph with its notions of a man's being gored by an animal and his ending up in a pit at another's hands, determines the sequence of the rules (animal that gores a man, human culpability for a pit). Only then is the need for extending the range of some rules recognized.

Another observation is in order about the sequence of the rules. The preceding rule is about an offense involving a pit. The lawgiver, we observed, necessarily substituted a fatal mishap to an animal for a fatal mishap to a person. It is therefore understandable why this rule, which continues a focus on a dangerous animal, returns to an example of another animal as victim.

It is well recognized that this rule in Exod 21:35, 36 is remarkably similar to LE 53, in both its formulation and its resolution of the problem.[38] In support of Meir Malul's view that this particular biblical rule is derived from the cuneiform, literary tradition,[39] I would observe that it owes nothing in its formulation to a biblical, literary tradition. Its subject matter, while linking with the issue of a dangerous animal in the Joseph story, is quite tangential to that particular development. In other words, this rule

[38] See Reuven Yaron, *The Laws of Eshnunna* (Jerusalem: Magnes, 1969), 192–200.

[39] Meir Malul, *The Comparative Method in Ancient Near Eastern and Biblical Legal Studies,* AOAT 227 (1990), 134–52.

more than almost any other in the Book of the Covenant stands apart from any biblical tradition.

Why do we not find an owner's liability for damage done by his animal extended to damage done by his slave? Such an extension is not found discussed until later Talmudic times (*Mishnah Yadaim* 4:7). It would occasion no surprise if there had been a clause to this effect already at the time of the *Mishpatim*. The explanation for its omission is again the narrow focus on the dangerous animal that Joseph's brothers concocted. This focus is ultimately the reason also for the unique, topsy-turvy nature of Talmudic jurisprudence when it assigns a man to the category of an ox attested to be dangerous (*Mishnah Baba Qamma* 2:4–6).

[4]

Jacob's Problems
(Part Two)

The lawgiver's procedure whereby a matter in one generation is traced back to a comparable matter in a preceding generation accounts for his return, after following Joseph's story, to more of Jacob's problems. Among these problems of Jacob are those with Laban, with his own sons, with Shechem, with Dinah, and with the Hivites. These interactions generate issues that are ruled upon in the following laws: animal theft, thief's death; damage to field and vineyard; deposit; hire; seduction; witchcraft; bestiality; sacrifice to other gods; oppression of the weak; loans; cursing authority; and no delay in offerings.

Theft of Animal, Manslaughter of Thief
(Exod 22:1–4)

1 If a man shall steal an ox or a sheep, and kill it or sell it; he shall restore five oxen for an ox, and four sheep for a sheep. 2 If a thief be found breaking up, and be smitten that he die, there shall be no blood shed for

him. 3 If the sun be risen upon him, there shall be blood shed for him. He shall make restitution; if he have nothing, then he shall be sold for his theft. 4 If the theft be found in his hand alive, whether it be ox, or ass, or sheep; he shall pay double.

Sources (Gen 31:1–43; 37:31). Joseph's brothers, for wrongful purposes, took an animal belonging to their father, Jacob. In the preceding generation Jacob was accused of taking Laban's animals and was almost slain during the night in leading them away.

The topic of theft is very much a feature of both the Jacob/Laban and Joseph narratives. The topic comes up in the arrangement Jacob made with Laban about the care of the latter's animals (Gen 30:32, 33), and it also emerges in the alleged theft of Joseph's divining cup (Gen 44:1–16). Indeed, as B. S. Jackson points out, the same terminology is found in both law (Exod 22:4) and narrative (Gen 44:16).[1]

An aspect of the Jacob/Laban (not the Joseph) narrative may have provided the main motivation for the presentation of the rule in Exod 22:1–4. A major complication

---

[1] B. S. Jackson, *The Mishpatim* (forthcoming). He is skeptical about the judicial aspect of the rules in the Book of the Covenant. He thinks they are geared to the needs of instruction rather than to the needs of institutional adjudication. For example, he notes that Exod 22:4 markedly lacks such a judicial aspect and, interestingly from my point of view, he notes that this same feature is present in the way the two parties to the dispute about Joseph's cup agree about culpability. He suggests, however, that the narrative may contain a literary allusion to the rule in the *Mishpatim*. If he means the rule as it is formulated there, I cannot agree. If, however, he means a preexisting form of the rule I have no objection.

about the rule is that it includes within its compass a quite different rule about a householder's liability for the death of a thief. If the two rules belong together originally we have to make sense of the combination. The following possibility—I rate it no higher than that—might be considered.

Joseph's brothers appropriated an animal, not for the usual reason, personal gain, but to conceal the offense of stealing a person, Joseph. The incident in which Joseph's brothers took the animal prompted the lawgiver to turn his attention to the first occurrence of the issue of animal theft in the nation's history. Jacob, the nation's first ancestor, secretly stole away from Laban's household and took with him wives, children, and animals. When Laban caught up after a seven-day pursuit, it was nighttime and his manifest resolve was to harm Jacob. Divine intervention in the form of a dream saved Jacob (Gen 31:24). He was informed the next day (v. 29) as to how fortunate he had been. The entire episode, we might stress, had its specific origin in Jacob's arrangement with Laban to acquire flocks for himself. When the agreement was made, Jacob discussed with Laban the issue of theft of the animals (Gen 30:32, 33). When Jacob did very well out of the arrangement Laban's sons had their suspicions, and Jacob took the hint that he should clear out with all his acquisitions (Gen 31:1, 2).

As commentators rightly stress, the narrative brings up a variety of legal matters.[2] Theft of animals is one. Jacob informs Laban that when he was shepherding for him and animals were stolen at night or during daylight he, Jacob,

---

[2] See, e.g., Gerhard von Rad, *Genesis* (Philadelphia: Westminster, 1972), 306–13.

bore the loss himself (v. 39). This specific issue of a shepherd's liability is, as we shall see, touched on in a succeeding rule (Exod 22:12).

What is not explicitly raised in Laban's encounter with Jacob is the issue of whether or not Jacob himself can be accused of the theft of Laban's animals. Laban openly states at one point that all the flocks Jacob has in his possession are in fact Laban's (v. 43). The narrator pursues his own aims and does not follow through on Laban's claim. One can see how the particular issue of theft of livestock comes up and can be explored by the lawgiver. Moreover, the awkward combination of topics in his legal construction can be related to the narrative.

The rule first states the sanction for theft of an ox or a sheep when the animal has been killed or sold—fivefold restitution for the ox, fourfold for the sheep. Before we learn what the sanction is (twofold restitution) should the thief be found with the stolen animal still in his possession, or what it is (sold into slavery) should the thief not have the means to provide restitution, we are given a rule about the death of the thief during the commission of his offense. There is no denying the awkwardness of this particular rule's formulation. Two observations might be made.

First, the concern with the topic of assault—in this instance, assault on the thief by the owner of the animals—is consistent with the sustained interest in this topic in the preceding rules. Second, the narrative about Jacob and Laban does in fact present us with this very topic. Jacob went off with animals that Laban had some claim to and was overtaken by him. Laban would, it is implied, have attacked Jacob if there had been no divine intervention. The attack, it appears, would have occurred at night (Gen 31:24, 29). Jacob learns during daylight hours about this danger to his life. So the distinction between an attack at night, when only supernatural assistance saved Jacob, and a confrontation during daytime, when there is a lesser threat to the culprit, comes through in the narrative. The distinction in the rule, which has to discount the possibility of divine action, is between the excusable slaying of the thief at night and a culpable slaying during daytime. The lawgiver, shifting his perspective to that of Laban, may have judged it excusable if someone in Laban's position killed a thief when he came upon him at night, but not so when confronting him during the day. The lawgiver contemplates a situation in his rule that is different from Laban's tracking down Jacob, namely, when the thief is caught in the initial stages of his action. The reason would be that the situation in which a supposed thief is confronted well away from the scene of the crime is much less open to legal control.[3]

The suggestion might be made that the first statement in the rule about theft of an animal, where it has been killed or sold, is a response to the topic as first raised by Joseph's brothers' wrongful slaughter of their father's animal. The theft of animals is also a concern in Jacob's dealings with Laban, and the issues raised by these dealings come under review in the next part of the rule. The switch in focus from one incident to the other results in the confusing way in which the subject matter of the rule has been set down. There is lack of continuity of focus between the first part of the legal construction and the

---

[3] See David Daube, *Studies in Biblical Law* (Cambridge: Cambridge University Press, 1947), 201–13; B. S. Jackson, *Theft in Early Jewish Law* (Oxford: Clarendon, 1972), 215–18.

latter part about the animal's turning up in the thief's possession, and how he will have to pay double or, if he has nothing, be sold for his theft.[4]

It is again noteworthy that if the hypothetical issue of Jacob's theft of Laban's animals is explored, one can also raise the issue of Jacob's standing vis-à-vis Laban. If Laban's claim to all the animals in Jacob's possession could be upheld (Gen. 31:43), then Jacob would be in no position to pay restitution.

The specific problem in the rule's construction is that the thief is understood to have been slain either at night or during the day, but the lawgiver goes on to state, "He should make restitution," in the instance where he is caught red-handed. The difficulty is certainly present in the text if we read it in its own terms without regard to any external source. Once, however, we read it against the backdrop of Laban's tracking down Jacob, the problem is lessened. Jacob came close to losing his life, but in the event did not. Only supernatural assistance saved him and a lawgiver has to discount it. Consequently he rules on the hypothetical issue where the thief does indeed suffer death at the hands of the owner. He returns to the story itself, which is about Laban's catching Jacob with the animals. He then sets down the ruling about the thief who has the animals in his possession.

---

[4] Raymond Westbrook also distinguishes between the thief of Exod 22:1, who has to pay five oxen or four sheep for his offense, and the burglar in Exod 22:2, 3 who might be sold. He introduces yet a third offender, namely, an innocent possessor of stolen animals (Exod 22:4); *Studies in Biblical and Cuneiform Law* (Paris: Gabalda, 1988), 111–28.

Damage to Field and Vineyard
(Exod 22:5, 6)

> 5 If a man shall cause a field or vineyard to be eaten, and shall let his beast loose, and it feed in another man's field; of the best of his own field, and of the best of his own vineyard, shall he make restitution. 6 If fire break out, and catch in thorns, so that the shocks of corn, or the standing corn, or the field, be consumed; he that kindled the fire shall surely make restitution.

Sources (Gen 37:31–33; 41:56–42:7). The brothers presented evidence to Jacob that they were not liable for the destructive action of a beast. On the occasion they were absolved of any culpability, but in the long term their guilt in disposing of Joseph brought about, at heaven's hand, the devastation of the land of Canaan in which Jacob resided. Jacob, portrayed as the victim of their misdeed, eventually received compensation for his loss.

The question of the brothers' liability for the destruction done by a beast is implied by the evidence they presented to Jacob that a beast had killed Joseph. Reuben's concern about Joseph's welfare also points to this dimension.[5] The development in the story can therefore be viewed as presenting the hypothetical issue of a force in nature that causes destruction, but responsibility for the action lies with a human agent. Both rules give practical expression to the issue. Indeed, if in the first of the two rules the animal is intentionally let loose by its owner to

---

[5] See Daube, *Studies in Biblical Law*, 12.

feed in another's land, as S. M. Paul argues,[6] of all the rules about animals causing damage this one comes closest to the brothers' action with an animal because of the deliberate nature of the act. These links between the Joseph story and the rule might be the only ones that can be claimed. Some further observations may be in order, however, if we continue to keep in mind the larger context of the story. I stress the conjectural character of what follows.

The fact that agricultural land is the focus of both rules is interesting in light of the famine that Jacob's family suffered. There is a sense in which Jacob's land was devastated by heaven because of his sons' misdeed. We have noted before, for example, Judah's punishment at the hands of heaven for his treatment of Joseph and how this larger perspective is the one common to both the lawgiver and the redactor of the narrative material in the book of Genesis. In order to construct a rule, the lawgiver cites devastation of another's land by, first, someone's beast and, second, fire. The example of the beast would tie in to the preceding rules about damage caused by a beast, and, more specifically, to the brothers' offense against their father: the lie about the beast having consumed Joseph, which led to a famine striking the land so that Joseph would regain his rightful place in his family. We might also recall that the pharaoh's dream, an omen of the famine, had to do with grazing animals that ate what they normally did not (Gen 41:1–8).

If the situation described in the rule should be viewed as inspired by as close a parallel as possible to heaven's

---

[6] S. M. Paul, *Studies in the Book of the Covenant in the Light of Cuneiform and Biblical Law* (Leiden: Brill, 1970), 110.

visitation of famine upon Jacob's land, we might account for some apparent difficulties in its formulation. It refers first to how someone's own field or vineyard is grazed over and then to how damage is done to a neighbor's field. We might wonder why the scene envisioned was confined solely to the grazing of the neighbor's field without reference to his vineyard also, especially when compensation to him consists of the produce of both field and vineyard. Conceivably, the explanation is that when the lawgiver thinks of the offender he anticipates Israel's future in the land, where fields and vineyards are available to the Israelite, but in thinking of the victim he concentrates on what happened to Jacob in Canaan where crops of the field only are in focus.

The example of the fire would constitute the closest parallel to what in nature, through indirect human agency, causes a famine-like effect. The example would be all the more appropriate if the notion of heaven's wrath was in the lawgiver's mind. Fire is frequently a metaphor for Yahweh's anger, and Moses predicts that, in the new land, if Israel fails to heed his commandments Yahweh's anger will cause drought and famine (Deut 11:17).

Jacob was compensated for the devastation to his agricultural land by receiving food laden on beasts ($b^{e^c}ir$), the promise of the good of the land of Egypt (Gen 45:17, 18), and the invitation to dwell (with his grazing animals) in the best of it (*meṭab*, Gen 47:6, 11). It is perhaps noteworthy that in the rule the term used for the damage-causing animal is the rare term $b^{e^c}ir$ and that compensation consists of the best (*meṭab*)[7] of field and vineyard. Critics have long been puzzled by the requirement that the sanction

---

[7] The term is found only once more (1 Sam 15:9, 15).

for causing loss to another's source of food should be the *best* from his own sources. With no basis in the text they assume that the entire crop had been consumed by the offending animal.[8] By contemplating Jacob's compensation, the lawgiver is possibly influenced in his choice of sanction for his hypothetical legal construction. If the link is less specific it is at least noteworthy that there is this shared language between the Joseph story and these rules. Another term, quite uncommon in the Pentateuch, found in the preceding rule about the thief who slaughters (*ṭabaḥ*) the stolen animal, turns up also in the account of Joseph's actions to cause his brothers to recall their offense against him (Gen 43:16).[9] I suggested that that rule about the theft of the animal may have had in focus the brothers' wrongdoing in killing an animal to make it appear that Joseph had been the victim of a wild beast.

Deposit (Exod 22:7–9)

> 7 If a man shall deliver unto his neighbour money or stuff to keep, and it be stolen out of the man's house; if the thief be found, let him pay double. 8 If the thief be not found, then the master of the house, shall be brought unto the gods [*ᵉlohim*], to see whether he have put his hand unto his neighbour's property. 9 For all manner of trespass, whether it be for ox, for ass, for sheep, for raiment, or for any manner of lost thing, which another challengeth to be his, the cause of both parties shall come before the gods; and whom the gods shall condemn, he shall pay double unto his neighbour.

[8] This view goes back to the LXX and the Samaritan version.
[9] Note too the same terminology in Exod 22:4 and Gen 44:16.

> *Source* (Genesis 31). The dispute between Jacob and La-
> ban revolved around Laban's claim to what was in
> Jacob's possession after he fled from Laban's household
> "with all that he had" (v. 21). At one point Jacob as-
> serted, "Whereas thou hast searched all my stuff, what
> hast thou found of all thy household-stuff? Set it here
> before my brethren, and thy brethren, that they judge
> betwixt us both" (v. 37).

From the role of Joseph's brothers as herdsmen in their
dealings with Joseph, the lawgiver, always seeking out
the earliest occurrence of some problem, turns his attention to Jacob in his role as a herdsman with Laban. Regarding the switch in subject matter of the rules, it is
noteworthy that, if Jacob and his entire family's departure
for Egypt comes into focus in the preceding rule, so his
earlier departure with his entire family for Canaan is the
focus of this rule about deposited goods and livestock. In
each instance in the pertinent tradition, Jacob's compensation for past wrongs done to him is in focus. When the
pharaoh generously received Jacob's family in Egypt, the
topic of employment as herdsmen in the pharaoh's household was raised (Gen 47:6). Five of Joseph's brothers informed the pharaoh that the occupation was one that had
a history in their family (vv. 2, 3). A cursory reading of
the laws at this point in the code suggests a transition
from the topic of assaults by animals to matters mainly
concerned with herdsmen (Exod 22:7–15).

The first rule in focus does not involve animals, but the
subsequent ones do. The reason is that the topics drawn
from the narratives present themselves in just this way.
The extraordinary theft of Joseph by members of his own

household determined a large number of the preceding rules. One generation back, an equally extraordinary theft, Rachel's theft of her father's household gods, brings up the issues that are found in the rule about deposit.

The wider context of this theft is the dispute about what in Jacob's household belongs to Laban. The latter manifestly believed that he had a claim to some of the goods in Jacob's possession—perhaps to all of them: "All that thou [Jacob] seest is mine" (Gen 31:43; cp. v. 1). On the other hand, Jacob's wives, Rachel and Leah, claimed that certain things that had been their father's now belonged to them (Gen 31:16). At the same time they protested that their father had sold them and consumed their money. Manifestly, the two parties were at loggerheads and their respective positions constituted the stuff of a complex legal wrangle. When Jacob decided to leave the Laban household and settle in his own elsewhere, the narrative makes special reference to the fact that Rachel took her father's gods. Laban's pursuit of Jacob and his family ended with Laban's searching among Jacob's goods.

Although no motive for Rachel's action is provided, it can be observed that her misdeed removes the usual means by which the dispute between the two households might be settled. However that may be, it can be argued that the lawgiver, for the purpose of pursuing a legal problem that might be equivalent to Laban's challenging Jacob about the stuff (Gen 31:37, $k^{e}lim$, as in the rule[10]) in his possession, focuses on the role of household gods in

---

[10] Interestingly, the other term in the rule (and in Exod 22:11), $m^{e}la'kah$, in the uncommon sense of property with which one's occupation is concerned, is found in Gen 33:14 in reference to Jacob's flocks and herds. The only other comparable texts are 1 Sam 15:9 and 2 Chron 17:13.

the settlement of the kind of dispute that existed between them.

The rule, like those in LE 36 and CH 124, is about the relationship between two households when one gives over money or goods to the other. In a formal sense, this feature is lacking in the story, although Rachel and Leah's claim that what had been their father's now belonged in Jacob's household readily points to this legal topic. In any event, in ordinary life the arrangement cited in the rule constitutes a situation that is likely to bring out issues comparable to Laban and Jacob's dispute. What dominates the story, a daughter's theft of her father's gods, is not legislated for,[11] but by choosing the topic of deposit the lawgiver is able to raise the issue of theft within the context of two households involved with each other and to give a role to household gods. Where a thief cannot be detected, the only approach is a resort to the gods by way of a second-best attempt to recognize a wrong by putting psychological pressure on the householder, in whose possession the goods are alleged to be.

We should keep in mind that the lawgiver pursues certain topics—for example, assault and now theft—that reflect not the idiosyncratic aspect of a narrative but the more realistic circumstances of ordinary life. Failure to be alert to this often crucial difference between a story's bias and a law's understandably prevents any perception of a link between a rule and a narrative.

The next part of the rule approaches much closer the substance of Jacob's complaint to Laban. Jacob asked him what his trespass (*pešaʿ*, as in the rule) was; in particular,

---

[11] For discussion of the theft of divine property in the cuneiform codes, see Westbrook, *Cuneiform Law*, 121–23.

he challenged Laban to name which of the goods were his and to bring them before each of their households so that judgment could be made. Presumably if Laban had responded to this challenge, the household gods, if they had been available, would have been used in some capacity to pronounce a judgment.[12] In the rule they are so used. Often, because a narrative takes a different turn, the lawgiver is challenged to follow through on the unresolved issue raised by it.

Safekeeping of Animals (Exod 22:10–13)

> 10 If a man deliver unto his neighbour an ass, or an ox, or a sheep, or any beast, to keep; and it die, or be hurt, or driven away, no man seeing it: 11 Then shall an oath of Yahweh be between them both, that he hath not put his hand unto his neighbour's property; and the owner of it shall accept thereof[13] and he shall not make it good. 12 And if it be stolen from him, he shall make restitution unto the owner thereof. 13 If it be torn in pieces, then let him bring it for witness, and he shall not make good that which was torn.

[12] For example, by having members of each household testify in their presence. There is no need consequently to resort to Martin Noth's complicated notion that some legal assembly is somehow involved in administering an appropriate sanction (*Exodus* [Philadelphia: Westminster, 1962], 184).

[13] See Jackson, *The Mishpatim*. He argues that in v. 10 "driven away" is an interpretation and that v. 11 should be translated "the owner shall take it [*scil.*, the carcass or mutilated animal], and he [the shepherd] shall not pay."

Source (Gen 31:38–54). Jacob recalled his twenty years of service under Laban as a keeper of his animals, and recounted the terms and conditions under which he worked.

The links between this rule and the narrative about Jacob's dispute with Laban are especially revealing. For example, it is somewhat puzzling why this rule is formulated after the preceding one, under which the present rule could easily be subsumed.[14] It is not so puzzling when we observe that immediately after Jacob's complaint to Laban about the search among his household goods, he broadened his complaint to refer to his dealings with Laban in the past twenty years. He pointed out to Laban how well he had cared for his animals: he had not stolen any of them by way of feeding himself; any that had been torn by wild beasts he in fact did not bring to him, to be absolved, it is implied, of liability for them; and Laban himself had made him liable for any animal stolen from him whether during daylight or during nighttime (Gen 31:38–40).[15] It is precisely these issues that are formulated in the rule, no doubt because they turn up in the context

---

[14] See Paul, *Studies*, 93, for the long history of puzzlement over these two similar rules. H. J. Boecker, *Law and the Administration of Justice in the Old Testament and Ancient East* (Minneapolis: Augsburg, 1980), 170, has to argue that Exod 22:9 is a generalized legal observation that has been added at some point to the Book of the Covenant.

[15] Commentators have long wondered why restitution is required in the case of the theft of an animal but not in the case of deposited goods (Exod 22:8). Laban's position may have been assumed to be in fact the rule in regard to a herdsman. See Paul, *Studies*, 93 n.2. The distinctions Paul cites by Rabbinic authorities are most likely theirs and not those of the biblical lawgiver.

of an actual dispute in the nation's past, and it is natural to pose the question, what should the rule be for future generations of Israelites?

Equally revealing of the link between law and narrative is that instead of the household gods playing a role in the resolution of the dispute, as in the preceding rule, there is resort to an oath of Yahweh between the disputants. In the story the resolution of all the difficulties between Jacob and Laban turns on an oath of Yahweh between them (Gen 31:49).[16] It appears that the lawgiver, alert to both the use of household gods and the invocation of Yahweh, simply decides to make use of both agencies. Such a procedure suggests that the formulations of the rules are scribal exercises, responses to the question of how, in light of what goes on in the history of Laban's dealings with Jacob, the disputes between them might be resolved. A factor in accounting for the role of the oath to Yahweh may be that, at that point where it is invoked in the narrative, Jacob's future life in his own cultural and religious setting is anticipated.

Liability of Borrower (Exod 22:14, 15)

> 14 And if a man borrow [aught] of his neighbour, and it be hurt, or die, the owner thereof being not with it, he shall surely make it good. 15 But if the owner

[16] Paul, *Studies*, 93, speculates about the use of different source material in which the oath before Yahweh "would be a modernizing of a pre-Israelite formulation." His speculation is shared by most commentators and illustrates how they render the material needlessly complicated.

thereof be with it, he shall not make it good. If a hired labourer [is its borrower], it came with his hire [wage].

Source (Gen 30:25–31:1). After Jacob had served Laban for fourteen years, he came to an arrangement whereby he would earn wages for a further spell of service to his father-in-law. The wages were to come from Jacob's use of Laban's animals.

The rule continues—an object of the verb "to borrow" is never expressed and has to be understood from the preceding rule—to take up issues that arose between Jacob and Laban over the complications surrounding Jacob's acquisition of Laban's daughters as wives. When Jacob first broached the subject of departing to his own country with his wives and children, Laban wanted him to stay because he had brought gain to Laban's stock (Gen 30: 27). They came to an agreement whereby Jacob would again serve Laban and receive his wages, the price of his hire, by again looking after Laban's flock.

The arrangement, however, was to be different from any previous one. The account of their agreement is not altogether clear, but David Daube lays out its major aspect.[17] Jacob would not take any wages this time for keeping Laban's animals ("Thou shalt not give me any thing," Gen 30:31), but would borrow them and use their reproductive services to acquire a flock of his own. In particular, he would take only newly born animals that were spotted and speckled. Remarkably, moreover, Jacob had

---

[17] Daube, *Studies in Biblical Law*, 16, 17; similarly, S. R. Driver, *Genesis*, WC, 9th ed. (London: Methuen, 1913), 277–78. For the problems in the account, see von Rad, *Genesis*, 297–302. The NEB is quite wrong. The main problem centers on the expression in Gen 30:32, "And [such] shall be my hire." In my view it cannot refer to what Jacob has just said but to what he is about to say (in v. 33).

Laban remove from the main flock animals of this rather rare kind. Laban readily agreed to such a bargain. In the likely course of nature the flock was not going to produce spotted and speckled animals. In the end it did, but such a surprising outcome was owing to Jacob's "genetic" engineering.

The lawgiver observes the nature of this arrangement and proceeds to set down a two-part rule. The first part is a general rule about the borrowing of an animal, presumably for a variety of common uses, hauling, plowing, and the like. It is the second part of the rule that concentrates on the particular situation of Jacob's arrangement with Laban. The statement, literally, "If a hired labourer it comes with his hire," is about the specific matter in the narrative. The statement has always caused great difficulty.[18] Yet once we relate it to Jacob's situation with Laban, its sense describes exactly their arrangement. If we translate the plain meaning, "If a hired labourer [is its borrower], it [the animal] comes with his hire [wage]," the sense refers in particular to the agreement whereby Jacob acquired Laban's animals by way of payment for his service. Indeed the statement's language is reminiscent of the language of Jacob's agreement with Laban. Jacob refers to the outcome of their agreement: "So shall my righteousness answer for me *when it [the time] shall come concerning my hire*" (Gen 30:33).

What the lawgiver has done in this part of his rule is to take up what is not discussed in Jacob's agreement with Laban, namely, the issue that he covers in the first part of his rule about injury or death to the animal when the owner has let it out to the borrower. Presumably, his judgment is, in David Daube's paraphrase, "If he [the

[18] See Paul's discussion, *Studies*, 95, 96.

borrower of the cattle that has suffered damage or died]
be a labourer [employed and paid by the owner of the
cattle], it shall be set against his hire [he shall make
amends up to the amount of his wages]."[19] Like the formulation of so many of these rules, the first section of it is
for a more normal situation than Jacob's—borrowing animals for general purposes; and the latter part reflects the
narrow bias of the tradition that prompted the legal
topics. Recognition of its dual character, because of the
use to which the narrative is put, obviates the need for the
tortuous speculations commentators resort to in order to
reconcile both sections. Thus the rule does not state,
"And if a man borrow [an animal]," and then, "And if
the man borrow a hired laborer [to work the animal]"; it
distinguishes between borrowing by a person who is not
a servant and borrowing by a hired servant.[20]

Seduction (Exod 22:16, 17)

16 And if a man entice a maid that is not betrothed, and
lie with her, he shall surely endow her to be his wife.
17 If her father utterly refuse to give her unto him, he
shall pay money according to the bride-price of virgins.

Source (Genesis 34). Dinah, Jacob's daughter, was seduced by Shechem who then sought to make her his

---

[19] Daube, *Studies in Biblical Law*, 17.
[20] The former sense is, e.g., J. P. Hyatt's, *Exodus*, NCBC (Grand
Rapids: Eerdmans, 1980), 240. We have noted before, in regard to
the slave laws in Exod 21:2–11, how Jacob's situation with Laban
prompted the lawgiver to introduce distinctions in status into his
rules.

wife. Despite negotiations about a bride-price he was refused her.

The preceding rules focused on Jacob's dealings with Laban. Many of these dealings centered on Jacob's payment in services, a bride-price, for his two wives, Rachel and Leah. Indeed, Laban's final concern was for the welfare of his two daughters. In particular, he wanted assurance from Jacob that he would not afflict or humble (*'innah*) them should he take wives in addition to them (Gen 31:50). The tradition that next raises the topic of marriage is in Genesis 34, the next stage in Jacob's life, and provides the subject matter, not just for this rule about marriage to an unbetrothed girl who has been seduced (and humbled, *'innah*, Gen 34:2), but for a succession of rules. In what is a typical procedure, going from an issue in one generation to a comparable one in the next, the lawgiver moves from one father's concern about the humiliation of his daughters to another's concern about the humiliation of his (only) daughter.

The rule takes up the issue from the tradition about Jacob's daughter, Dinah, and her seduction by Shechem, the prince of the Hivites, who then sought to pay a bride-price and make her his wife. One reason the rule is founded on this story is that this incident is the first in the nation's history where the topic of a virgin's seduction appears. A central feature of the story is the refusal of the Israelites to give Dinah to Shechem. This too is the special bias in the rule, the father's refusal to give his daughter to her seducer. Such a narrow bias is always a telling sign that, if a comparable one exists in a narrative, the influence is likely to be in the direction of story to law. It is just not realistic to assume that the incident about Shechem's seduction of Dinah has been made up in order to illustrate a specific bias in some rule.

As is the nature of a story, it is idiosyncratic: the seducer was a Canaanite, and spurious negotiations over a bride-price were a cover for killing him.[21] Moses, we are to believe, takes up the topic for an Israelite society: not a foreign seducer but an Israelite one is denied her, although the rule's formulation, it might be noted, does not in fact exclude the development in the story. In it the bride-price was negotiable. Shechem offered to pay as much as Dinah's father and brothers might ask (Gen 34:11). The rule recognizes a current rate of value for a virginal girl which the seducer is required to pay should the father refuse to give him his daughter.

David Daube argues that the rule, looked at in its own terms, assumes a negotiable bride-price in the initial dealings between the father and the seducer. He speculates that the reason for the father's refusal is an economic one. The father sets the price so high that the seducer cannot or will not pay it. The father nonetheless collects one sum from him (the current rate) and can look forward to another sum from a future suitor.[22] While this set of circumstances may well be an example of the kind of situation to be reckoned with in such matters, it does not account for the rule's formulation, its *ratio legis*. However we might speculate about the specific reasons for the father's refusal, it might be best, in light of the rule's link with the

[21] In this regard the role of deception is similar to its role in Jacob's dealings with Laban about the latter's animals, the subject matter that prompted the preceding rule.

[22] See Daube's review of L. M. Epstein, *Sex Laws and Customs in Judaism* (New York: Bloch, 1948), in *Book List of The Society for Old Testament Study*, 1950, 54.

story, to suggest that the rule's intent is to prevent within Israelite society any deception or hostility comparable to that which arose between the parties in Genesis 34. The lawgiver places a check on the dealings between the two parties because, should they break down, he provides a monetary settlement. An economic solution to a problem has this capacity to sidestep uniquely personal issues in a dispute.[23]

Witchcraft (Exod 22:18)

Thou shalt not suffer a witch to live.

Source (Genesis 34). Dinah took it upon herself to visit the foreign Canaanite women. While among them she was seduced by a Canaanite prince, Shechem.

For this rule, so fateful in the history of witchcraft in the Western world, we are again to assume that Moses evaluated Israelite tradition. The first suggestion, or potential example, in this history of an Israelite woman's contamination by evil foreign influence was Dinah's presence among the Canaanite women. She it was who took herself into their midst, and who was seduced, "treated as though she were a harlot" (Gen 34:31), by one of their

---

[23] No wonder psychoanalysts compare money to feces: "both the result of specifics dissolving into formless mass"; David Daube, "Money and Justiciability," *ZSS* 96 (1979), 15. Daube further comments, "Justice, too, could be said to be faecal, in a high degree denying the uniqueness of things . . . finds expression in abstract rules, to be administered indifferently, Book of Common Prayer, evenhandedly, Shakespeare, ending where mystery begins, Burke."

distinguished males. So, on the one hand, in placing herself among Canaanite women and, on the other hand, in taking on the status of a harlot, Dinah suggests an identity that is akin to a certain kind of foreign woman met with elsewhere in biblical tradition. The combination of sorcery and harlotry becomes proverbial for pernicious influence on the Israelites by foreign women, Jezebel, for example (2 Kings 9:22). Such a proverbial view underlies the personification of Nineveh as a harlot who is expert in witchcraft (Nah 3:4).

It is the seer Moses who is alert to the potential danger in the case of the first Israelite daughter and consequently constructs the prohibition against a sorceress. The death penalty for her corresponds to the punishment of Shechem, which was determined not by his seduction as such, but by his being an uncircumcised Canaanite—with all that that represented in religious terms—who had seduced a daughter of Israel.[24] Indeed, the extreme development in the story is owing to this anti-Canaanite bias. The story itself is not explicit in its negative evaluation of Dinah's presence among the Canaanite women. What reveals its stance, however, is the subsequent notice about Jacob's instruction after the slaughter of the adult male Hivites. Jacob had to order that, because of the incorpora-

---

[24] S. R. Driver raises the long-standing issue as to whether the narrative in Genesis 34 is one in which individuals really stand for tribes. He points out that, after the conquest, Israelites and Canaanites dwelt in Shechem side by side (Judges 9). In that there is almost a complete identity of expression between Gen 33:19 and Judg 9:28, the name Shechem that signifies the place in the latter text may in Genesis 34 be really a personification of the inhabitants of the place. Consequently, we may not be dealing with the sexual seduction of Dinah by Shechem, but with the religious seduction of Israel by a Canaanite tribe. See *Genesis*, WC, 307–8.

tion into his tribe of the surviving Hivite women and children, the foreign gods in the midst of all the people be put away (Gen 35:1–4). Also pertinent in revealing the narrator's stance is the further notice that God destroyed any Canaanite city in the vicinity of Jacob and the people (v. 5). The inhabitants of these cities would, as Jacob himself had pointed out (Gen 34:30), automatically have aligned themselves with their fellow Canaanites who had been slain by Simeon and Levi.

By relating the law to the story we can explain why it is about a female offender only. This text is in fact the only one in biblical material that has the feminine form "sorceress" (m*kaššepah). The other texts use either the masculine form or the term "sorceries."[25] The common view that sorcery was especially a female interest may not be so accurate.[26]

A sure indication that later Israelite history is anticipated in these rules,[27] especially the awareness of idolatrous Canaanite influence, is to be seen in the code's epi-

[25] See the listings by Driver, *The Book of Exodus*, CBSC (Cambridge: Cambridge University Press, 1911), 229–30.

[26] Even the evidence from the Neo-Assyrian period (900–600 B.C.), which might suggest that the sorceress was more prominent than her male counterpart, requires much more rigorous analysis. See Sue Rollin, "Women and Witchcraft in Ancient Assyria (c. 900–600 B.C.)," in *Images of Women in Antiquity*, ed. Averil Cameron and Amelie Kuhrt (London: Croom Helm, 1983), 34–45. Later Talmudic statements require their own analysis in terms of time and place, e.g., *Babylonian Sanhedrin* 67a, "Because mostly women engage in witchcraft."

[27] The rule about cultic prostitutes in Deut 23:17, 18 covers different generations of Israelite involvement with Canaanites beginning with the incident in Genesis 34. See C. M. Carmichael, *Law and Narrative in the Bible* (Ithaca: Cornell University Press, 1985), 240–43.

logue. It explicitly warns about the confrontation of the Israelites with Canaanite religion and mentions, among others, the Hivites (Exod 23:23, 24).[28]

Bestiality (Exod 22:19)

Whoever lies with a beast shall surely be put to death.

Source (Genesis 34; 49:5–7). Shechem, the son of the "Ass" Hamor, lay with Dinah, the daughter of the "Ox" Jacob/Israel.

The rule prohibits bestiality, and we would be hard pressed to know why such a practice might invite condemnation. The English writer Laurie Lee observed that "quiet incest" flourishes where the roads run out.[29] So too is it with bestiality. It would be anachronistic to introduce later notions of natural and unnatural, such as we find in Philo, into this particular rule.[30] It is just not likely that what herdsmen sometimes did occasioned this prohibition. The participial form, "Whoever lies," can include a female offender too. She is openly cited in the prohibition in Lev 18:23 and 20:16.

Again the way a narrative is used to raise topics ex-

---

[28] Contrary to almost all commentators ("One of the most difficult problems arises from the complete omission in vv. 20–32 of any mention of the preceding laws," writes B. S. Childs, *The Book of Exodus: A Critical, Theological Commentary* [Philadelphia: Westminster, 1974], 461), I see a substantial link between the code's epilogue (Exod 23:20–33) and the preceding laws.

[29] Laurie Lee, *Cider with Rosie* (London: Penguin, 1959), 206.

[30] Philo, *De specialibus legibus* 3.37–50. The characterization of the coupling in Lev 18:23 as confusion (*tebel*) may, however, come close.

Jacob's Problems (Part Two)

plains the rule's formulation. Shechem, the son (*shechem*, shoulder) of the ass, Hamor (Hebrew for ass), seduced and lay with (*šakab* as in the rule) the daughter of the ox, Jacob, whose group is compared to the animal, the ox, precisely in reference to its troubles with the Canaanites because of what was done to Shechem (Gen 49:6).[31] The figurative meaning in the story, and in Jacob's deathbed comment on it, elicits the lawgiver's prohibition: no sexual commerce between a man or a woman and an animal. The death penalty corresponds to Shechem's fate and is intended to include any Canaanite male or female who may like Shechem become involved with an Israelite "ox," or any Israelite male or female who may like Dinah become involved with a Canaanite "ass." Such a development calls for an extreme response, precisely because of the religious attitude that motivated Simeon and Levi in

---

[31] Jacob's condemnation of Simeon and Levi's action against the Hivite group reads: "For in their anger they slew a man, and through their goodwill they hamstrung an ox." The slain man is Hamor ("Ass"), the representative head of the Hivites slaughtered by Simeon and Levi. This same action had from Jacob's point of view the baneful effect of weakening his own people, the house of the Ox: hence the parallelism of the poetical lines. To hamstring an animal is to weaken it and is an activity associated with what goes on between two warring groups (Josh 11:6, 9; 2 Sam 8:4). Jacob is being sarcastic when he tells Simeon and Levi that they did a good thing, as they certainly believed they did, by slaughtering the Hivites. Instead the consequence was to render their own people vulnerable to the vengeful attacks of the other Canaanite groups. The term *ʿiqqer* "to hamstring" reveals a typical feature of all these sayings in Genesis 49—a play on *ʿakar* in Gen 34:30: Jacob's complaint there that Simeon and Levi have brought trouble on him. Jacob refers to himself but he stands for his entire house, as is made clear in his final comment about "I and my house." For the ox, domestic or wild, as a figure for the house of Israel, especially as regards its military prowess, see Deut 33:17; Num 23:22, 24:8.

Genesis 34, and is shared by the author (or redactor) of that story and the lawgiver.

The rule should not be separated from its meaning in the context of the anti-Canaanite sentiment of the story: no sexual involvement between an Israelite and a Canaanite.[32] The term *b'hemah*, "beast," typically refers to those animals owned and used by humans, such as the ox and ass; it should indeed be confined to these two because of the rule's inseparable link with the story.[33] In summary form, the rule might be best paraphrased as: a Canaanite, like Shechem, who lies with an Israelite "ox," or an Israelite, like Dinah, who lies with a Canaanite "ass," shall be put to death.

---

[32] It is probably going too far to suggest, as does Umberto Cassuto, *A Commentary on the Book of Exodus* (Jerusalem: Magnes, 1967), 290, that the prohibition is anti-idolatrous in the sense that Canaanite culture celebrates, for example, Baal's intercourse with a heifer (in order to avoid death as a result of the devices of Mot, the king of the netherworld). For the text, see G. R. Driver, *Canaanite Myths and Legends* (Edinburgh: Clark, 1977), 72 ll. 17–22. Cassuto, followed by other commentators, avoids a plain meaning for the prohibition—that is, they do not view it as condemning bestiality as such, but in a religious context. The prohibition in Deut 22:10, about not plowing with an ox and an ass together, also focuses on the incident in Genesis 34 but from another angle. See C. M. Carmichael, *Law and Narrative*, 195–97, 203. Contrary to J. L. Kugel, *In Potiphar's House* (San Francisco: Harper, 1990), 26 n.4, the metaphorical meaning of this law is original to it and not acquired at some point prior to Ben Sira, "Happy is he who lives with an intelligent wife, and does not plow with ox and ass" (Sir 25:8a).

[33] The term is not used figuratively in the Old Testament, presumably because of its inclusive character. In the context of the rule it is intended to refer to the "ox" and the "ass," and having done so the figurative meanings have then to be read.

166

The difference in formulation between the two rules about the sorceress who is "not to live," and the rule about the person lying with a beast, who "dying, shall die," may be accounted for in light of their shared background. The former, as B. S. Childs rightly points out, is a term for the sacred ban (Num 31:15; Deut 20:16; 1 Sam 27:9–11), the extirpation of idolatrous agents.[34] Dinah's contact with the Hivite women only suggested the later problem of actual idolatrous influence, and the sanction against the sorceress focuses on such later developments. Shechem, on the other hand, this "ass," does die for his offense against Dinah and the more concrete "shall surely die" may echo his fate. Underlying each rule is the concern with idolatry, but in the case of Dinah the lawgiver ranges beyond the details of the story.

If my interpretation of the prohibition against bestiality is correct, we have to assume that the lawgiver had before him the story of Shechem and Dinah. Moreover, because the laws he sets down are part of a narrative history, we should draw the somewhat obvious conclusion that each law was to be understood in relation to its relevant story. When the laws were formulated they were integrally linked to the narratives: in other words, the laws were never intended to be read independently of the narratives *at this early stage*.

Sacrifice to Yahweh Only (Exod 22:20)

> Whoever sacrificeth unto any god, save unto Yahweh only, shall be utterly destroyed.

[34] Childs, *Exodus*, 477.

Source (Gen 35:1–4). Certain Hivites, a group belonging to the Canaanites, were incorporated into the house of Jacob/Israel. Jacob, alert to their presence and possible influence, instructed all in his midst to put away any foreign gods that might be among them, and to prepare to worship his god at Bethel.

After the incident involving Shechem, Jacob was instructed to build an altar at Bethel to "the God that appeared unto thee [Jacob] when thou fleddest from the face of Esau thy brother" (Gen 35:1). That god was Yahweh (Gen 28:13). Jacob received further instruction to put away the foreign gods that were present in his midst, no doubt because of the influx of the Canaanite women and children. In this context the prohibition against sacrificing to any god, save to the god Yahweh who helped Jacob with Esau, is singularly appropriate.[35] The penalty of extermination (*ḥerem*) for the offense is in line with the treatment of the male Hivites by Simeon and Levi.

Once this rule is seen as a response to a matter in the traditions available to the lawgiver, it can no longer be

---

[35] Some manuscripts of the LXX and the Samaritan text have condemnation of sacrifices to other gods, without any reference to Yahweh. Albrecht Alt, *Essays on Old Testament History and Religion* (Oxford: Blackwell, 1966), 112 n.73, claims that this formulation of the rule was the original one. Such a reading, however, would be an attempt to undo what appears to be a surprising juxtaposition, namely, altars to Yahweh alongside altars to other gods. The MT would represent the *lectio difficilior* and be readily explained in light of the development described in Gen 35:1–4. The text of the MT reads awkwardly: "Whoever sacrifices unto the gods shall be destroyed, except to Yahweh alone." This formulation, however, fits its context exactly: the focus is on the Hivite gods and then on the recognition that these incomers must worship Yahweh.

used in support of the early dating for the Book of the Covenant. Interpreters, assuming that it is a product of a time when the Israelites were mixing with the Canaanites, postulated a date during the period of conquest. The rule, so the argument goes, belongs to a time when Canaanite influence was still a problem for those urging a distinctive form of Israelite religion. It is plain, however, that such a period of time could just as readily reach well into the history of the monarchy; indeed, it could be as late as Josiah's time, the seventh century. Once it is understood that these rules are judgments inspired by the lawgiver's evaluation of the past, the criteria for dating the rules *so formulated* change. Critics have thought that the period of time to which the laws relate must be the time of their origin. They have made two errors: failure to recognize the archaic factor at work, in particular, the attribution of the laws to Moses, and failure to distinguish between a rule that might exist (there will be exceptions) in some form or another at an early period, and its formulation at a much later time.

The rule brings into the open the religious dimension that is a factor in the inspiration for the two preceding rules. The participle (*zobeah*) can include male or female. Both Israelite males and Canaanite females (and their young males) were potential offenders in Genesis 35.[36]

[36] Insofar as other critics see a link between this rule and the two preceding ones (bestiality and witchcraft) in terms of anti-Canaanite bias, they observe in a general way what I claim can be quite clearly specified. B. S. Childs, e.g. (*Exodus*, 478), speculates that because sacrifice to other gods might involve child sacrifice (to be associated with the Canaanites, Deut 12:31), this possible feature would indicate the close connection with the two preceding rules, both of which he links to antagonism to the Canaanite world.

Oppression of a Stranger (Exod 22:21)

> Thou shalt neither vex a stranger, nor oppress him: for
> ye were strangers in the land of Egypt.

Sources (Gen 34:29; Exod 3:7–17). The Hivite women
and children became captives of the house of Jacob/Is-
rael and consequently of low status in their new social
environment. The Israelites themselves were later to
experience a similar form of subjugation when they
lived among the Egyptians.

Having responded to the religious problem posed by
the Hivite women and children, the lawgiver turns to a
sympathetic consideration of the social problems occasioned by their incorporation into the Jacob group. This
observation provides substance to Umberto Cassuto's
general comment that "since the preceding paragraph con-
tained drastic laws against alien customs, the Bible wishes
to indicate at once that this opposition is directed only
against the customs, and not against the foreigner."[37] In
specific terms, the history of Jacob and his family (that is,
the beginnings of Israel) in their interaction with the
Hivites is under scrutiny.

The language of the rule, because of the reference to
Egypt, suggests that the lawgiver switches from the example of the possible oppression of the incorporated Hivites by the Israelites to the example of the Israelites
having been the object of oppression in Egypt. The Israelites were slaves incorporated into Egyptian society. The
Hivites were slaves incorporated into the Jacob group, in-

---

[37] Cassuto, *Exodus*, 291.

deed the first example to suggest the problem of oppression. The laws reveal an interest in historical parallels, because Moses looks back to the previous experiences of his people with the intention of addressing similar problems among future Israelites. The rule about the oppression of the stranger is a product of this process. The switch from the singular "thou" to the plural "you" in reference to the experience in Egypt may well reflect the conscious switch to a certain period of time in Israel's history. The "you" form in the Deuteronomic laws is typically used when Moses supposedly appeals to the common experience of himself and his audience.[38]

The verb *yanah*, "to vex," has a general application. The only time the term *lahas*, "to oppress," is used of the oppression of the Israelites in Egypt is in Exod 3:9: Yahweh will deliver them from it and give them the land of, among others, the Hivites (Exod 3:8). Indeed, this context provides the first description of the problem of Israel's oppression in Egypt. Consequently, it is no surprise to find the lawgiver switching to this particular context in his scanning of the problem of oppression in a later generation of the sons of Israel. It is noteworthy that in Moses's encounter with the deity on a sacred spot Yahweh informs Moses that he is the god of Jacob. In other words, the narrator, like the lawgiver, links both periods of history.

Martin Noth presumes that the second verb in the prohibition is a secondary addition.[39] He does not ask what might have prompted it. Again, however, we can readily

---

[38] See C. M. Carmichael, *Law and Narrative*, 19, 20, 127, 130, 230.

[39] Noth, *Exodus*, 186.

account for its specific use by noting how the lawgiver has gone from the episode about the incorporated Hivites to the one about the Israelites in Egypt. The sole use in the exodus story of the term *laḥaṣ* in the same context about the acquisition of the land of the Hivites is as clear an indication as we might hope for of how the lawgiver works.

Oppression of Widow and Orphan (Exod 22:22–24)

> 22 Ye shall not afflict any widow, or fatherless child. If thou afflict them in any wise, and they cry at all unto me, I will surely hear their cry: And my wrath shall wax hot, and I will kill you with the sword; and your wives shall be widows, and your children fatherless.

> *Source* (Gen 34:25–29). Simeon and Levi slew all the adult male Hivites with the sword and a consequence was that an underclass of Hivite widows and their children was created among the Israelites.

The rule is inspired by the fate of the Hivite women and (fatherless) children, who became part of Israel.[40] The penalty in the rule is death by the sword for the fathers and husbands who do the oppressing, precisely the fate that befell the Hivite males. The extreme, almost bizarre, nature of the penalty is readily explained in light of this background. The use of the plural address in the initial prohibition might be explained by the fact that in the his-

---

[40] The term *yatom*, "orphan," although not always clear, refers to a fatherless child.

torical episode about the Hivites there are a number of victims.

The ethical sensitivity of the lawgiver is remarkable and is comparable to that of the redactor of the story about the Hivites in Genesis 34. Jacob was furious about Simeon and Levi's having put the Hivite males to the sword. His fury was motivated by political considerations. Simeon and Levi's action was motivated by anti-Canaanite, religious ones and meets with the approval of both the story's redactor and the lawgiver. The lawgiver nonetheless sees beyond the issue of idolatrous influence and focuses on the social problem of the incorporation of the Hivite women and children.

Loans (Exod 22:25–27)

> 25 If thou lend money to any of my people that is poor by thee, thou shalt not be to him as a creditor, neither shall ye lay upon him interest. 26 If thou at all take thy neighbour's raiment to pledge, thou shalt deliver it unto him by that the sun goeth down: For that is his covering only, it is his raiment for his skin: wherein shall he sleep? And it shall come to pass, when he crieth unto me, that I will hear; for I am gracious.

Sources (Gen 33:18, 19; 34:10, 21; 35:2). Jacob entered into a business transaction with the Hivites when he bought a parcel of land from them. Further discussions with Hamor the head of the Hivites took place about trade arrangements between both groups, but these ended with the annihilation of the adult male Hivites by Simeon and Levi. There remained the problem of the economic well-being of the surviving Hivites in their new social and national setting.

Hamor proposed that the Hivites and the Israelites conduct business in a mutually advantageous way (Gen 34:10). Such a commercial arrangement—recognized in Deut 23:20 for trade between Israelites and (certain) foreigners—was vitiated because of Simeon and Levi's action. But these Hivite women and children, having changed their religion and ethnic identity, became part of the Israelite nation, and they had to exist economically. Their status, and the fact that husbands and fathers were not available to provide for them, suggest the example of the poor who need loans to survive. The judgment is that these new members of Israel should not come under the proposal originally suggested by Hamor. They did not have their previous means—it was appropriated by Simeon and Levi (Gen 34:28, 29)—and they could not engage in ordinary commercial transactions.

In stating the meaning of the law in this way, I am claiming that this "historical" background is indeed the motivation for its formulation. I am not claiming, however, that the rule is solely concerned with the incorporated Hivites. Characteristic of rulemaking at all times and places (and most easily observed in the history of ancient law) is a tendency to generalize. This lawgiver's survey embraces successive generations well into the history of the kings.

The example of the garment (śimlah) in pledge may be inspired by the requirement that was imposed on the Hivite newcomers, who had to change their garments (śimlah, Gen 35:2).[41] Where would they have obtained new ones? All their wealth had been taken from them

---

[41] In Exod 22:9 the spelling for garment is śalmah, yet in Exod 22:26 the spelling is śimlah, exactly as in Gen 35:2:

(Gen 34:29). They would have had to obtain them from established Israelites. In any event, their garments would be their sole possession, the only thing they could give by way of a pledge should they need a loan. Crying is common to this law and the preceding one—an indication of similar derivation.

Cursing Authority (Exod 22:28)

> Thou shalt not revile God [*'elohim*], nor curse the ruler of thy people.

Source (Gen 35:1–4). After the slaughter of the adult male Hivites, Jacob was required to make an altar to his god and to prepare his people to worship. Among his people was the new underclass of the surviving Hivites whose allegiance to their new leader, Jacob, and his god was coerced.

The Hivite newcomers, having been required to put away their gods and worship Jacob's god (Gen 35:2, 3), had reason in their new situation to curse the god(s) (*'elohim*) of the Israelites and to revile the ruler (*nasi'*) who had replaced their old and honored one, Hamor (*nasi'* in Gen 34:2).[42]

---

[42] Martin Noth's much-discussed meaning for *nasi'* as a reference to some leader of an assumed pre-monarchical sacred federation is irrelevant to this rule, and consequently to the attempt to date the Book of the Covenant by means of this understanding of it; *Exodus*, 187–88. R. E. Clements, *Exodus*, CBC (Cambridge: Cambridge University Press, 1972), 146, also comes out firmly for some pre-monarchical type of leader. I agree but on the basis of quite different "historical" considerations.

When Josephus and Philo understood the reference to be to heathen gods, they no doubt were thinking of the circumstances of their own time and place.[43] Consequently, we would consider their interpretation anachronistic. Be that as it may, if we put ourselves in the position of the incorporated Hivites, from their perspective the Israelite god(s) were foreign deities.[44] In this light Josephus and Philo were right to give the sense of foreign gods to the term *ᵉlohim*.

Umberto Cassuto's intuition was sound when he suggested that this rule was placed after the preceding one because it was the disadvantaged person who was likely to curse God. He compares Isa 8:21 about just such a likelihood (the term *melek* and not *naśiʾ* is used).[45]

Non-delay of Offerings (Exod 22:29, 30)

> 29 Thou shalt not delay to offer from the fulness of thy harvest, and of the outflow of thy presses; the firstborn of thy sons shalt thou give unto me. 30 Likewise shalt thou do with thine oxen, and with thy sheep; seven days it shall be with his dam; on the eighth day thou shalt give it me.

Source (Genesis 35). At Bethel Jacob was under an obligation to worship his god, but before he acknowledged him by presenting an offering he buried Rebekah's

---

[43] Philo, *Vita Mosis* 2.26.205; *De specialibus legibus* 1.53; Josephus, *Contra Apionem* 2.237; *Jewish Antiquities* 4.207.

[44] Recall how, in formulating the slave laws in Exod 21:2–11, the lawgiver put himself in the position of the foreigner Laban in his dealings with Jacob.

[45] Cassuto, *Exodus*, 293.

nurse, Deborah. After the act of worship Jacob, accompanied by all his people and livestock, journeyed on from Bethel. Rachel died in giving birth to Benjamin. There follows a listing of all of Jacob's sons born to his various wives.

A fuller paraphrase of events in Jacob's life is called for at this point. Jacob eventually returned to Bethel, the place of religious significance and where, in Gen 28:20–22, he had made the binding vow to give the tenth of all that he had should he return there in peace. God kept his side of the agreement: he caused a terror to befall the surrounding Canaanite inhabitants so that Jacob returned to Bethel unharmed. God instructed Jacob to make an altar (Gen 35:1), but Jacob first attended to changing the religious orientation of the Hivites. It is their new situation that prompts the preceding rule about cursing God and a ruler. Jacob built an altar, but before he acknowledged God by giving him offerings, the burial of Rebekah's nurse, also at Bethel, intervened. Only after God appeared to him, changed his name from Jacob to Israel, blessed him with the blessings given to Abraham, and repeated the promise of the land to his descendants did he present a drink and oil offering.[46]

The rule focuses on the delay. It provides a fine example of how the lawgiver is alert to a matter not given attention in the narrative. We know from the injunctions in Deut 23:21 and Eccles 5:3 that delay in the payment of

[46] S. R. Driver makes a case for attributing these verses about Jacob's change of name etc. (vv. 9–13, 15) to P. The view does not affect my argument. E's account has the sequence: construction of altar, burial of Deborah, the libation at some sacred stone. See Driver, *Genesis*, WC, 309–10.

vows, in the example of these two texts, is a matter of some moment.[47] The topic is a proverbial one in that it concerns the keeping of a promise. The lawgiver sees in the gap between Jacob's presumed readiness to present offerings at the newly constructed altar and his eventual payment precisely this problem of delaying an obligation. We can assume such readiness on Jacob's part because of his original commitment at Bethel when he vowed to pay to God a tenth of all that he had been given (by way of agricultural produce only, it can be presumed).

The rule anticipates the time when the land will be inhabited and refers to the requirement to give of its fruits; it also, harking back to Jacob's drink and oil offering, requires the outflow of its wine and oil presses. The term *dema*ᶜ—found only in this text in Exod 22:29—is used by way of including both of Jacob's liquid offerings. The term, from a verb meaning "to weep," refers to the trickling of oil and wine. The reference to the outflow of the presses could presumably have been included in the term *mᵉleʾah*, "full produce," and hence its separate mention invites attention. The terseness of the language—in Hebrew, "thy fullness and thy trickling" is all we read—is not an indication of archaic rules in the sense in which S. R. Driver and Umberto Cassuto understand it, namely, very old ones.[48] Rather, the terseness is due to the lawgiver's focus on the ancient Jacob's drink offerings and the related, wider concern with the tithe of the future land's produce.

---

[47] The rule in Deut 23:21 is inspired by the example of the delay in Jephthah's payment of his vow (Judg 11:30–40); C. M. Carmichael, *Law and Narrative*, 246–50.

[48] Driver, *Exodus*, CBSC, 234, and Cassuto, *Exodus*, 294.

What follows (in Gen 35:16–26) is the birth of Benjamin to the dying Rachel, a reference to the other son born to her (Joseph, the one who would acquire the right of the firstborn), the sexual offense of Jacob's firstborn son, Reuben, and then a comprehensive listing of Jacob's sons, including a reference to Reuben as the firstborn.[49]

These are Jacob's descendants, the inheritors of the promise to Abraham (Gen 22:17; 35:12). In keeping with that promise, the lawgiver judges, God has a claim to an Israelite firstborn, as he has a claim to the first of the harvest and the presses. Taking up the topic of what an Israelite owes to the deity from the fruit of the womb, the lawgiver has probably recalled the original incident in which the deity first asserted the claim, namely, his request that Abraham sacrifice Isaac. The deity's claim to an Israelite's firstborn son was presumably viewed as established then. As a result of Abraham's acknowledgment of the claim, God had promised to multiply his descendants (Gen 22:15–17). In the rule the use of the verb "to give" for both the human and animal firstborn—a source of puzzlement to interpreters[50]—would then be explained in

---

[49] The listing of the sons is generally attributed to P. If the lawgiver is not himself responsible for it, if he did not have it before him in his traditions, the topic of Jacob's offspring is still very much to the fore in the J material. If this view of the makeup of Genesis 35 is sound, note that both the lawgiver and the priestly writer proceed in similar fashion.

[50] See Childs, *Exodus*, 479–80. Those who seek to interpret the rule as originating in a remote past of the Israelites assume a direct link between the rule and some set of historical circumstances. My assumption is that the rule is read out of an *account* of some such set of circumstances (Abraham's sacrifice of Isaac). When that "reading" took place is the actual historical origin of this particular rule.

light of the quite literal requirement of the offering of Isaac to the deity. In any event, the repetition of the promise to Jacob at Bethel, his drink and oil offerings there, and the different notices about his offspring prompt the lawgiver to tack on the rule requiring the giving of the firstborn to God.

The sequence of topics in the rule might justifiably occasion puzzlement—the agricultural requirement preceding the human and animal—but again the narrative sequence provides illumination. Moreover, another puzzling feature is solved when we note the link between law and narrative. The rule switches from a focus on delay in presenting agricultural produce to, simply, the requirement to offer human firstborn with no concern expressed about a delay in offering them. The reason is the lawgiver's switch from the notice about Jacob's oil and drink offering, after the inferred delay owing to the burial of Deborah, to the notices about Jacob's sons.

Jacob came to Bethel with his many animals (Gen 33:13, 17). In the rule similar claims are laid on an Israelite's ox and sheep.

What comparable rule existed at the time of this reading is what the legal historian would like to know (and cannot).

[5]

Joseph's Problems
(Part Two)

The lawgiver turns again to Joseph's problems with his brothers. Beginning with his rule about torn animal flesh, the lawgiver takes up issue after issue in the dispute between them and sets down rules accordingly. There is a parallel to his procedure, the same dispute being in focus, in a series of Deuteronomic laws (Deut 24:17–25:3, 25: 13–16).[1] This phenomenon, where a tradition is examined from different angles, is well illustrated in the three decalogues of Exodus 20, Exodus 34, and Deuteronomy 5.

Previously, the lawgiver focused on the issue of assault in the brothers' dealings with Joseph. In the following series of laws he ranges more widely and takes a look at many different aspects, not just of the brothers' treatment of Joseph, but also of Joseph's treatment of his brothers after they came to Egypt to obtain food from him. The laws are: torn flesh; duties of witnesses; avoidance of par-

---

[1] See C. M. Carmichael, *Law and Narrative in the Bible* (Ithaca: Cornell University Press, 1985), 278–303.

The Origins of Biblical Law

tiality to the poor in the resolution of a dispute; an enemy's beast; bribes; and oppression of sojourners.

Torn Flesh (Exod 22:31)

> And ye shall be holy men unto me. And ye shall not eat any flesh that is torn [by beasts] in the field; ye shall cast it to the dog.
>
> *Source* (Gen 37:18–33). Joseph's brothers conspired against him and caused their father to conclude that a wild beast had torn him to pieces. In fact, they killed an animal of the flocks in order to convey the false notion that a wild beast had been preying in their midst.

The preceding rule is about animals kept separate, then slaughtered for the deity, and consequently constituting holy things. Jacob's animals and the altar at Bethel were in focus, as had been Jacob's sons in the initial part of the rule. The rule about torn animal flesh focuses on an incident involving both his sons and his animals.

The sons slaughtered one of their father's flock in order to deceive him into thinking that a wild beast had torn Joseph to pieces—a singularly unholy act, cutting off a descendant of Abraham, Isaac, and Jacob. Instead they should be men consecrated to Yahweh. The story concerns who in Jacob's family would emerge as the possessor of the power associated with the firstborn. The brothers' action against Joseph was motivated by his claim to it as expressed in his dream. This interest in primogeniture, especially in regard to giving the firstborn to

God, arose in the preceding rule.[2] In presenting the torn coat as evidence of Joseph's demise, the brothers were suggesting that Joseph's flesh had been torn. The words of the law, "flesh in the field, torn [flesh]," reflect this background. Ordinarily, in the experience of shepherds a wild beast kills one of their animals and the question of their eating it, should the beast have been scared away, will present itself. The lawgiver, as is typical, turns to this more normal situation—although the language may point to its background in the Joseph story[3]—and declares such flesh not suitable for consumption by Israelites. It has to be thrown to the dog (singular). From Job 30:1 we learn of sheepdogs, dogs of the flocks (ṣo'n). It is tempting to suggest that the reference in the rule relates to the possibility that Joseph's brothers had a dog to help them with their flocks (ṣo'n), even to guard against predators. Or, alternatively and more likely, the lawgiver thinks simply

---

[2] In light of the lawgiver's focus, the link between the Joseph narrative and the preceding genealogical material in the book of Genesis deserves more emphasis in assessment of the structure of Genesis.

[3] Terms from ṭarap are used in both law and narrative. Critics point to the apparent awkwardness of the Hebrew "flesh in the field, torn [flesh]," e.g., B. S. Childs, *The Book of Exodus; A Critical, Theological Commentary* (Philadelphia: Westminster, 1974), 450. The language may be the outcome of retaining the link between the law and the narrative: the law can refer to both situations, human and animal. The term ṭ'repah is used elsewhere (in Gen 31:39) to mean a torn animal and presumably could have been used by itself in this rule in this way, because it was automatically understood to refer to animal flesh. By adding "flesh in the field," the lawgiver drew attention back to the literal significance of torn flesh, that is, human or animal, and thus a reminder of the torn Joseph.

of a shepherding situation comparable to that of the brothers.

The puzzling initial reference to "holy men"—all the more puzzling in that it is stated first—is probably a response to the brothers' wrongful action and its related lie about an animal predator. They separated Joseph from Israel for perverse reasons, but God saw to it that his separation served good ends. The holiness that is required by the rule stands in contradistinction to the deceitful action of the brothers when they presented the torn coat to their father.[4] It is conceivable, however, that the two parts of the rule, as its language tends to indicate, should not be so closely linked. The first part focuses on the brothers' misdeed, and the second part solely on the example of torn animal flesh that is suggested by the brothers' action. The rule's plural formulation may reflect the concern with the brothers.

False Report (Exod 23:1)

Thou shalt not utter a false report: put not thine hand with the wicked to be a witness of violence.

Source (Gen 37:18–20). The brothers issued a false report about Joseph's violent fate.

The rule takes up, because of the preceding rule about

[4] The commonly expressed view—see, e.g., S. R. Driver, *The Book of Exodus*, CBSC (Cambridge: Cambridge University Press, 1911), 235–36—that the term "holy" here is confined to a ceremonial, ritualistic sense turns out to be wrong in light of the larger context from which the injunction issues.

torn flesh, from the remark of Joseph's brothers: "Then we shall say that a wild beast devoured him" (Gen 37:20). There is no joining particle between the two parts of the rule, between the prohibition against uttering a false report and the condemnation of a conspiracy. The reason is that the two actions of the brothers, concocting a falsehood and each testifying to its truth, belong together. The term 'ed-ḥamas literally means a "witness of violence."[5] It very accurately conveys what the brothers were doing: putting their hands on Joseph's coat to splash it with blood and claim that he had been a victim of violence. To conceal their own wrongdoing, they falsely accused a wild beast of a violent act. The rule's focus, as its language reveals, is not on someone (in this instance an animal!) who would be wronged by the false accuser, but on the latter's utterances. Critics misplace the rule's focus when they claim its purpose is, in Noth's words, "to protect the poor and the weak against a partial judgment in favour of the rich and the powerful."[6]

Collusion (Exod 23:2)

Thou shalt not turn aside after many to do evil; neither shalt thou speak in a cause to turn after many to incline to crookedness.

[5] While the term ḥamas can take on the meaning of malice, evil in general, its link to destructive physical assault is often its prominent feature. Herbert Haag is alert to this aspect in Exod 23:1 but is misleading when he states that the false accuser "plans or commits ḥamas through his appearance as 'ed"; TDOT 4:484.

[6] Martin Noth, Exodus (Philadelphia: Westminster, 1962), 188, followed by J. P. Hyatt, Exodus, NCBC (Grand Rapids: Eerdmans, 1980), 245.

Source (Gen 37:18–33). The brothers, with the exception of Reuben, conspired to slay Joseph. Changing their minds, they decided to sell him but nonetheless tell their father that he had met a violent end.

The two parts of the sentence follow the development about the ill-treatment of Joseph—each brother, with the important exception of Reuben, was influenced by the other. "Thou shalt not turn aside after many to do evil" observes how "they saw him afar off, and before he came near to them they conspired to kill him" (Gen 37:18). The brothers then had to change their approach of eliminating him directly by devising the scheme to make their father believe a wild beast had killed him. "Thou shalt not speak in a cause [the false "legal" report to their father] to turn after many to incline to crookedness." The legal tenor of both this rule and the preceding one is not owing to a concern with the local courts in ancient Israel, as almost all critics assume,[7] but to the brothers' need to clear themselves of any responsibility for Joseph before the *iudicium domesticum* of their father.

That Reuben did not go along with his brothers in their evil machinations highlights all the more the concern of the rule, namely, that a person might be influenced by others. It is also noteworthy that the sequence of the rules—first the false report and then wrongful influence—reflects the flow of the narrative, first the account

---

[7] Umberto Cassuto, e.g., refers to giving evidence in a court (*A Commentary on the Book of Exodus* [Jerusalem: Magnes, 1967], 296); so too Driver, *Exodus*, CBSC, 236; Noth to statements and judgments in a legal assembly (*Exodus*, 189); Werner Richter to the conduct of judges and leading circles in the judicial organization (*Recht und Ethos* [Munich: Kosel, 1966], 123).

of the brothers' conspiracy and then the information that Reuben did not go along with them (Gen 37:21, 22).

Wrongful Partiality to the Poor (Exod 23:3)

> Neither shalt thou countenance a poor man in his cause.

Source (Gen 37:22–27). "And Reuben said to them, 'Shed no blood; cast him into this pit that is in the wilderness, and lay no hand upon him;' that he might rid him out of their hands, to deliver him to his father again" (Gen 37:22).

"Then Judah said to his brothers, 'What profit is it if we slay our brother and conceal his blood? Come, let us sell him to the Ishmaelites, and let not our hand be upon him, for he is our brother, our own flesh.' And his brothers heeded him" (Gen 37:26, 27).

The dispute between Reuben and the other brothers was settled because the acquisition of money appeared to be a satisfactory resolution of the matter. Reuben's proposal to his brothers was presumably intended to convey to them that they should not shed Joseph's blood but let him die of natural causes because he would not be able to get out of the pit. It is the narrator who conveys Reuben's real intention, to eventually take Joseph from the pit and restore him to their father. The brothers (discounting Reuben) were partial to Judah's solution because Joseph's life would be saved and they stood to gain financially. Their partiality, however, meant that the wrong remained, despite the appearance of favor to both parties, Judah and his brothers on the one hand, Joseph on the other. In the event no favor was done one party, because Midianite traders intervened, and the favor done the other was an intolerable wrong.

The rule requires that someone not adorn (*hadar*, honor, countenance) a poor man in his dispute.[8] To be partial to him will be a satisfactory resolution for him, but such partiality does not address the wrong, of which he may be culpable, at the heart of the dispute. The combination of honor to the person and the fact of his poverty is a curious one. It is the reason interpreters have tried to emend the text to read "great" for "poor."[9] Avoiding such an arbitrary change, we may find illumination from noting that one brother, Judah, took the initiative in deciding what to do with Joseph. The fact that his other brothers, with presumably the exception of Reuben, responded positively to him means in fact that honor was conferred on him. Judah was not only usurping the position of authority that Reuben as the eldest son enjoyed, but in disposing of Joseph he was also usurping someone whose destiny it was, because of the content of

---

[8] The example of a poor person who may have committed a wrong is to be distinguished from the example of the poor man in Nathan's parable (2 Sam 12:1–6) and the example of the widow in the parable of the Unjust Judge, where it is assumed that their cases are sound (Luke 18:1–8).

[9] The common attempt to emend the text of this rule, to read *gadol* for *w^edal*—one is not to be partial to a great man in his lawsuit (see the listing for *hadar* in BDB, 214)—is unwarranted in light of the rule's origin in the dispute between Reuben and his brothers, and in light of the similar rule about partiality to the poor in Lev 19:15. The use of the particle *w* at the beginning of the rule indicates the continuation of the lawgiver's judgment on the brothers' treatment of Joseph.

his dreams, to become the leading member of his family. Interestingly, in his farewell speech Moses refers (Joseph's preeminence being long established) to Joseph's firstborn as a firstling bull that has majesty (honor, *hadar*, Deut 33:17).

As for the notion of poverty, it is perhaps derived from the contrast between a shepherd who comes into money, because of the sale of Joseph, and the usual situation of a shepherd, namely, low economic status.[10] Certainly the low status of the conspiring brothers was thrown into sharp relief when they, sitting down to eat bread, beheld the Ishmaelite traders from Gilead whose camels were laden with spices, balm, and myrrh (Gen 37:25). The mere fact that Judah proposed a means of acquiring some money raises the issue of their economic class. The prospect of unlawful enrichment for lowly shepherds was raised but came to nothing, because of the intervention of the Midianite traders (Gen 37:28), and such a reversal of expectations typically prompts the lawgiver to pursue a topic.

[10] On the low status of a shepherd (admittedly the evidence is from later times), see Joachim Jeremias, *Jerusalem in the Time of Jesus* (Philadelphia: Fortress, 1969), 303–12. The term *dal* is only found elsewhere in the Pentateuch in the Joseph story (Gen 41:19, "poor cows") and three times in P. On the basis of other biblical texts, H. J. Fabry points out that the *dal* appears to refer to those perpetually obliged to make a daily living by hard work, and who are not independent (*TDOT* 3:219). The term comes into its own in the Wisdom literature. It is from this background that the lawgiver approaches the legal and ethical issues raised by a reading of the Genesis narratives. The Testament of Judah cites, in addition to Judah's love of drink and fornication, the lure of money (13:3–8, 16:1, 17:1, 18:2, 19:1, 2).

A Personal Enemy's Straying and Broken-Down Animals (Exod 23:4, 5)

> 4 If thou meet thine enemy's ox or his ass going astray
> thou shalt surely bring it back to him again. 5 If thou
> see the ass of him that hateth thee lying under its bur-
> den, and wouldest refrain from leaving [it] to him,
> thou shalt surely leave with him.

Source (Gen 37:14–30). Joseph, wandering, eventually
found his brothers shepherding their animals. The
brothers sought to slay Joseph, but Reuben had them
cast him into a pit, hoping to rescue him and return
him to Jacob later. Reuben proved unsuccessful.

Joseph should have been restored to his father. Reuben's solution was the correct one. He would have restored him even though he also hated Joseph. The rule
concerns a personal enemy's straying (*taʿah*) ox or ass. Joseph in Gen 37:15 was found wandering (*taʿah*) in the
field.[11] Joseph's mission was to go and see how his
brothers and their father's flocks were faring. The association with a straying animal is readily made and enables
the lawgiver to render the exceptional example in the
story into a more mundane one for the purposes of a rule.[12]

---

[11] In the Pentateuch *taʿah* (*qal*) is only found elsewhere in Gen
21:14 (Hagar).

[12] This law and the one about torn animal flesh in Exod 22:31
provide examples where initial attention is on a human being, Joseph,
and a switch is then made to the animal world. Contrariwise, animals
in fables, while retaining their essential characteristics, are endowed
with human speech and human motivation so as to convey a message
about the human world. In Jacob's pronouncements about his sons in

Although there is no need to force the correspondence, we might note that the brothers' antagonism to Joseph was owing to their father's attitude and consequently their enmity was also directed against him. The ox and the ass, but not sheep or goats, are cited perhaps because the lawgiver, in switching from the human to the animal world, chooses animals that work together with man.

A second time when Joseph was helpless in the pit Reuben intended to lift him out and take him back to their father. The development suggests—if we assume a switch from the human to the animal world—the example of the broken-down donkey and, because the master is hated, the need for an injunction to help out. The double rule is thus readily explained by the dual development in the narrative.

Much discussion has been engendered by the awkwardness of the language (ʿazab, "to leave") in v. 5. Alan Cooper rightly criticizes the usual attempts to translate it, for example, the RSV's "You shall refrain from leaving [ʿazab] him with it, you shall help him to lift [ʿazab] it up." His own attempts founder on a failure to understand that the rule belongs to the sphere of morality and not of law.[13] If

---

Genesis 49 he likens them and their ways to animals. In Moses's comparable pronouncements in Deuteronomy 33 Joseph is compared to an ox (v. 17). In the law about cultic prostitution in Deut 23:17, 18 the male homosexual is identified with a dog. In the law against plowing with an ox and an ass (Deut 22:10), the ox stands for an Israelite, the ass a Canaanite. The composers of the laws are not a separate group from the composers of the narratives, proverbs, and the like.

[13] Alan Cooper "The Plain Sense of Exodus 23:5," *HUCA* 59 (1988), 1–22. See note 4, Chapter 3. He also acknowledges his arbitrary treatment of the prepositions lᵉ and ʿm, (16 n. 69). Moreover,

the Hebrew of v. 5 is reliable, what is most interesting is that the language uncannily tunes into Reuben's predicament with Joseph. In the rule the plain meaning of the language is that the owner's enemy sees the problem the owner is having with his donkey, and, remarkably, instead of ignoring it because of his hatred of him, "refrains [holds back] from *leaving* [the burden] to [*l^e*] him." Why, in the ordinary course of human conduct, would the person feel so positively disposed to his enemy?[14] Translators and critics misconstrue the meaning (and misuse the preposition *l^e*) by turning a comment about a disposition into a command: "You shall refrain from leaving him with it" (RSV). The puzzle is solved if we assume that the lawgiver is thinking of Reuben's stance vis-à-vis Joseph.

Reuben suggested to his brothers that Joseph be thrown into a pit, but his aim was to lift him out eventually and return him to their father. That never happened. Reuben was not around when Joseph was lifted from the pit by Midianite traders (Gen 37:28–30). The lawgiver may well be focusing on Reuben's failure to live up to his responsibilities. The language of the rule could then be viewed as, at one point, addressing itself to the situation Reuben found himself in: he had not wanted to leave Joseph in the pit—he refrained from leaving him—and, so the lawgiver judges, should have actually accompanied him back to their father. "And thou wouldest refrain from leaving [the burden] to him [the ass's owner]"

---

he interprets the first part of the injunction about the straying animal one way, and the second part about the broken-down (or, as he would have it merely resting) beast in a contrary way.

[14] Cooper thinks that the opposite attitude prevails, namely, he is intent on mischief.

would correspond to Reuben's disposition not to leave
Joseph to his fate. The final part of the rule, "Thou shalt
surely leave with ['m] him," would correspond to Reuben's intention to have Joseph restored unharmed to
Jacob. We have noted before—for example, in the rule
about assault (Exod 21:18, 19)—how its language betrays
a focus on, as it happens, this same tradition.

The placement of this rule at this point is invariably a
matter for comment by critics who either suggest dis-
placement[15] or a tenuous link with the context.[16] Again,
however, the contents of the narrative determine the
seemingly unrelated topics that appear in sequence in the
laws.

Wronging the Poor (Exod 23:6)

> Thou shalt not wrest the judgment of thy poor in his
> cause.

Source (Genesis 42). Joseph, established as vizier in
Egypt, received his brothers in their quest for food to
alleviate their family needs back in Canaan. Concealing
his identity from them, Joseph sought by unfair means
to pay them back for their injustice to him.

The focus continues to be the dispute between the
brothers. The term *'ebyon*, "poor," has the sense of those

[15] Driver, for example, *Exodus*, CBSC, 237.
[16] Noth, for example, suggests that the enemy refers to someone
with whom there is a legal dispute (*Exodus*, 189).

193

lacking material necessities.[17] Joseph's brothers came to Egypt to obtain food because of the famine in their own country, but Joseph, in disguise and pursuing his dispute with them, pronounced judgment upon them that in fact they were spies come to view "the nakedness of the land." As a consequence of this false accusation, he put them in prison (Gen 42:5–20)—a wresting of justice. The rule opposes Joseph's action.

The rules in the Book of the Covenant focus on relations between Joseph and his brothers and hence we do not find rules at this point taken up with Joseph's problem with Potiphar's wife.[18] There is, as we have already noted, a concentration on the ins and outs of the running dispute between them.[19] Critics have understandably been

---

[17] The term is found in the Pentateuch only in Exod 23:6, 11, and seven times in Deuteronomy, a fact consistent with the view that the Deuteronomist is responsible for the rules in the Book of the Covenant. As G. J. Botterweck points out, the *'ebyon* in Exod 23:11 is "clearly contrasted with the landowner: whereas the landowner can live off the produce of the foregoing years during the seventh year while the land lies fallow, the *'ebyon* is forced to eat that which grows wild on the fallow ground in the Sabbatical Year, because he has no property or produce" (*TDOT* 1:30). The brothers' need for the produce of Egypt is differently based from Judah's need for money, and hence the use of the term *dal* in regard to the latter (in Exod 23:3) but the term *'ebyon* in regard to the former.

[18] For such rules, see Carmichael, *Law and Narrative*, 206–9, 215–18, 280–81.

[19] Maren Niehoff finds it somewhat astonishing to note how in late antiquity the biblical Joseph enjoyed great popularity among Jewish interpreters in contrast to "the rather insignificant role which Joseph plays in the shaping of Israelite religion"; "The Figure of Joseph in the Targums," *JJS* 39 (1988), 234–50. This common view about the supposed lack of influence of the Joseph story on other biblical material has to be jettisoned. D. B. Redford speaks of

ready to claim that the rules seem in no order whatsoever: for example, this rule about wresting justice is similar, it is claimed, to Exod 23:2. They imagine the accumulation of diverse rules that come from different periods of time. They can hardly be impressed with how ancient scribes worked with their material. The entire picture changes when we view the rules as issuing from judgments on developments in the narrative.

False Accusation (Exod 23:7)

Keep far from a false matter; and the innocent and righteous slay thou not: for I will not justify the wicked.

Source (Genesis 42). The disguised Joseph wrongly accused his brothers of being spies. His intention was to bring judgment on them for another offense of which they were indeed guilty.

---

the "virtually complete silence of the rest of scripture on the subject of the Joseph story. The romanticized hero of the Genesis story almost never appears elsewhere in the Old Testament outside Genesis and the first chapter of Exodus." This assertion becomes a prop for dating the story around 650–425 B.C.; *A Study of the Biblical Story of Joseph* (Leiden: Brill, 1970), 249–50. J. L. Kugel's comments are curiously uncritical in *In Potiphar's House* (San Francisco: Harper, 1990). At one point he says Joseph "eschews revenge and hatred" (14) and his virtue is supreme. Yet he refers to Joseph's "intrigue with their [the brothers'] grain sacks" (22), saying that "if he [Joseph] does arrange things so as to give his brothers a scare or two along the way—well, a reader most likely feels that this is only justified in view of their earlier misconduct" (13).

Joseph's false scheme—accusing them of being spies, imprisoning them in order to pressure them into bringing Benjamin to Egypt—was intended to make them recognize their own wickedness in selling him into slavery. In this matter of spying, however, they were innocent and, in fact, were engaged in a righteous cause (to obtain food for their family), and Joseph was the one resorting to wickedness. Spying would have been a capital offense: note "By the life of Pharaoh surely ye are spies" (Gen 42:15); also Joseph tells them explicitly what they must do to avoid death (Gen 42:20). If the charge of spying had been upheld, the innocent would have forfeited their lives.

Critics rightly wonder why this injunction seems to repeat the similar one in Exod 23:1. They suggest that the former is addressed to witnesses, the latter to judges.[20] The solution, however, is that the injunction in Exod 23:7 focuses on Joseph, who in getting back at his brothers is himself doing what they did. The rule in Exod 23:1, on the other hand, was prompted by the brothers' false report to their father about Joseph's fate. Again links to narrative tradition produce more concrete results than does the usual mode of linking the laws to inferred differences in social and legal circumstances at some undetermined point in the life of ancient Israel.

"For I will not justify the wicked" seems a curiously unnecessary statement. The LXX changed it to "And

---

[20] Cassuto, for example, *Exodus*, 298–99. J. I. Durham (*Exodus*, WBC 3 [Word Books: Waco, Texas, 1987], 331) criticizes this view as too restrictive: both can apply to anyone with a determinative role in a legal proceeding. He does not address the problem of apparent duplication.

thou shalt not justify the wicked"—an indication that the translators saw the problem. They presumably read the sentence as extending the sense of the preceding one: to do injustice to the innocent probably entailed a simultaneous justification of wrongdoers. The *lectio difficilior*, however, should be upheld. The MT reading presumably refers to those against whom a false charge is made. They are guilty of some offense but not of the particular charge against them. This is precisely the position of Joseph's brothers, whose wickedness would in the end be visited upon them. Indeed this was their reaction after Joseph's false charge about their being spies: "We are verily guilty concerning our brother" (Gen 42:21).[21] The rule, if we narrowly confined it to its background inspiration, could be read as an address to Joseph: "Keep thee [Joseph] far from a false charge [that your brothers are spies]; and the innocent and righteous [your brothers in their quest for food to alleviate famine in their family] slay thou [Joseph] not: for I [Yahweh in my overall control of events] will not justify the wicked [your brothers because of their original offense against you]."

Wrongful Gifts (Exod 23:8)

And thou shalt take no gift: for the gift blindeth the open-eyed, and perverteth the words of the righteous.

Sources (Gen 42:25–38; Exod 18:14–26). In selling grain to his brothers, the disguised leader Joseph misused the

[21] The language about justifying (the righteous and) the wicked is found in Deut 25:1. The focus is again on the dispute between Joseph and his brothers. See Carmichael, *Law and Narrative*, 285–91.

money they had paid for the grain to make them realize their offense in having him sold into slavery. Moses, in order to deal with offenses by the Israelites, appointed judges who would eschew gain when deciding for one disputant against another.

Joseph, the victim of his brothers' wickedness, schemed to pay them back. His placing money in their cornsacks was a gift with a twist, a means to win a dispute. Joseph's aim was to bring his undoubtedly righteous case against them to a successful conclusion. The brothers themselves had brought gifts to the disguised Joseph, as well as double the amount of the money that had turned up in their sacks, in order to gain his favor should he bring up the subject of the money (Gen 43:11, 12, 25, 26).

The brothers' original offense had been to plan to sell Joseph who, as the standing sheaf of grain in his dream, had anticipated his eventual superiority over them and thereby aroused their hostility. In return, Joseph as their superior in Egypt provided them with grain and, in order to concentrate their minds, the very money they thought they had paid for it.[22] The use of money in this deceptive way is like Joseph's false accusation that is the subject of the preceding law; and in both instances the lawgiver adopts an ethical stance condemning the kind of deception committed by Joseph.

What Joseph did with the money was not bribery. The situation depicted was a topsy-turvy one. He was not

---

[22] On the role of Joseph as the sheaf of grain in his dream, its significance for the entire story, and its impact on the law of the forgotten sheaf in Deut 24:19–22, see Carmichael, *Law and Narrative*, 278–88.

seeking a favor from the recipients of the money; rather he was trying to trip them up in order to make them realize their guilt in having him sold into slavery in Egypt. He was like a prosecutor of justice who seeks a conviction by underhanded means.

The clue to a correct understanding of the rule is the lawgiver's typical procedure of finding in another generation a situation comparable to the one depicted in Joseph's. Noting Joseph's deceptive use of money in his pursuit of justice, but unable to formulate a rule that would address itself to Joseph's ploy, the lawgiver turns to the next comparable occasion in Israelite history when the issue of correct procedure in pursuing justice arose. That occasion was the exodus from Egypt when Moses, like Joseph in so many ways, had authority over his brother Israelites. His father-in-law Jethro (a Midianite, a band of whom had originally sold Joseph to the Egyptians) instructed him on the best way to administer justice: Moses should communicate certain rules and appoint some men to judge most cases at law (Exod 18:20–22).

In that Moses is thought of as giving the rules in the Book of the Covenant, and in that one of their consistent features is that he as the lawgiver often ranges over similar developments in succeeding generations, the rule about bribery can be read as one of those he addressed to the appointed judges. As most critics have readily observed, the rule has every appearance of constituting an address to judges. Most noteworthy is that one criterion in Moses's selection of judges is that they must hate unjust gain (*beṣaʿ*, Exod 18:21), that is, a bribe (cp. 1 Sam 8:3; Prov 1:19; 15:17; 28:16).[23]

---

[23] This is the term Judah uses in Gen 37:26 in reference to gaining

In sum, Joseph's deceptive practice with the money was too idiosyncratic to prompt a comprehensible rule. The lawgiver consequently turned to the next occasion when one Israelite had judicial and political authority over his fellows. That occasion was Moses's appointment of judges who would eschew unjust gain in their administration of justice. Hence the lawgiver, Moses, formulates a rule against bribery. On quite other grounds, I have tried to show that the almost identical rule in Deut 16:19 also takes us to Moses's selection of judges when counseled by his father-in-law, Jethro.[24]

The language of the rule may owe something to the story: the brothers' eyes were not open, surprisingly not even on the second occasion (because they had been drinking, Gen 43:34), when the steward attended to their sacks. By contrast, with a bribe, in the more ordinary situation contemplated by the rule, the recipient knows

---

profit out of Joseph. Joseph's return of the money in the brothers' sacks was to remind them of this fact. See C. M. Carmichael, "Moses and Joseph," *S'vara* (Forthcoming).

[24] Carmichael, *Law and Narrative*, 86–90. I also note (299–303) that the rule about false weights and measures (Deut 25:13–16) was prompted by Joseph's trickery in the transaction about the grain, but that the rule required a more obvious instance of fairness in such dealings as occurred on a comparable occasion later (the exact provision of food to the starving Israelites at the time of the exodus, Exodus 16). In other words, the procedure is identical to the way the rule about bribery in Exod 23:8 has come to be formulated. The question arises whether these narratives that are explicitly concerned with justice (e.g., Exodus 16 and 18) already revealed this interest in justice at the time when the lawgiver turned to them, or whether the interest is a result of the process that underlies the presentation of the laws. In other words, was the intent of these narratives to show that God and Moses exhibited the highest regard for justice in contrast to Joseph, whose supreme position as vizier was not synonymous with such regard?

the nature of the gift: his eyes are open and, unlike Joseph's brothers, he pretends not to notice what is really going on. We cannot say whether the gift in the rule is a monetary one, but it probably is.

Joseph is depicted as righteous, but his remark, communicated through his steward, about the return of their money was a perversion of the words of a righteous man. He had his steward claim that their god had given them "treasure in their sacks." Note that he was saying that the money was theirs to keep: it had been a gift but not of the usual kind. The reference in the rule to the perversion of the words of the righteous is difficult to make sense of, but perhaps less so in light of Joseph's deception. The term "words" in effect refers to someone's case or cause (as is made clear in Exod 24:14, in the direction to the people to bring their "words" [for judgment] to Aaron and Hur).[25] Again, we might note that Joseph was pursuing his cause against his brothers. I repeat, however, that because of the highly idiosyncratic nature of Joseph's ploy, the rule is not a straight comment on it. Rather his deception has triggered the proverbial concern about bribes (Prov 6:35; 17:8, 23; 21:14). Hence Moses switches to the concern about bribes that confronted him in administering justice in his own time.

Oppression of Sojourner (Exod 23:9)

> Also thou shalt not oppress a sojourner: for ye know the heart of a sojourner, seeing ye were sojourners in the land of Egypt.

[25] See Driver, *Exodus*, CBSC, 256.

Sources (Genesis 42–44; Exodus 3). When his brothers came as sojourners to Egypt, Joseph used a variety of underhanded means to trip them up in revenge for their offense against him. The brothers' experience of oppression in Egypt was but a foretaste of what was to happen to the succeeding generation under an oppressive pharaoh.

Joseph's return of the money to his brothers was but one element in a pattern of oppressive treatment of persons who were sojourners in a foreign land. The gift of the money was not to the usual end of gaining favor but to torment them. Other elements in the pattern are: false accusations that they are spies, putting them in prison for three days, letting them return to their own land but leaving one of them (Simeon) bound in prison in Egypt, repeating the action of returning their money, concealing the cup in Benjamin's sack, and causing distress by insisting on keeping Benjamin in Egypt.

Joseph's oppression of his brothers was motivated by his desire to make them remember that they had caused him to be sold into slavery in Egypt. When Judah takes the initiative in appealing to Joseph not to have Benjamin retained in Egypt, we are meant to recall Judah's role as the one responsible for selling Joseph. When he urges Joseph that he, Judah, become a bondman in Egypt (Gen 44:33), he is visiting upon himself the offense against Joseph. Or more accurately, in line with the religious perspective of the story, God brings judgment upon Judah. From this perspective Joseph is but an instrument in the deity's hands in the working out of justice. The lawgiver, however, has to discount such a providential role in ordinary life and lay down standards of conduct that would apply to someone like Joseph in his pursuit of justice. We are furnished with an example of how the deity's role in human affairs, while affirming proper values, is not helpful in making human beings responsible for their conduct.[26]

The issue of the sojourn and eventual slavery of the sons of Jacob in Egypt begins with the Joseph story but becomes an overriding issue a few generations later. The same verb, laḥaṣ, in the figurative sense of "to oppress" is used in Exod 3:9 (only here and in the two rules in Exod 22:21, 23:9) in reference to the later pharaoh's oppression of the Israelites. It is used right at the beginning of the story: God's revelation to Moses that he is the god of Abraham, Isaac, and Jacob—and Joseph too, we might add—and that he is responding to Israel's dire needs (Exod 3:6–9). Both periods of history come under review in the rule. A characteristic of the lawgiver is, as frequently noted, to range over similar developments in succeeding generations.

We can explain why this rule is so similar to the preceding one in Exod 22:21: each takes up similar issues in different narratives (Exod 22:21 focuses initially on the incorporated Hivites). This explanation avoids the barren notion that the ancient lawgiver simply added rules to already existing ones without regard to the fact that he might be repeating himself. It is not a matter of this kind of redundancy but of similar responses to recurring patterns in the history of the nation. History repeats itself, historical writing imitates historical writing, and this awareness of repetition and imitation deepens human reflection and evokes similar comments and warnings.

[26] For another example, see Carmichael, *Law and Narrative*, 270.

[6]

Israel in Egypt

Joseph's brothers and father, the entire house of Israel, migrated from Canaan to Egypt, survived the famine, became slaves, sought and obtained liberation, and anticipated life in the land of Canaan. Their various experiences, first under the leadership of Joseph and then under that of Moses, are reflected in a range of rules: the fallow year; seventh-day rest from labor; invocation of other gods; annual pilgrimages; and sacrifices and offerings.

The Fallow Year (Exod 23:10, 11)

> 10 And six years thou shalt sow thy land, and shalt gather in the increase thereof: 11 But the seventh year thou shalt let it rest and lie still; that the poor of thy people may eat: and what they leave the beasts of the field shall eat. In like manner thou shalt deal with thy vineyard and with thy oliveyard.

Source (Gen 41:33–47:26). Worked out in a systematic way, Joseph's agricultural program in Egypt was designed to help out his fellow Israelites in need as well as the Egyptians themselves.

This rule too has reference to the Egyptian experience, not to what H.-J. Boecker calls a "cultic purpose the original significance of which has been lost."[1] The rule concentrates on grain and only at the end cites a similar consideration about grapes and olives. We can explain this priority by the lawgiver's response to the significance of the Joseph story. The purpose of the brothers' sojourn in Egypt was to obtain food in the form, not of grapes or olives, but of grain, because of the famine in Canaan. Joseph's agricultural policy in Egypt was in effect: during seven years of growth a fifth each year had been set aside for the coming years of want (Gen 41:34). After the famine Joseph instituted a comparable, permanent agricultural policy in Egypt (Gen 47:24).[2]

The rule in Exod 23:10, 11 is puzzling. How are the landowning Israelites to obtain food in the seventh year? The assumption is inescapable that they would have to adopt a policy similar to Joseph's policies in Egypt in anticipation of what is to happen to them in the seventh year.[3] When the rule states that the land's produce will be

---

[1] H.-J. Boecker, *Law and the Administration of Justice in the Old Testament and Ancient East* (Minneapolis: Augsburg, 1980), 91.

[2] *t^ebu'ah* (harvest, increase) in the rule and in Joseph's later rule, comparable to his one in Gen 41:34, namely, "And it shall come to pass, in the increase, that ye shall give the fifth part unto Pharaoh," Gen 47:24. On some problems of the narrative, see Gerhard von Rad, *Genesis* (Philadelphia: Westminster, 1972), 408–10.

[3] In contrast to Lev 25:6, 7: not just the poor as in Exod 23:11, but all are to be provided from the land in the sabbath year. One indication of the later character of the institution of Lev 25:2–7 is

gathered in each year, we should understand the process to include some arrangement whereby a fraction of it is set aside for the coming fallow year. The fact that in the seventh year the wild beasts are to consume what the poor do not rules out, in contrast to the corresponding regulation in Lev 25:6 ("And the sabbath of the land shall be meat for you; for thee, and for thy servant"), any resort on the part of the landowners to the same (seventh year) source of food. Remarkably, critics in their discussion of the rule in Exod 23:10, 11 do not raise the issue of where the non-poor would obtain their own provisions that year. B. S. Childs simply states that it is difficult to imagine how the people coped if the whole land were subject to the rule.[4] Even if the question of any link to the Joseph narrative was put aside, we might speculate that a policy similar to Joseph's in Egypt would have to be in effect.

The curiously impractical nature of the rule—it would have made more sense to have called for provision for the poor each year[5]—should make us alert to its unexpected

---

that the rule is no longer written up with the grain as primary focus; vines receive equal attention. It seems to be typical of the Levitical lawgivers that they no longer understand the rationale behind existing rules. They interpret them in their own terms in an often narrowly rational way. See C. M. Carmichael, "Forbidden Mixtures," *VT* 32 (1982), 411–12.

[4] B. S. Childs, *The Book of Exodus: A Critical, Theological Commentary* (Philadelphia: Westminster, 1974), 482. Cp., however, n. 17, chap. 5.

[5] J. P. Hyatt rightly questions the practical reasons suggested by other scholars; see *Exodus*, NCBC (Grand Rapids: Eerdmans, 1980), 247. As usual, S. R. Driver (*Exodus*, CBSC [Cambridge: Cambridge University Press, 1911], 239) lays out the issues in masterly fashion: is it a year common to the entire land, or, more prac-

origin. The significant element, evoking the notion of famine, is the fallow year with its lack of provision because there is not the usual cultivation of the land. The periodic nature of the institution also serves to recall the periodic character of the time in Egypt, namely, seven years of plenty followed by seven years of want. This observation does not exclude the further one that the idea of the rest from active cultivation in the seventh year may be modeled on the institution of the seventh-day rest from daily work. The sabbath, we might note, is the issue in the next rule.

The rule against oppressing the poor (the sojourner) that precedes the rule about the fallow year is set against both the time when the brothers, seeking corn, were oppressed by Joseph and the later time of the Israelite enslavement in Egypt, when God intervened and promised to deliver them from bondage and to bring them into a land "flowing with milk and honey" (Exod 3:8). The land was that of Canaan, the one the brothers lived in but that would in future become their descendants', and would presumably not be subject to famine (unless there was disobedience of the kind cited in Deut 11:17) because it was "a good land and a large" (Exod 3:8). The rule about

---

tically, "one varying with the different properties, and reckoned in each from the year in which it first began to be cultivated?" He is wrong, however, in claiming that Lev 19:23–25 supports the interpretation of Exod 23:10, 11 along practical lines. The focus of Lev 19:23–25 is on the first entry into the land and the planting in that first year, not on cultivations in different successive years. J. I. Durham rightly points out that Lev 25:1–7 (sabbath rest for the land) "clearly implies a general sabbath year every seventh year following entry into the promised land" (*Exodus*, WBC 3 [Word Books: Waco, Texas, 1987], 332).

the fallow year can be viewed as the equivalent of what Joseph legislated for in Egypt. Like his program, the rule's intent is directed toward the needs of those in want. In the tradition about Joseph in Egypt the deity is the one ultimately directing matters. Although the two situations, in Joseph's Egypt and in the future Canaan, are different, the lawgiver is under an obligation to set up some institution that will have the Israelites commemorate God's first provision of food for needy Israelites.

So many biblical institutions, the passover, for example, have the aim of historical commemoration. The curious institution of the fallow year can be explained on this basis. Only those occasions, however, that occurred in Moses's own time are ever explicitly cited in support of the relevant institution.

Sabbath Day (Exod 23:12)

> Six days thou shalt do thy work, and on the seventh day, thou shalt rest: that thine ox and thine ass may rest, and the son of thy handmaid, and the stranger may be refreshed.

> *Source* (Exod 5:4–19). The Israelites in Egypt constituted labor gangs whose daily tasks were of the most onerous and increasingly oppressive kind. The increase in their workload was a direct result of their request to go on a pilgrimage, which was interpreted as a request to rest from their labors.

The formulation of this rule is marvellously revealing of the lawgiver's use of an existing tradition. The emphasis in the rule is on cessation from work for those whose lives are virtually synonymous with hard toil. The rule is prompted by that feature of the exodus narrative—introduced in Exod 1:11, 3:7—focused on Israel's enslavement and hard toil under Egyptian taskmasters. The term for work in the rule, *ma'śah*, is different from the term in the sabbath rule in the decalogue (Exod 20:11) and is indeed the one used to describe the work of the Israelites under their taskmasters (Exod 5:5, 13). We have moved from the hardship of Israel's experience of famine in Egypt, which was closely linked to Joseph's (and his brothers') history of enslavement, to the next episode of hardship, the larger experience of slavery in Egypt. Typically, because of the lawgiver's interest in succeeding generations, and in line with the exodus narrative itself (for example, Exod 3:8), the rule anticipates the later settlement in the land of Canaan.

The rule is about a rest from work on the seventh day and its focus reveals the link to the experience in Egypt. In particular, the lawgiver would have noted that in Egypt there was an emphasis on the Israelites' daily tasks (Exod 5:13, 19). Moreover, when they requested to go on a three-day pilgrimage to worship their god, the pharaoh interpreted the request as an excuse to rest (*šabat*) from work (Exod 5:5). The result was an increase in the tasks imposed on the Israelites—the opposite of a rest from their labors. The lawgiver, reacting to this aspect of Israel's oppression in Egypt, requires of the Israelites in their land that they should rest (*šabat*) every seventh day. Presumably the rule about the sabbath is already known to the lawgiver, and the incident with the pharaoh is what prompts this particular formulation of it. How revealing the link is between the sabbath rest and the religious festival that was requested by the Israelites is a question that has to be kept open. Texts such as 2 Kings 4:22, 23; Isa 1:13; Hos 2:11; and Amos 8:5 suggest that the sabbath was an occasion not just for an intermission from labor and trade, but for religious observance, including sacrifices and revelries.

Another indication of the evocation of the experience in Egypt is that in the rule the son of the bondwoman is singled out as one who is in need of rest from work. Like the Israelite slaves in Egypt whom the pharaoh would have willingly kept in perpetual bondage, the son of the bondwoman is a perpetual slave in Israel.

A puzzle is why the ox and the ass are given consideration first, or even at all. The explanation appears to lie in the lawgiver's concern to evoke the closest parallel in his own time to the hard labor that characterized the situation of the Israelites in Egypt. From this perspective the ox and the ass epitomize such labor, and the house slave and an alien, who are next cited, represent similar if not such intense employment. Perhaps too that feature in the narrative that told how the Israelites came to be denied any assistance in making bricks (Exod 5:7–13) prompted awareness of the normal role of animals in assisting humankind with daily tasks. However that may be, the regard for the ox and the ass makes no sense as an ordinary feature of the rule. If there is to be a seventh-day rest that extends to every person and slave in the community, it is redundant to spell out that the domestic animals have to be rested too—yet their needs are given first mention. The rules in the Book of the Covenant, focused as they are meant to be on future life in the new land, are freighted with associations drawn from significant developments in the past. This rule about the sabbath rest, like those about passover, provides a model illustration.

Naming Other Gods (Exod 23:13)

> And in all things that I have said unto you take ye heed:
> and make no remembrance of the name of other gods,
> neither let it be heard out of thy mouth.

Source (Exod 3:13–17). In communicating to the people
the momentous change about to happen to them, how
they can expect to go to a new land inhabited by other
peoples, Moses brings up the problem of ignorance
about the name he will use of the deity who has made
himself known to him at the burning bush.

This rule and the remaining ones concern aspects of the
exodus, but they also anticipate, as does the narrative itself, later life in the land. Original happenings or developments typically invite attention. In the deity's first ex-
change with Moses when the bush burned but was not
consumed, the issue of God's name surfaced.

Moses wished to know what name to use of God when
he spoke to the people: "And God said unto Moses, *I am
that I am*: and he said, Thus shalt thou say unto the children of Israel, *I am* hath sent me unto you" (Exod 3:14).
The opening part of the rule, "In all things that I have
said," might be illumined in light of the frequent use of
the verb "to say" (*'mr*), both in Exod 3:14 and in the narrative's preceding verse ("Behold, when I [Moses] come
unto the children of Israel, and shall say unto them. The
God of your fathers hath sent me unto you: and they shall
say to me, What is his name? what shall I say unto
them?"). The deity adds to his remarks by instructing
Moses to say to the people, "Yahweh God of your fathers, the God of Abraham, the God of Isaac, and the

God of Jacob hath sent me unto you: this is my name forever, and this is my memorial [*zeker*] unto all generations." Noteworthy are the links to the past and future generations, precisely the feature that shows up in so many of the rules. Also noteworthy is that, although the rule's context, the Book of the Covenant, requires us to read it as an utterance of Moses, it in fact reads like a rule uttered directly by Yahweh. What accounts for this impression is Yahweh's address to Moses at the bush. We might also note that in the rule the use of "you" ("Take ye heed") before the switch to "thou" ("thy mouth") may also reflect the plural address in the narrative. In other words, the singular form of address is the predominant one in the Book of the Covenant, but the plural form sometimes intrudes because of its use in a narrative.

The reason for Moses's negative statement in his rule is the pressing need to counter the appeal of other gods in later generations, when the Israelites, as anticipated in the context of Exodus 3, will live in "the place of the Canaanites, and the Hittites, and the Amorites, and the Perizzites, and the Hivites, and the Jebusites" (Exod 3:8; cp. 3:17 and note Josh 23:7). His rule draws out the implications of Yahweh's pronouncements in Exod 3:14–16. The rule uses the verbal form of *zakar* when it prohibits an Israelite's calling to mind the name of other gods ('*elohim*). Its use might be owing to the emphasis on Yahweh, the god(s) ('*elohim*) of the fathers, as the only name to be brought to mind by the Israelites at all times. The reference in the rule to what comes out of the mouth is likewise interesting in light of the discussion between God and Moses about how God will be with his mouth, likewise with Aaron's, and how Aaron will be a mouth for Moses (Exod 4:10–16). Aaron's later apostasy with the golden calf is probably also a factor in the rule's negative formulation.

Rules, we have noted, are typically formulated by way of bringing out what is implicit in an aspect of a tradition. The reference in Exod 3:18 to the god of the Hebrews, who had commanded the Israelites to sacrifice to him in the wilderness, signifies that god as opposed to the gods of the Egyptians—and to those of the Canaanites, because of the anticipation of encountering them (Exod 3:17). The preceding rule about the sabbath was directly linked to the Israelites' request to go and worship their god in the wilderness. Instead of granting the request, the pharaoh, interpreting it as an excuse to rest from work, increased their daily tasks. The specific request about the worship of the god of the Hebrews in another place is thus the context for the formulation of both the sabbath rule and the succeeding rule about the identity of the god the Israelites are to recognize when they eventually settle permanently in one place.[6] This same request to go on a three-day pilgrimage (*ḥag*) to meet their god in the wilderness is likewise what prompts the listing in the next rule of the three annual pilgrimages in Israel's settled state.

Three Annual Pilgrimages (Exod 23:14–16)

14 Three times thou shalt keep a feast unto me in the year. 15 Thou shalt keep the feast of unleavened bread: thou shalt eat unleavened bread seven days, as I commanded thee, in the time appointed of the month Abib,

---

[6] Critics, e.g., Driver (*Exodus*, CBSC, 241) and Hyatt (*Exodus*, NCBC, 247), are at a loss to explain the position of the injunction against naming other gods in the sequence of rules.

for in it thou camest out from Egypt; and none shall
appear before me empty. 16 And the feast of harvest,
the first fruits of thy labours, which thou hast sown in
the field; and the feast of ingathering, which is the end
of the year, when thou hast gathered in thy labours out
of the field.

Source (Exod 5:1). Moses and Aaron reported to the
pharaoh that their god required them to make a pilgrimage to him in the wilderness.

The repeatedly stated purpose of the deliverance from
Egypt is that the Israelites, having served under an oppressive master, might serve God through sacrificial worship. In the context of the instruction about the name of
God—the context out of which was fashioned the preceding rule against uttering the name of foreign gods—there
are two references to this anticipated outcome (Exod
3:12, 18). The Israelites' immediate plan is directed toward their first pilgrimage (*ḥag*, Exod 5:1, 10:9), the
three-day trek into the wilderness. The annual pilgrimages (*ḥaggim*), after the settlement in the land of Canaan, represent the fulfillment of the wish first stated in
the exodus narrative to go and worship their god. The
rules, we have noted, are geared to this future, as the
code's epilogue makes explicit (Exod 23:20–33). Each of
the three feasts concerns agricultural crops. One reason
why no other type of sacrifice, such as those that require
animal offerings, is mentioned at this point—they come
up in the next and final section of the code—may be that
the lawgiver has in view Joseph's agricultural policy in
the service of the pharaoh and of his own people.[7] The

---

[7] In light of the lawgiver's stance, there is consequently no sup-

requirements for the Israelites in their own land, in the service of their own god, represent the final development in a providential process that began with Joseph in Egypt.

Another reason the three annual *pilgrimages* are set down together may be that, because of the aspect of travel, they highlight part of the exodus narrative in which the Israelites are required to go on a three-day journey to sacrifice to their god (Exod 3:18, 8:27). That narrative itself at one point cites the need for future instruction in serving Yahweh (Exod 10:26). Moses, in his rules, gives that instruction.

There is explicit reference, in regard to the feast of unleavened bread, to the exodus from Egypt. Moses, we are to believe, addresses an audience that had direct experience of the events in Egypt and so he can speak openly about it. That God speaks personally in the rule ("unto me") is, similar to what occurred in the preceding rule, a probable consequence of the interchange between God and Moses in the exodus narrative about the incident of the burning bush. Moreover, as S. R. Driver notes, the words "As I commanded thee" appear to refer to the narrative account of the instructions Moses laid down on the actual occasion of the exodus from Egypt (Exod 13:6).[8] The link between law and narrative has come into the open. In that narrative account the observance of the feast of unleavened bread "shall be for a sign unto thee upon thine hand, and for a memorial [*zikkaron*] between thine eyes, that Yahweh's law may be in thy mouth" (Exod 13:9). The preceding rule's concern was (1) that the name

---

port for the common suggestion (see B. S. Childs, *Exodus*, 484) that the silence about the passover festival indicates the originally independent character of the feast of unleavened bread.

[8] Driver, *Exodus*, CBSC, 242.

of other gods should not be brought to mind (*zakar, hiph.*), apart from, it is implied, Yahweh's; and (2) that one should be careful about what comes out of one's mouth.

The surprising requirement in the rule that none shall appear empty before Yahweh reflects the result of the discussion between Moses and the pharaoh in Exod 10:24–26. The pharaoh at last permitted the Israelites to go on pilgrimage and serve Yahweh, but said that their flocks and herds should remain behind. Moses countered by declaring that they were bound to present sacrifices and burnt offerings. S. R. Driver wonders why the requirement not to appear empty is stated after the rule about the feast of unleavened bread and not after the following two rules about the two other annual pilgrimages, harvest and ingathering.[9] The reason is that the rule's attachment to the feast of unleavened bread is again owing to the influence of the exodus story. The requirement takes up Moses's response to the pharaoh that the Israelites must appear before Yahweh with something to offer. The feasts of harvest and ingathering point forward to Canaan and not back, as with the feast of unleavened bread, to Egypt.[10]

---

[9] Driver, *Exodus*, CBSC, 242–43.

[10] Similar considerations apply to the crux singled out by Childs, *Exodus*, 614. He wonders why in the similar set of rules in Exod 34:18–20 the two rules in Exod 23:15 (unleavened bread, not to be without an offering) are placed in, respectively, Exod 34:18 and 34:20 (not 21 as Childs indicates). The intervening rule about the firstborn is appropriately placed in the context of Exod 34:18–20 because of the use of the exodus narrative (see discussion of the decalogue of Exodus 34).

Males before Yahweh (Exod 23:17)

> Three times in the year all thy males shall appear before the Lord Yahweh.

Source (Exod 10:8–11). In the negotiations between Moses and the pharaoh about the Israelites' projected pilgrimage, Moses wanted all of his people to go on the pilgrimage but the pharaoh insisted that only the males should fulfill the duty.

A quite specific aspect of the exodus narrative is relevant to this rule. The pharaoh, presumably suspicious of Moses's intentions, was prepared to let only the male Israelites go and worship their god (Exod 10:11). Such a restriction was not acceptable to Moses, precisely because his aim was the liberation of the nation from Egyptian sovereignty. In his rule for the settlement in the land he recognizes the validity, not of a restriction as such, but of a divine requirement, one that may well have had the weight of custom behind it but is nonetheless prompted by this aspect of the exodus story. Pharaoh's statement, "Go now ye that are men, and serve Yahweh; for that is what ye desire," may well mean that the pharaoh was understanding the Israelite norm correctly. The lawgiver consequently looks beyond the particular historical circumstances and infers the norm.

S. R. Driver rightly wonders why this rule is almost identical to the one expressed in v. 14, "Three times thou shalt keep a feast unto me in the year."[11] The redundancy is explained, not according to Driver's view as a norm

---

[11] Driver, *Exodus*, CBSC, 244.

taken over from Exod 34:23—one would wish to know why the compiler of the material in Exod 23:14–17 so proceeded—but as a response to the issue raised by the pharaoh. The use of the term $r^e galim$, literally "feet," for "times" in v. 14, as against $p^{a^c}amim$ in v. 17, may conceivably reflect the aspect of travel, which is more prominent for the rule in v. 14.

The unexpected use of the term 'adon, "Lord," has a parallel in Exod 15:17: Moses celebrates the triumph over the Egyptians and anticipates the final goal of settlement in Canaan at "the sanctuary, O Lord, which thy hands have established."[12] S. R. Driver remarks, "The title 'Lord' is an indication that these pilgrimages are to be observed as marks of homage and respect to Jehovah, as Sovereign of the land."[13] We have just noted that the pharaoh's claim to sovereignty in opposition to the Israelites' wish to worship their god in the wilderness is the specific context for the presentation of the rule.

Sacrifices (Exod 23:18)

Thou shalt not offer [lit. slay] the blood of my sacrifice with leavened bread; neither shall the fat of my sacrifice remain until the morning.

Source (Exodus 11–13). The final plague in Egypt when the slaughter of the Israelite firstborn of man and beast was avoided by the sacrifice of the passover lamb.

[12] Driver, Exodus, CBSC, 139.
[13] Driver, Exodus, CBSC, 244.

The climax of the exodus story prompts the three final rules in the Book of the Covenant. We can therefore address the important question why it ends with these particular rules.[14] The lawgiver focuses on that part of the tradition that tells of the crucial moment when the Israelites were about to leave Egypt. We have noted just how closely he tunes into that period of time: he sets down rules that reflect some aspect of it followed by further ones that reflect conditions in the future occupation of the land. The request that the Israelites be permitted to go on a pilgrimage was met, at one point in the negotiations, with a response that they might go but their flocks and herds should stay behind. Moses insisted, however, that they had to take their animals because they would not know what sacrifices would be required of them until they reached their destination. Moreover, even the pharaoh must provide sacrifices and burnt offerings for the occasion.

The lawgiver, while he does not accept the pharaoh's idea of a pilgrimage without animal sacrifices, sets down the three Israelite annual pilgrimages that involve crops and then turns to animal sacrifices. His procedure is always to have the rule reflect some aspect of Israel's history. In that he is dealing with the nation's struggle with the pharaoh his focus is on what actually transpired: prior to any feast that Israel might hold in the future was the climactic occasion of Israel's (passover) sacrifice to avoid the destruction that Yahweh visited upon the firstborn of Egyptian man and beast. That sacrifice and that destruction were the prelude to the momentous event of Israel's

---

[14] We might recall how the climax of the Adam and Eve story prompts the final rule (about coveting) in the decalogue.

release from the pharaoh's control. Sacrifices in the future—certainly the one that came to be known as the passover sacrifice—must somehow incorporate aspects of that occasion.[15] So important was the occasion in question that details of how the Israelites were to observe a commemorative sacrifice, namely, the passover, were given as part of the narrative history (Exodus 12, 13).

In the rule in Exod 23:18 the incompatibility of mixing the blood from the sacrifice with the leaven is intended to bring to the hearer's mind the situation in Egypt. Blood from the slaughtered lamb on the dwellings of the Israelites guaranteed life for them, just as the avoidance of leaven also ensured their survival (Exod 12:3–29). The blood represents life, the leaven in this context death, and so the two must not be mixed.[16] The peculiar language of the rule about slaying the blood may reflect the rule's commemorative intent,[17] just as the enjoined absence of leaven plays the same function. To speak, as the rule does, about "slaying the blood" implies that the blood is

[15] It is not clear if the rule in Exod 23:18 should be confined, as the one in Exod 34:25 explicitly is, to the passover sacrifice. Driver thinks not (*Exodus*, CBSC, 245). My assumption is that the passover sacrifice is in focus.

[16] On the role of the distinction between life and death in the formulation of a considerable number of biblical laws, see C. M. Carmichael, "On Separating Life and Death: An Explanation of Some Biblical Laws," *HTR* 69 (1976), 1–7; "A Common Element in Five Supposedly Disparate Laws," *VT* 29 (1979), 129–34.

[17] Nowhere else do we find "blood" as the object of the verb "to slaughter" and, as Menahem Haran points out, a solution to the puzzle proves elusive. He makes a tentative proposal, but probably skirts the problem, by understanding "blood" as adjectival in force, and translates "bloody sacrifice." See "The Passover Sacrifice," *Studies in the Religion of Ancient Israel* (Leiden: Brill, 1972), 98.

synonymous with life. To commemorate passover the blood must retain its association with life. To "slay" it, by offering leaven with it, is to destroy that important association.

The attached rule about not leaving the fat of the sacrifice overnight likewise has regard to the climactic incident in Egypt. Indeed, it is attached because of its analogous significance. The consumption (presumably by fire to Yahweh) of the fat before morning recalls again Yahweh's response to the Israelites' sacrifice to him at the time of the final plague. Their lives were spared because of the pre-midnight sacrifice and they avoided the death that came to the Egyptians from midnight till morning (Exod 12:8–10, P; 29–34, J). The lawgiver deduces the nature of the rule from that historical sacrifice: because Yahweh brought death to the Egyptian firstborn at midnight it can be inferred that the fat of the sacrifice on the occasion had been consumed by midnight. Reflection on what is not stated in the tradition but can be inferred is a typical motive for formulating a rule.[18] The tradition contains matters that require amplification and this is Moses's role. The fat as the most esteemed part of the animal is singled out as especially requiring total consumption before midnight. Indeed, the evidence of such texts as Exod 29:12, 13; Lev 3:16, 17; 7:22, 27; 8:14–30; Num 18:17, where there is the closest association between blood and fat, suggests, as J. I. Durham rightly observes, that both convey notions of "the very essence of life."[19]

[18] The later P instruction is equally alert to the issue when it requires that nothing of the sacrifice should remain until morning, but, should some do so, it has to be consumed by fire (Exod 12:10).

[19] J. I. Durham, *Exodus*, WBC, 333–34.

Firstfruits (Exod 23:19a)

> The first of the firstfruits of thy land thou shalt bring
> into the house of Yahweh thy God.

Source (Exodus 11–13). Again the occasion of the final
plague in Egypt and its consequences.

In order to understand the placement of the rule about
firstfruits, we have to consider again the rule about the
firstborn in Exod 22:29, 30. The final plague in Egypt
raises the issue of Yahweh's claim to the Israelite firstborn, as is demonstrated, for example, in the explicit link
forged between the event and the claim in other contexts
(Exod 13:15; Num 3:13, 8:17). The underlying belief is
the notion of Yahweh's power to give life and to take it
away, to make a distinction between life and death.

The rule about the human and animal firstborn in Exod
22:29, 30 was formulated, not by way of commentary on
the Egyptian incident, but in the context of the birth of
sons to Jacob. In that context the focus was on the blessing of fruitfulness in the womb that Yahweh bestowed on
the patriarchs (Gen 35:11). That tradition does not go on
to cite a requirement that the Israelites must acknowledge
such fruitfulness by giving their firstborn to Yahweh, but
it is precisely this implicit aspect of the tradition that
prompts the rule.

We must always bear in mind the lawgiver's interest in
origins. The requirement about the firstborn can be
linked to developments in the lives of the patriarchs, and
these developments take precedence over the later one
concerning the firstborn at the time of the exodus. This

222

priority explains why the lawgiver does not set down his rule about the firstborn when he comes to the focus on them in the exodus account. Instead, in that the lawgiver also looks ahead to life in the new land, Yahweh's claim to the firstfruits, because they constitute a manifest indication of his giving life, is seen as parallel to his claim to the Israelite human and animal firstborn. Hebrew *bikkurim*, "firstfruits," is cognate with *bᵉkor*, "firstborn."

The lawgiver's interest in the history of his nation—which means that often, as in regard to this rule about firstfruits, he links one period of time to another—may explain the unexpected reference to "the house of Yahweh thy God." The pertinent link is with Jacob's vow in Gen 28:20–22, with its reference to the house of God and the anticipation of future offerings there. The lawgiver is doing what the redactor of the biblical material in general is doing. This redactor sometimes openly cites historical periods, for example, the patriarchal (Exod 3:6), or implies one when he anticipates the settlement in Canaan (for example, Exod 15:17).

Evidence in support of this link with Jacob's vow at Bethel is to be found in its sequel in Gen 35:6–15. This sequel—about Deborah's death and burial, which delayed Jacob's payment of a drink and oil offering at the newly constructed altar at the house of God—prompted the presentation of the rule in Exod 22:29, 30 about the avoidance of such a delay. That rule anticipates, as does the narrative (Gen 35:11, 12), Israel's future fruitfulness in the land and consequently calls for no delay in offering from the fullness of the harvest (as well as drink and oil offerings). It likewise states the requirement to offer human and animal firstborn.

S. R. Driver regards the rule about the harvest in Exod

The Origins of Biblical Law

22:29, which he argues must refer to the firstfruits only,[20] as parallel to the rule in Exod 23:19a: "The two laws probably belonged originally to two different collections, and both were preserved on account of the difference in their form."[21] There is in fact a difference in substance too in that Exod 22:29 concerns a delay in offering, whereas Exod 23:19a simply states the requirement. What accounts for their similarity is not the difference in sources, as Driver speculates, but rather the responses on the part of the lawgiver to whatever narrative history he is working with. In formulating his rules he, like the redactors of the narratives themselves, takes stock of parallel issues and developments in the history of his nation.

However we account for the language about the "house of Yahweh thy God," it is worth noting again that the rule about the firstfruits in Exod 22:29 is juxtaposed with the requirement about human and animal firstborn. It is another indication that the concern with the firstfruits in Exod 23:19 can be readily related to a simultaneous interest in the firstborn of man and beast, especially as regards their role at the time of the final plague in Egypt.

Kid in Mother's Milk (Exod 23:19b)

Thou shalt not seethe a kid in his mother's milk.

Source (Exodus 11–13). Again the final plague in Egypt.

[20] Driver, *Exodus*, CBSC, 234. The LXX makes the link explicit. Driver rightly observes that the rule could not possibly refer to the whole of the harvest's produce.
[21] Driver, *Exodus*, CBSC, 246.

There is an obvious link, as S. R. Driver notes, between the rule about offerings from the harvest (firstfruits) in Exod 22:29 and the rule about firstfruits in Exod 23:19a.[22] The former is followed by the requirement to offer human and animal firstborn and includes the injunction that the young of the oxen and the sheep should remain seven days with the mother and be handed over to Yahweh on the eighth (Exod 22:29). As for the rule about firstfruits in Exod 23:19a, it is followed by the prohibition against boiling a kid in its mother's milk. It is surely reasonable to infer that the formulation of this prohibition can be related to the rule about the firstborn in Exod 22:29. The young animal receives sustenance from the mother's milk for seven days and, we might speculate, the owner proceeds to prepare it for sacrifice on the eighth day by cooking it in the same milk. That the prohibition against so cooking it has to do with a sacrifice is also indicated by its context: the rules that precede concern sacrifices. That it is focused primarily, if not necessarily solely, on the offering of the firstborn is also indicated by its context: the rule that immediately precedes concerns firstfruits.

Why the prohibition at this particular point in the *Mishpatim*? The slaughtered young is to be separated totally from its living mother, a strict separation of life and death. Boiling the dead kid in the mother's milk would entail the undesirable mixing of life and death. The rule is set down at this point so that a parallel is forged with the event at the exodus. The firstborn of the Egyptian beasts were slaughtered but not their mothers. The rule, like the preceding ones, would serve a commemorative function.

---

[22] Driver, *Exodus*, CBSC, 246.

This function would be comparable to the one spelled out in, for example, Exod 13:8: "And thou shalt shew thy son in that day, saying, This [no leaven] is done because of that which Yahweh did unto me when I came forth out of Egypt" (cp. Exod 13:14). The purpose of the kid law would be to set forth an example of the reality of separating life from death and to relate this separation to Yahweh's comparable action in Egypt. The focus on the mother's milk serves to bring this reality to consciousness, namely, the living mothers but the slaughtered young.

In rules about the giving of the firstborn to God, where the association with the exodus is made (Exod 13:15), the emphasis is on the firstborn and not on their mothers. This much less emphasized aspect of the climactic events in Egypt, that the mothers live but the offspring die, is the cue for the lawgiver.

The observation that the context of the kid law in Exod 23:19 is sacrificial matters, but in Deut 14:21 it is food matters,[23] can be explained by the different narrative backgrounds that have prompted the two presentations of the law. The presentation in Exod 23:19b is based on Yahweh's sacrifice of the Egyptian firstborn, whereas in Deut 14:21 the background incident is from a much later time, namely, the famine in the reign of a king of Israel when human mothers cooked and ate one of their sons (2 Kings 6:25–31).[24] We have already noted how the two virtually

---

[23] See David Daube, "A Note on a Jewish Dietary Law," *JTS* 37 (1936), 289–91.

[24] See C. M. Carmichael, *Law and Narrative in the Bible* (Ithaca: Cornell University Press, 1985), 68–72.

identical rules about oppressing a sojourner in Exod 22:21 and 23:9 are responses to different narratives.

The rule against cooking a kid in its mother's milk is made to function like a proverb, and proverbs are often designed to gain the hearer's attention. We might speculate that the practice of cooking the animal in the mother's milk was probably a typical one in ordinary life,[25] and to prohibit a customary practice is to compel reflection on what is ordinarily taken for granted—and consequently to derive significance from the content of the prohibition. In the example of the kid in the mother's milk the significance, as already indicated, revolves around the interplay between notions of life and death. Once such universal meaning is obtained the proverbial type rule can be applied to different situations. Consequently, the three times that it is cited it is made to apply to different historical incidents: mothers and young at the time of the final plague in Egypt (Exod 23:19b); the supernatural significance accorded to the golden calf (Exod 34:26b); and mothers and young in a famine during the time of the monarchy (Deut 14:21). The law of the bird's nest in Deut 22:6, 7, in which the mother bird is let go but the young are taken for food, provides an almost identical parallel to the rule about the kid in its mother's milk.[26]

[25] Ancient and modern examples exist in the Middle East of cooking a young animal in the mother's milk; see Driver, *Exodus*, CBSC, 247.

[26] See C. M. Carmichael, "On Deuteronomic Legislation—Sparing the Mother Bird," *LawHR* 2 (1984), 287–99.

Afterword

I no longer accept the view that the *Mishpatim* constitute the earliest codification of biblical law. They reveal all the marks of being a Deuteronomic product and consequently, if the Deuteronomic laws are to be dated around the sixth century, I would date the *Mishpatim* then too. I do so because my guess is that the Deuteronomic process of working with the traditions in Genesis, Exodus, Numbers, Joshua, Judges, Samuel, and Kings is probably one that took place after the Babylonian exile. I have become skeptical about the historical accuracy of events as related in 2 Kings 22 about the reign of King Josiah. The primary feature of the "historical" books is their Deuteronomic stamp. To serve his own religious and ideological needs, the Deuteronomist interferes with the past, making events happen that never happened, or never happened in the way he describes them. This phenomenon is such a pervasive one in antiquity (it is common at all times) that any attempt to write an objective history runs up against the complex, sophisticated character of ancient narrative writing.[1]

The question arises: if the *Mishpatim* are a Deuteronomic composition, why was it a separate composition from the (laws of the) book of Deuteronomy?[2] The answer is that the rules of the *Mishpatim* take up issues in the lives of the first ancestor of the nation, Jacob, of his favored son, Joseph, and of Moses. In other words, the rules focus on matters from the beginning of the nation, Israel, until the moment when Moses delivers them. The book of Deuteronomy, on the other hand, while always interested in the beginnings of some issue in the life of the nation, going back even to Abraham on a number of oc-

---

[1] For a useful perspective, see Averil Cameron, ed., *History as Text: The Writing of Ancient History* (London: Duckworth, 1989). The etiological character of tales such as those involving Jacob with Esau, the daughters of Lot with their father is probably no less true for the tale of Josiah's reign. Such narratives are attempts to explain or justify existing situations (relations between Israel and Edom, Israel with the Ammonites and Moabites, Israel in exile). The use of historical narration in relating such matters is a clever device not just to communicate the ideological point but to buttress it. The law book that happened to turn up in the temple treasury in Josiah's reign is not just a "plant," as Joseph Blenkinsopp suggests (*Wisdom and Law in the Old Testament* [Oxford: Oxford University Press, 1983], 96), but the account of its turning up is likewise largely an invention to bolster the position of the Deuteronomic stance. We might compare how the story of the golden calf in Aaron's time (Exodus 32) is, whatever kernel of historicity might be present, largely an invention for the purpose of anticipating the use of the calves in King Jeroboam's time. Consequently, Jeroboam's use of them at Bethel and Dan to oppose the political power of King Rehoboam in Jerusalem (1 Kings 12:25–33) could be condemned by appeal to "past" authority.

[2] Graham Davies, Cambridge University, who kindly read part of my manuscript, posed this question.

casions, covers issues that arise in the period of the Judges
and the Kings. Moses, delivering his farewell address,
hands on leadership for the life of his nation and consequently anticipates the nation's future. Consider, for example, the law about kingship in Deut 17:14–20. Moses
draws a parallel between the crisis of leadership that he
"sees" will arise in Samuel's time, when the people requested a king (1 Sam 8:4–9), and the crisis in his own
time when Aaron constructed the golden calf in response
to the people's request for new leadership. At the same
time he anticipates the first occasion when the issue of kingship arose in Israel, namely, Abimelech's reign in the period
of the Judges (Judg 9:1–6): hence the curious prohibition
against appointing a king who "is not thy brother." Again,
too, he anticipates the supreme moment of kingship in Israel, Solomon's reign, and takes account of his shortcom-
ings (the multiplication of horses, silver, gold, and wives).[3]

What is most interesting to observe is that the epilogue
to the *Mishpatim* (Exod 23:20–33) anticipates precisely the
problems of that period of time that the initial rules of
Deuteronomy 12 address, namely, Canaanite religious influence.

Laws and Proverbs

There is a sense in which the laws are miniature narratives.[4] They belong to a process of composition that oc-

[3] See C. M. Carmichael, *Law and Narrative in the Bible* (Ithaca:
Cornell University Press, 1985), 97–101.

[4] Or more precisely, they resemble etiological myths, that is, in-
ventions *ex post facto* in which there is (usually) the kernel of a

curred before the formalization of courts and court procedure, before the establishment of an institutionalized judiciary. Their formulation is most like the process by which proverbs, maxims, gnomic sayings, witticisms come into existence, for example, the proverbial expression "to eat sour grapes" from Aesop's fable of the fox and the grapes. The imaginative element that is characteristic of storytelling is carried over into the rules themselves; for example, matters in the human world are transferred to those in the animal. What the biblical rules encapsulate are judgments, frequently those attributed to God, that are implicit in a narrative. Biblical narratives, it is worth recalling, have themselves undergone a process of reflection, refinement, critical appraisal, and didactic orientation. The formulation of the laws is a similar process that has probably gone hand in hand with the process that has shaped biblical narrative.

The link between the laws and proverbs requires further elucidation. The laws resemble proverbs in that they encapsulate matters in a story.[5] There is a resemblance too in that, just as a sage searches for the universal aspects of

---

long-existing rule. Interestingly, the etiological elements found in some narratives (for example, the explanation for the prohibition against eating a certain part of an animal's hip joint that is embedded in the story about the angel wrestling with Jacob [Gen 32:30]) have a similarly indirect relationship to the thrust of the narrative as do some laws to their narrative source. On the link between such elements and the narratives in which they are inserted, see Gerhard von Rad, *Genesis* (Philadelphia: Westminster, 1972), 319.

[5] On this aspect of proverbs, see Archer Taylor, *The Proverb* (Cambridge: Harvard University Press, 1931), 27–32; C. M. Carmichael, "Forbidden Mixtures," *VT* 32 (1982), 394–415; and David Daube, "A Quartet of Beasties in the Book of Proverbs," *JTS* 36 (1985), 380–86.

Afterword

conduct and expresses them in proverbs, so the lawgiver
scans his records for recurring patterns of conduct from
generation to generation and formulates his laws. Even
more pertinent is the observation that the laws are like
proverbs, parables, and fables in their adaptability: they
are made to apply to different situations.

The proverb that points to the failure to uphold the
principle of individual responsibility, "The fathers have
eaten sour grapes, and the children's teeth are set on
edge," in Jer 31:29, 30 has a different application from the
same saying found in Ezek 18:2. The law about individual
responsibility for an offense (Deut 24:16) is formulated in
response to the incident in Genesis 34 where an innocent
father, Hamor, is put to death along with the true offender, his son Shechem. The same formulation is applied
to a quite different situation in 2 Kings 14:1–6: the vengeance visited upon those who slew Amaziah's father when
only the culprits, not their sons, were executed. The fable
of the thistle and the cedar ("The thistle that was in
Lebanon, sent to the cedar that was in Lebanon, saying,
Give thy daughter to my son to wife: and there passed by
a wild beast that was in Lebanon, and trode down the
thistle") is directed awkwardly—the setting is a purely
military confrontation—against Amaziah at this time (2
Kings 14:8–10); it is an application of a fable probably
formulated for the situation of Hamor and Shechem in
Genesis 34.[6]

The rule prohibiting the consumption of an animal that

---

[6] See David Daube, *Ancient Hebrew Fables* (Oxford: Oxford University Press, 1973), 19, 20, and Carmichael, *Law and Narrative*,
272–76. Note how the fable upholds the principle of individual responsibility—only the father, the offender, is slain.

has died naturally (Deut 14:21) is set down against the background of the famine in King Joram's reign (2 Kings 14:24–31), whereas the formulation in Exod 22:31 prohibiting the consumption of an animal that has been torn by a wild beast is posed against the background of the Joseph story.[7] One of the most interesting examples of a law that is used like a proverb to illuminate different situations is the prohibition against boiling a kid in its mother's milk. Its citation in Exod 23:19 appears to have a commemorative function, recalling how the Egyptian firstborn beasts died but not their mothers; the citation in Exod 34:26 may have regard to the supernatural significance that was attributed to the golden calf in Exodus 32; and its citation in Deut 14:21 may apply to the incident of the mothers who consumed one of their sons during the famine in the reign of King Joram (2 Kings 6:25–31).[8]

Practical Application of the Laws

The question of the apparent realism of the rules has to be addressed. This realism should be attributed to a process in which the lawgiver takes up, not the idiosyncratic

---

[7] For the former formulation, see my *Law and Narrative*, 68–72; for the latter, see discussion of this rule under Exod 22:31.

[8] Ordinarily, we tend to conclude that different applications of a law signify different authors. I am suggesting that where laws are made to function like proverbs this conclusion should be resisted. Philo provides an example of an author who expresses different views by means of the same law. See David Daube, "Two Jewish Prayers," *RJ* 6 (1987), 186. We might recall how a place-name such as Mahanaim or Penuel has different explanations attached to it and, again, different authors may not necessarily be involved. Cp., however, von Rad, *Genesis*, 312, 314.

issues of a story, but the closest possible parallels to those issues in ordinary life. This process would explain why the rules appear to be an outgrowth of societal problems.[9] Although there may be some scope for assuming that the lawgiver intended to influence his contemporary world, it should be stressed that the disorder in the arrangement of the rules is a telling indication that this kind of influence was limited. The ideal nature of some of the rules, for example, the periodic rest for the entire land every seventh year (Exod 23:10, 11), also points in the direction of such limitation. Should the rules' formulations be dated to the time of the exile, or to a time shortly before, when the end of the nation was perceived to be inevitable, their influence on existing legal ways was presumably minimal. Indeed, what was being consolidated was the nation's body of tradition, the correct interpretation of which in the form of rules and judgments was considered vital for a continuing sense of nationhood.

Law in the Narratives

Insights into the laws obtained by linking them to the narrative traditions prompt us to pay renewed attention to the narratives' own jurisprudential aspects. For example, the juxtaposition of one story with another, espe-

[9] Raymond Westbrook observes for the cuneiform codes a process whereby laws are set down as if they constitute actual cases but are in fact theoretical discussions of a matter that originally might have been an individual case. The case chosen was preferably borderline in character, "since the law in the ordinary case could also be derived from it by implication"; *Studies in Biblical and Cuneiform Law* (Paris: Gabalda, 1988), 4, 123.

cially in the book of Genesis, often reveals an interest in retributive justice. Jacob's cheating Esau out of the right of primogeniture by exploiting Isaac's blindness meets with its own precise form of retribution. Laban underhandedly substitutes his elder daughter for the younger one on Jacob's wedding night, when it is dark and Jacob is, no doubt, blind drunk (Gen 29:22).[10] Comparably retributive is the action of Jacob's elder son, Reuben, in lying with his father's concubine—no doubt at night when Jacob would be blind to it. The result is that Jacob, again being paid back for his offense against Esau, has to deny his own firstborn the right of primogeniture (Gen 49:3, 4). Judah's initiative in having Joseph sold into slavery in Egypt, and consequently causing his father to think that his favorite son is dead, has its terrible retribution when Judah loses his two sons, Er and Onan (Genesis 37, 38).[11] It is no accident that these narratives are quarried so extensively by the lawgiver in both the *Mishpatim* and the book of Deuteronomy.

What the laws do—they hark back to issues in ancient history and make judgments upon them—some narratives may also do. An example is the etiological account of how Moses came to set up Israel's judicial system (Exodus 18). That narrative takes up from the failure of the first generation of the sons of Jacob to resolve disputes in their midst.[12]

[10] See David Daube, "Fraud on Law for Fraud on Law," *OJLS* 1 (1981), 51–60.

[11] See my analysis in *Women, Law, and the Genesis Traditions* (Edinburgh: Edinburgh University Press, 1979), 57–73.

[12] See C. M. Carmichael, "Moses and Joseph," *S'vara* (forthcoming).

Afterword

The story of Ruth (not, so far as I am aware, quarried
by any biblical lawgiver) looks back to the patriarchal traditions—the link is sometimes spelled out (Ruth 4:12)—
and obliquely criticizes the acts of Israel's ancestors. Boaz
acts responsibly in regard to the levirate duty owed to
Ruth, in contrast to Judah who does nothing for Tamar.
If we compare the threshing floor scene in Ruth with Judah and Tamar's encounter at Enaim, we find that Boaz
like Judah cannot recognize the woman who lies with
him. Boaz, however, unlike Judah inquires who she
might be. Ruth identifies herself, but Tamar keeps her
identity a secret. Judah and Tamar's dealings are covert
and masked, Boaz and Ruth's open and honest. The narrator of the story of Ruth brings out the economic aspect
of these dealings, an aspect that is only implicit in Genesis
38. The (nameless) nearer kinsman in the book of Ruth
openly expresses his fear of losing his inheritance should
he give conception to Ruth. In Genesis 38 Onan's fear of
losing his inheritance to the son he might engender is
only to be inferred from his action of spilling seed on the
ground. The first Moabite woman in the Bible makes her
nearest relative drunk in order to have intercourse with
him (Gen 19:30–38). Ruth, a Moabite of a later generation, only partially mirrors the conduct of her Moabite
ancestor. She lies down beside Boaz only when he is already drunk.[13]

Just as a legal formulation in the different collections of
laws is determined less by a real-life influence and more
by a literary precursor in the form of a story, so a literary
precursor, more than a real-life background, appears to

[13] See Carmichael, *Women*, 76–83.

determine the details of a story like Ruth's.[14] Boaz is one generation older than Ruth because Judah is a generation older than Tamar. Ruth's mother-in-law, Naomi, cannot have a child herself. This aspect of the story may have been influenced by the fact that in Genesis 38 Judah's wife, Bathshua, dies, the implication being that she could no longer produce a child to make up for the loss of Er and Onan. The made-up names of the characters in the book of Ruth—for example, Mahlon ("Sickly") and Qilyon ("Weakly")—are one pointer that no living reality is being depicted.

Selection of Topics

A major result of this study is that we can explain why certain topics are found in the code, while others that might have been expected to show up do not. Umberto Cassuto comments on the selective character of the rules; for example, there is a rule on seduction but not on adultery or rape.[15] N. M. Sarna states, "The entire field of commercial law is for all intents and purposes non-existent. There is all but total silence surrounding such matters as merchants, sales, contracts, pawns, pledges, sureties,

[14] Note how an ancient custom about the conveyance of land has to be explained to the reader (Ruth 4:7). The topic of literary precursors is an enormous one. See the illuminating remarks about rhetorical imitation in Greco-Roman literature, which are also pertinent to biblical and ancient Near Eastern, in T. L. Brodie, "Luke 7, 36–50 as an Internalization of 2 Kings 4, 1–37: A Study in Luke's Use of Rhetorical Imitation," *Bib* 64 (1983), 459–64.
[15] Umberto Cassuto, *A Commentary on the Book of Exodus* (Jerusalem: Magnes, 1967), 288–89.

Afterword

and partnerships."[16] The point is that the choice of topics depends on what occurs in the "case" at issue, namely, the problems that show up in a narrative. There are, for example, no rules on real property—ownership, acquisition, and alienation of houses and land (topics common in other ancient legal codes), because the Jacob-Laban and Joseph stories that are under scrutiny in the *Mishpatim* neither raise nor suggest any particular issues in regard to them. Meir Malul comments that for the Near Eastern legal traditions, "the phenomenon of incompleteness of the law corpora constitutes one of the strongest arguments for proving their literary, rather than legal, nature."[17] The same observation applies to the biblical legal tradition.

Audience

The original audience for the mode of lawmaking we are observing was probably an elite, scribal circle. In this setting narrative art was developed, the language of legal formulation and proverbial saying was cultivated, and collections of laws and proverbs were made. The aesthetic pleasure of such activity should be stressed, especially if it is novel in character.[18]

[16] N. M. Sarna, *Exploring Exodus: The Heritage of Biblical Israel* (New York: Schocken, 1986), 170.

[17] Meir Malul, *The Comparative Method in Ancient Near Eastern and Biblical Legal Studies, AOAT* 227 (1990), 123 n.13.

[18] Cp. the remark of J. J. Sheehan, *German History 1770–1866* (Oxford: Clarendon, 1989), 144: "Since we live in a culture awash with printed matter, we may find it difficult to share that sense of awe and wonder that books produced in intellectuals." He is refer-

The final shaping of the material in the context of its narrative setting, namely, the Pentateuch, may however betoken a change of audience.[19] The fictional element in this literary activity, namely, that Moses is the author of the laws, may point away from the original scribal setting to, in some sense, a more politically oriented one. It is remarkable that only incidents in Moses's own time are explicitly referred to while those that occurred in prior and later times are not mentioned. One wonders why. Is the aim to conceal criticism of the nations' ancestors, Abraham, Isaac, Jacob, and Joseph? The laws do focus on their actions, often with implicitly negative judgment upon them. We can assume that in the lawgiver's time these particular ancestors were revered, just as the traditions themselves extol Abraham, Isaac, Jacob, and Joseph when in some matters we might have expected otherwise. No negative judgment, for example, is hinted at in regard to Abraham's deception about his wife's status, nor is Joseph censured for his treatment of his brothers in Egypt.

The question of criticism of the ancestors is, however, more complex than might appear. Jacob openly criticizes certain of his sons, for example, Reuben, Simeon, and

---

ring to the age that marks the beginning of a consciously German literary and philosophical culture. On a playful aspect of some rules in Celtic codes, see Phillip Grierson, *The Origins of Money* (London: Athlone, 1977), 17.

[19] Cp. how the parables in the gospels have undergone a change of audience (often with a significant change of meaning); see Joachim Jeremias, *The Parables of Jesus* (New York: Scribner, 1955), 23–31. For rules that start out for an elite but are eventually applied to everyone, see David Daube, *Ancient Jewish Law* (Leiden: Brill, 1981), 82, 83.

Afterword

Levi (Gen 49:3–7). He criticizes Judah severely but by means of irony (Gen 49:8–12). Criticism of Jacob himself shows up in a subtle way by means of the juxtaposition of the traditions about him—the same is true for Judah—so that the discerning reader can pick up how sometimes an ancestor is paid back in his own coin for something untoward that he has done. The critical spirit that is already at work in the presentation of the traditions becomes more fully developed in the work of the lawgiver in his examination of them. He nonetheless preserves the tendency to criticize the leading ancestors in an indirect way.

Once the laws were taken out of their scribal setting, in which the laws and the narratives were scrutinized together, and presented to the national consciousness—at what time we do not know—the result was the gap between the two that later tradition has lived with. What was the point of such a disparity? I can only speculate that the national identity required, on the one hand, the preservation of the tales about the less than virtuous ancestors and, on the other hand, some means, namely, the rules, of coming to terms with the ancestors' ways should anyone choose to extol them uncritically.

Priestly Laws

I observe no direct links between the *Mishpatim* and the (later) Priestly (P) material. What is revealing, however, and promises to be a new area of inquiry, is the indication that there is an equally interesting if different kind of link between Priestly laws and individual narratives. In brief, whereas the Deuteronomic method is to set down rules in collections independently of the narratives that inspire them, one Priestly method is to integrate the rule and the narrative. Examples are the story of creation and the institution of the sabbath (Gen 1:1–2:3); the flood story and the appended rules about blood (Gen 9:4–6);[20] the institution of circumcision in the time of Abraham (Gen 17:1–14); the passover rules in the context of the story of the passover (Exod 12:1–13); observance of the sabbath during the provision of manna (Exod 16:22–26); and, more complicated, rules about killing man or animal, or mutilating a person, in the context of the story about the man who blasphemed (Lev 24:10–23).[21]

I have given indications that the process of lawmaking went hand in hand with the redaction of Pentateuchal material.[22] If these observations prove worthy of further inquiry, they also promise a new way forward in understanding the literary origins of the Pentateuch.

[20] On just how closely these rules relate to the story of the flood, see C. M. Carmichael, "A Time for War and a Time for Peace: The Influence of the Distinction upon Some Legal and Literary Material," *JJS* 25 (1974), 58–63.

[21] See my discussion about the links with the story of Naboth (1 Kings 21), "Biblical Laws of Talion," *HAR* 9 (1986), 123–26.

[22] Not that I would separate the Deuteronomic writings, Joshua–2 Kings, in any analysis of the issue.

Index of Sources

References are to the numbering in the English versions.

Index

Index

245

Index

Index

Index

249

Index

Subject Index

Index

Fictional Moses, 4–7, 14, 24, 87, 169, 230, 239
Food laws, 133, 182–84, 194, 204–8, 226, 227, 231–33
Forgotten sheaf, law of, 4, 198

Gifts, 61, 197–201, 216
Graven images, 29–32, 48, 53–56, 60, 72
Greek Law, 6

Harlotry, 120, 122, 127–29, 161–63
Hire, 13, 156–58
Homicide, 10, 13, 15, 22, 38, 39, 45, 98–106, 124–31, 142–45
Household gods, 86, 87, 149–52
Hypothetical rules, 15–21, 127, 234

Incest, 93, 94, 164
Indirect causation, 117, 118, 136–39, 146–49
Individual responsibility, 118, 119, 123, 128, 135, 232
Intent, 102, 125
Irony, 165, 240

Justice, 161, 199, 200, 203

Kingship, institution of, 10–12, 23, 24, 31, 230

Law and religion, 2, 99, 100, 128, 145
Levites, 23, 32
Life and death, 60, 61, 69–73, 130, 220–27
Loans. See Borrowing
Lying, 43

Males, duties of, 62, 217, 218
Marriage, 39–42, 83–97, 108, 123, 156, 159
Medical expenses, 114–16, 136
Money, 15, 90, 116–19, 123, 134, 151, 160, 161, 187–89, 198–201
Murder. See Homicide
Mutilation, 121, 124–31

Name of God, 32–34, 48, 52, 53, 57, 60, 73, 75, 211–13
Nationalism, 18–21, 133, 234, 240

Oaths, 33, 155, 177, 178, 223

Parables, 232, 239
Parents: honor to, 13, 37, 38, 45, 64, 73, 113; attitudes toward children, 98, 106–8, 110
Perversion of justice, 12, 13, 184–89, 193–203
Pilgrimages, 36, 37, 56–67, 208–10, 213–18
Priestly laws, 3, 46–50, 205, 206, 221, 240, 241
Primogeniture, 11, 54, 58–62, 179, 180, 182, 183, 189, 222–24, 235
Procreation, 37–41, 50, 64, 113, 222, 236, 237
Property, 13, 151, 152, 238
Prophecy, 23
Proverbs. See Wisdom

Ransom, 61, 134, 135
Retribution. See Talion

Sabbath, 13, 23, 34–38, 45–50, 57–59, 62–65, 207–10
Sacrifices, 38, 67–73, 167–69, 218–27
Sale, 90, 109–13, 116, 120, 144, 145, 202
Satan, 32
School activity, 17, 19, 133, 134, 238–40
Seduction, 7, 13, 158–61, 237
Sequence of laws, 13, 113, 180, 193, 195, 203
Shame, 10, 42, 74–77, 159
Shepherds, 116, 118, 142, 143, 150, 183–92
Slavery, 3, 4, 11, 12, 15, 77–86, 99, 116–20, 125, 126, 129–31, 143, 170, 196, 203, 209
Sorcery. See Witchcraft
Sources of law, 16–23
Spying, 196

252

Library of Congress Cataloging-in-Publication Data

Carmichael, Calum M.
    The origins of Biblical law : the Decalogues and the Book of the Cove-
nant / Calum M. Carmichael.
        p.   cm.
    Includes bibliographical references and index.
    ISBN 0-8014-2712-6
    1. Bible. O.T. Exodus XXI, 2-XXIII, 19—Criticism, interpretation,
etc. 2. Ten commandments. 3. Law (Theology)—Biblical teaching.
4. Jewish law—Sources. I. Title.
BS1245.2.C37   1992
222'.1206—dc20   92-6908